D0261478

SPY PRINCESS

Spy Princess

The Life of Noor Inayat Khan

Shrabani Basu

Foreword by M.R.D. Foot

SUTTON PUBLISHING

First published in the United Kingdom in 2006 by
Sutton Publishing Limited · Phoenix Mill
Thrupp · Stroud · Gloucestershire · GL5 2BU

Reprinted 2006

British Library Cataloguing in Publication Data
A catalogue record for this book is available from the British Library.

ISBN 0-7509-3965-6

The extracts from *Between Silk and Cyanide* (1998) by Leo Marks on pp. 91–6 are reprinted by permission of HarperCollins Publishers Ltd.

Typeset in 11/13pt Sabon.
Typesetting and origination by
Sutton Publishing Limited.
Printed and bound in England by
J.H. Haynes & Co. Ltd, Sparkford.

To my sisters,
Nupur and Moushumi

A mermaid once went in a ship
Upon the stormy sea,
And as she sailed along, the
Waves arose and sprung in glee,
For on the ship she hung a lamp
Which gave a light so sweet,
That anyone who saw its glow
With joy was sure to meet.

Noor-un-nisa Inayat Khan (age fourteen),
The Lamp of Joy

Contents

Foreword

Holders of the George Cross are out of the common run; Noor Inayat Khan was even farther out of it than most. She was an Indian princess on her father's side; her mother was American. She was brought up in Paris, where she wrote and broadcast children's stories; she had a gentle character and the manners of a lady, but lived in no luxury. She fled to England in 1940, when the Germans invaded France, and worked as a humble wireless operator on Bomber Command's ground staff. She was plucked up into SOE, volunteered to go back to France in secret, survived for a few months in Paris but got betrayed, and was beaten up and murdered in Dachau.

What was an innocent like this doing with a pistol in her handbag? Why was she sent to France at all, in the teeth of reports that she was quite unfit to go? Why was the prearranged code that showed she was in German hands not believed when she sent it? These are some of the questions this book raises; to some of them it can provide answers.

There are books about her already, one by a close London friend of hers who detested SOE, one in French that does not pretend to be truthful. No other biographer had access, as this author did, to her recently released secret archive, and none till now was a compatriot. Shrabani Basu, London correspondent of a leading Indian newspaper, understands from inside what her heroine must have felt during the world war about the struggle for Indian independence. This is not a story to be missed.

M.R.D. Foot
Nuthampstead
September 2005

Acknowledgements

This book would not have been possible without the encouragement of many people who went out of their way to help me.

I would like to thank Noor's family, her brothers, Vilayat Inayat Khan and Hidayat Inayat Khan, who despite ill health and pressing work commitments for their Sufi orders, took the time to talk to me and give me details of Noor's life. Thanks to Hidayat for allowing me generous use of Noor's stories, poems, documents and family photographs. Sadly, Vilayat did not live to see the publication of the book. Thanks also to Noor's cousin, Mahmood Youskine, who filled me in with many interesting family details, and to David Harper, Noor's nephew, for his insights. I would have been lost without the warm and efficient Hamida Verlinden, from the Sufi Headquarters at The Hague, who helpd me with Noor's papers, and Martin Zahir Roehrs, Vilayat's assistant in Suresnes, who made every meeting possible. Thanks also to Amin Carp from East West Publications at The Hague for his help.

To Professor M.R.D. Foot for meticulously reading each chapter and helping me at every stage, I owe my heartfelt gratitude. I could not have asked for a better guide. I would also like to thank him for writing the foreword to this book.

I am indebted to Jean Overton Fuller, too, for sharing her precious memories of Noor and providing her insights into her friend's life. I am also grateful to her for allowing me to quote material from her book.

Thanks to Francis Suttill for sharing information with me about his father, Alain Antelme for all his inputs on his uncle and John Marais for sharing his memories of his mother and Noor. Their help has been invaluable.

In Dachau, I would like to thank my wonderful guide, Maxine Ryder, and Dirk Riedel from the Dachau Museum for his inputs. In

Delhi, thanks to Kamini Prakash from the Hope Project for showing me around Inayat Khan's tomb. In Calcutta, thanks to Mohammed Husain Shah, direct descendant of Tipu Sultan, for telling me about the family history, and in Moscow, thanks to Jelaluddin Sergiei Moskalew for his helpful inputs on Inayat Khan and the birth of Noor.

Thanks also to Phillip Knightley, Michael Dwyer, Heather Williams, Sarah Helm and Chris Moorhouse and John Pitt of the Special Forces Club for all their help and advice.

I am grateful to my commissioning editor at Sutton Publishing, Jaqueline Mitchell, for her invaluable guidance, patience and encouragement, and my editors Anne Bennett, Jane Entrican and Hazel Cotton for their meticulous work.

Thanks to my daughter, Sanchita, for French translations and Klaas Van Der Hoeven for German translations. And finally, my family for their much needed moral support. To everybody, I owe this book.

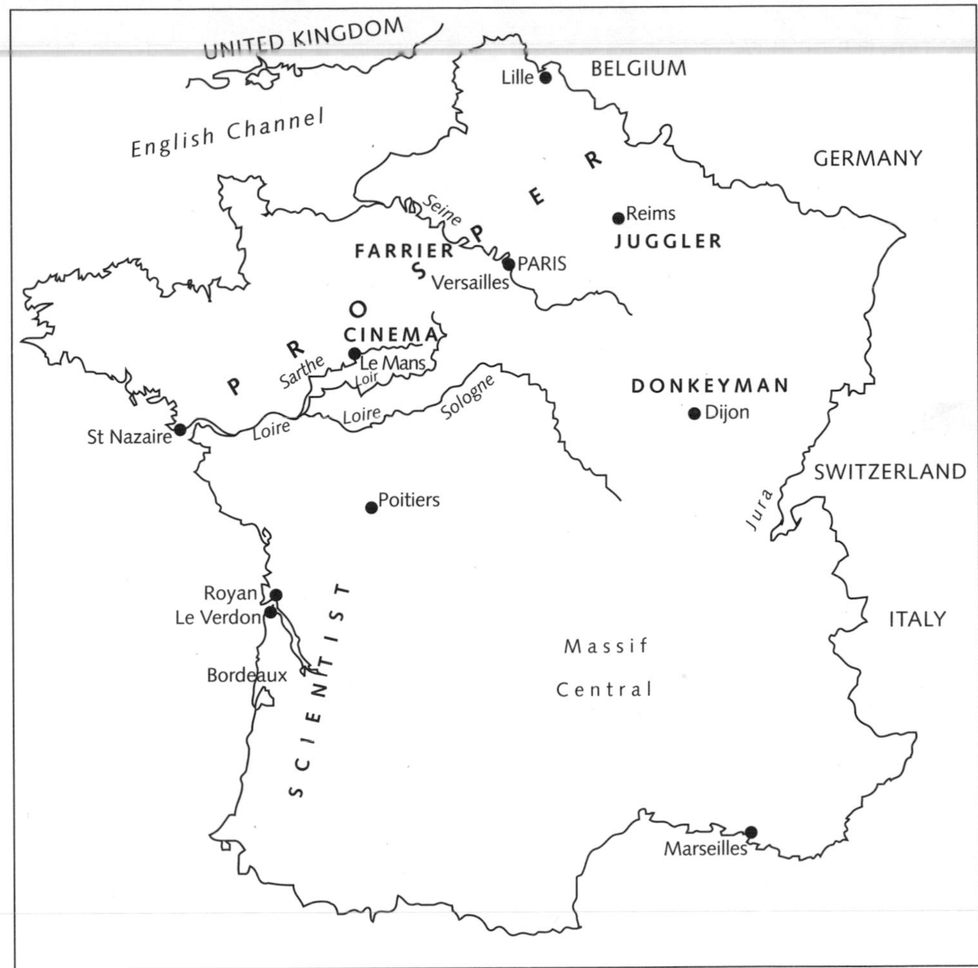

Map of France showing the areas covered by the Prosper and other connected circuits and sub-circuits.

Introduction

The lone gardener was working in the June sun clearing the weeds around Fazal Manzil, the childhood home of Noor Inayat Khan. It was a particularly hot day in Paris, a precursor to the heatwave that would sweep Europe in the summer of 2003. From the steps of Fazal Manzil, where the Inayat Khan children had often sat and played, I looked out over the hill towards Paris. The view was blocked by apartment blocks that have mushroomed in Suresnes. It was not quite the sight the children would have seen all those years back.

At eighty-seven, Pir Vilayat was a frail but impressive figure in his white robes. Walking with the help of a stick he took me to the living room with its large bay window. From here one could see the garden and the city beyond. It was in this room that he and Noor had decided that they would go to Britain and join the war effort. A large portrait of their father, Hazrat Inayat Khan, hung on the wall.

'Every day of my life I think of her. When I go for a walk I think of her, when I feel pain, I think of how much more her pain was, I think of her in chains, I think of her being beaten. When I am cold I think of her, I think of her lying in her cell with hardly any clothes. She is with me every day,' said Vilayat. It was a moving tribute from a brother.

I had first heard of Noor Inayat Khan many years ago in an article about the contribution of Asians to Britain. I was immediately drawn to the subject and read Jean Overton Fuller's *Noor-un-nisa Inayat Khan*, which was fascinating.

As an Indian woman myself, Noor's life held a natural attraction for me. How a Muslim woman from a conservative spiritual family went on to become a secret agent, working undercover in one of the most dangerous areas during the war, was something I wanted to study in detail. The fact that Jean Overton Fuller's book had been written over fifty years ago in 1952 made me feel it was worth making another attempt. Noor was an unlikely spy. She was no Mata Hari. Instead she was dreamy, beautiful and gentle, a writer of children's stories. She was not a crack shot, not endowed with great physical skills and a far cry from any spy novel prototype. Yet she went on to display such courage and fortitude in the field that she was presented the highest civilian honours – the George Cross (UK) and the Croix de Guerre (France). She was one of only three women SOE agents to receive the George Cross, the others being Violette Szabo and Odette Sansom.

The opening of the personal files of SOE agents in 2003 gave me the leads I had been looking for. Though the main players in the field, Noor's chiefs and associates at SOE – Maurice Buckmaster, Selwyn Jepson, Vera Atkins and Leo Marks – were all dead, I was confident that Noor's own files and the files of the agents who worked with her in the field would provide fresh material. In an area like the secret service there will always be gaps which cannot be filled. Meetings are held in secret and hardly any records kept. Most of Noor's colleagues were killed in France, murdered in various concentration camps, and few lived to tell their tale, making the job even more difficult. With the help of Noor's family – her brothers Vilayat and Hidayat, Jean Overton Fuller's account, SOE archives and other sources – I have tried to complete the jigsaw of Noor's life and her final road to death.

While working on this book, I realised that Noor has been romanticised in many earlier accounts with much information about her that is pure fantasy. She has been said to have been recruited while on a tiger-hunt in India. Her father, an Indian Sufi mystic, is said to have been close to Rasputin and invited by him to Russia to give spiritual advice to Tsar Nicholas II. She is said to have been born in the Kremlin. None of this is true, though much of it has been repeated in many seminal books on the SOE.

Noor was an international person: Indian, French and British at the same time. However, she is better known in France than in Britain or India. In France she is a heroine. They know her as Madeleine of the Resistance and every year a military band plays outside her childhood home on Bastille Day. A square in Suresnes has been named Cours Madeleine after her. She has inspired a best-selling novel *La Princesse Oubliée* (The Forgotten Princess) by

Laurent Joffrin, which has also been translated into German. Joffrin has given her lovers she did not have and taken her through paths she did not walk; it is a work of fiction.

Sixty years after the war, Noor's vision and courage are inspirational. I hope my book brings the story of Noor Inayat Khan to a new generation for whom the sacrifices made for freedom are already becoming a footnote in history.

Shrabani Basu
November 2005

Prologue

11 September 1944, Pforzheim prison, Germany

Her hands and feet chained together, classified as a 'very dangerous prisoner', Noor Inayat Khan stared defiantly at her German captors. Her dark eyes flashed at them as they tried to break her resistance. They had virtually starved her, keeping her on a diet of potato peel soup, struck her frail body with blows and subjected her to the dreaded Gestapo interrogation, asking her again and again for the names of her colleagues and her security checks. She had said nothing.

But at night, in the confines of her cell, she gave vent to her anger and pain. Fellow prisoners in neighbouring cells could hear her sobbing softly.

Kept in solitary confinement, unable to feed or clean herself, Noor's mind wandered off to her childhood days. The dark German cell seemed a world away from her childhood home in France where her father sang his Sufi songs in the evening and Noor played with her younger brothers and sister. Little 'Babuli', as her father used to call her, had come a long way.

She was now Nora Baker, a British spy, being tortured and interrogated in a German cell. Ten months had gone by since she had been captured in France. She had a chain binding her hands together and another binding her feet. There was a third chain that linked her hands to her feet so she could not stand straight.

Her father's words kept coming back to her, his gentle Sufi philosophy, but also his reminder to her that she was an Indian princess with the blood of Tipu Sultan in her veins. She called out silently to Abba to give her strength. And the great-great-great-granddaughter of Tipu Sultan, the Tiger of Mysore, held on, though she knew the end was near.

At 6.15 that evening the men from the Gestapo entered her cell again. Noor was told it was time to go. 'I am leaving,' she scrawled in a shaky hand on her food bowl and smuggled it out to some fellow French women prisoners. It was her last note. Still chained, Noor was led out of her cell and taken to the office.

At the prison office, Noor was met by three officials of the Karlsruhe Gestapo. She was driven in handcuffs to Karlsruhe prison, 20 miles away.

12 September 1944, Karlsruhe prison, Germany

Early in the morning, around 2 a.m., Noor met three of her fellow spies, Eliane Plewman, Madeleine Damerment and Yolande Beekman, at the Commandant's office. Noor had trained with Yolande in England. Josef Gmeiner, head of the Karlsruhe Gestapo, told them they were being moved. Still in handcuffs, the four young women were driven in Gmeiner's car to Bruchsal Junction to catch the express train to Dachau, 200 miles away. Their escorting officers, Max Wassmer and Christian Ott, gave them some bread and sausages for the journey.

After the confines of the prison, it felt good to be outdoors. There was a brief halt at Stuttgart where they boarded another train for Munich. The young women were given window seats in the same carriage and allowed to talk to one another. Naturally, they chatted animatedly. It was a pleasure for them to meet colleagues and speak English again. One of the women had some English cigarettes on her which she passed around. When they were finished, the German officer offered them some German cigarettes which they also smoked. It almost felt like a picnic.

On the way there was an air raid. The train pulled up at Geisslingen and waited for two hours. The women stayed calm as Allied aircraft flew overhead, even though they could hear the sound of the bombs. It had been three months since the Allies had landed in Normandy. The girls exchanged what information they had about the invasion.

At Munich they changed trains again. Their escorting officers made them board a local train for Dachau. It was midnight when the train finally reached the siding there. Still in handcuffs, the prisoners were ordered to walk the 2 kilometres to Dachau concentration camp.

13 September 1944, Dachau concentration camp, Germany

The air was cold as the young women prisoners struggled towards the camp with their bags. The first chilling sight was of the camp's searchlights, visible from afar. As the beams swept the area, the new arrivals could see the high walls of the camp, and the barbed wire. Built in 1933, it was the first concentration camp to be constructed by Hitler, close to his base in Munich, where thousands of Jews, gypsies and prisoners of war were to meet their deaths. Other camps, including Auschwitz, were built later with Dachau as the model.

Noor and her colleagues were taken through the main gate of the camp inscribed with the words *Arbeit Macht Frei* (Work Will Make You Free). The words were ironic because few walked free from Dachau. Over 30,000 people were exterminated here between 1933 and 1945.

As they entered the camp, they could see the line of barracks on their left. Inside, in rows of dirty bunk beds, lay the inmates, crammed like cattle, half starved and thinly clad, inhabiting a world somewhere between the living and the dead. Along the side of the barracks ran the electric fences covered with barbed wire and the deep trench which prisoners were warned not to cross. Further down was the crematorium. Outside it stood a single post with an iron hook. Here the Gestapo hanged their prisoners, often stringing them up from meat hooks with piano wire and leaving them to die slowly.

The four young women were taken to the main registration office and then led to their cells where they were locked up separately. In the early hours of the morning, the SS guards dragged Madeleine Damerment, Eliane Plewman and Yolande Beekman from their cells, marched them past the barracks to the crematorium and shot them through the back of their necks.

For Noor, it was to be a long night. As the prisoner who had been labelled 'highly dangerous', she was singled out for further torture. The Germans entered her cell, slapped her brutally and called her names. Then they stripped her. Once again she bore it silently. All through the night they kicked her with their thick leather boots, savaging her frail body. As dawn broke over the death camp, Noor lay on the floor battered and bleeding but still defiant. An SS soldier ordered her to kneel and pushed his pistol against her head.

'*Liberté!*' shouted Noor, as he shot her at point blank range. Her weak and fragile body crumpled on the floor. She was only thirty.

Almost immediately, Noor's body was dragged to the crematorium and thrown into the oven. Minutes later eyewitnesses saw smoke billowing out of the crematorium chimneys. Back in England that night, her mother and brother both had the same dream. Noor appeared to them in uniform, her happy face surrounded by blue light. She told them she was free.

ONE

Babuli

The story of Noor Inayat Khan began on New Year's Day in Moscow in 1914. As the frozen Moskva river gleamed in the reflected light of the green and purple domes of the Kremlin, a baby girl was born in the Vusoko Petrovsky monastery, a short distance from the Kremlin. The proud father was the Indian Sufi preacher Hazrat Inayat Khan, and the mother a petite American woman with flowing golden hair, Ora Ray Baker. They named their little girl Noor-un-nisa, meaning 'light of womanhood'. She was given the title of Pirzadi (daughter of the Pir). At home their precious little bundle was simply called Babuli.

Inayat Khan and Ora Ray Baker had arrived in the city of Moscow in 1913. For Inayat it had been a long journey from his home town in sunny Baroda in western India to the snowy splendour of the Russian capital. He had left India on the instructions of his teacher Syed Abu Hashem Madani to take Sufism to the west. Inayat was the grandson of Maula Baksh, the founder of the Faculty of Music at the University of Baroda, and Casimebi, the granddaughter of Tipu Sultan, the eighteenth-century ruler of Mysore. The family enjoyed a proud heritage as descendants of the Tiger of Mysore, as Tipu Sultan was known, who had fought bravely against the British.

Yet the family did not publicise this royal heritage, for political reasons. After Tipu Sultan had been killed fighting the British on the battlefield of Seringapatam in 1793, his family was forcibly removed from Mysore to prevent further rebellion in that area. The son of Tipu Sultan was also subsequently defeated and killed in Delhi fighting the British during the Indian mutiny of 1857. According to family legend his daughter, the 14-year-old princess Casimebi, was taken to safety by two faithful servants – Sultan Khan Sharif and Pir Khan Sharif. They were the sons of an officer who had served under Tipu Sultan. The princess was taken secretly to Mysore and her true identity concealed. Because she was of royal descent, Casimebi could marry only a person of noble standing, who carried royal honours and titles.[1]

As luck would have it, Inayat Khan's grandfather, Maula Baksh, went to Mysore in 1860 and sang at a competition before the Maharaja that lasted for eleven days. A skilled singer in both the North Indian classical style and the South Indian Carnatic classical style, Maula Baksh won the competition. The delighted Maharaja of Mysore presented him with a *kallagi* (turban ornament), *sarpesh* (turban), *chatra* (large umbrella), *chamar* (fly whisk) and the right to have a servant walk in front to announce him. When Maula Baksh received these emblems of royalty, the two retainers secretly arranged his marriage to Princess Casimebi.

Maula Baksh was now told of the secret of the princess's ancestry. Casimebi's heritage was talked about only in whispers (lest the British discover that the retainers had hidden one of Tipu's descendants). Maula Baksh and Casimebi then moved to Baroda (also known as Vadodara) in Gujarat at the invitation of the city's ruler. Here Maula Baksh started the Gyanshala or Music Academy, overlooking the lake, where it still stands.

Inayat's father, Rahmat Khan, a musician from the Punjab, came to Baroda and started teaching at the Gyanshala. He married one of Maula Baksh's daughters, Khatijabi, and moved into Maula Baksh's large family house on the edge of the town with its stables, large courtyard and separate women's quarters. It was in Baroda that Inayat Khan was born to Rahmat Khan and Khatijabi on 5 July 1882. Soon two more sons were born, Maheboob Khan and Musharraf Khan.

The house of Maula Baksh was an open one where all religions were tolerated and music rang out from each corner. Meals for forty to fifty people were cooked in the kitchen every day. The liberal, tolerant atmosphere of his maternal grandfather's house was to have a major influence on Inayat Khan and on his daughter, Noor.

Inayat Khan soon began to teach at the Gyanshala and travelled extensively, giving concerts in Nepal, Hyderabad and Calcutta. In Hyderabad he played for the Nizam and was initiated into Sufism by Syed Abu Hashem Madani. His teacher advised him to combine his music and his philosophy in order to bring about a better understanding between East and West.

After the death of his father Rahmat Khan, Inayat Khan decided to follow his teacher's advice. He had received an invitation to play in New York and he wrote to his brother Maheboob Khan and cousin Mohammed Khan asking them if they wanted to join him. They agreed immediately.

'*Dost chalo*' (Friend, let us go), Inayat Khan told his brother and his cousin as he used to do when they were young.[2] The men packed their instruments and sailed from Bombay in a small Italian ship in September 1910.

New York came as a shock to the musicians from Baroda. They were used to the leisurely life of the Gyanshala and the hectic pace of Manhattan took time to get used to. So did the weather and the food, but gradually they settled into their new surroundings. The group called themselves the Royal Musicians of Hindustan and began giving concerts at Columbia University. Soon they were recruited by the dancer Ruth St Denis, who took them on a tour of the country starting in Chicago.

At a lecture in the Ramakrishna Mission Ashram in San Francisco, California, Inayat Khan met a young woman called Ora Ray Baker. She was born in Albuquerque, New Mexico, in 1892 to a half-English and half-Irish father and a Scottish mother, both of whom had died when she was young. Ora Ray had then been brought up by her half-brother, a doctor. She was the niece of a Senator O'Brien and the granddaughter of one Erasmus Warner Baker, a solicitor. Ora Ray is believed to have been a distant cousin of Mary Baker Eddy, the founder of the Christian Science movement.

Ora Ray Baker was captivated by Inayat Khan's lecture. She approached him after the discussion and asked if she could interview him privately. He granted her request and the two soon fell in love.

But Inayat Khan knew his future was uncertain. He told Ora Ray that he was a dervish and did not know where his next meal would come from. Ora Ray Baker's family did not approve of the match, and neither did Inayat Khan's brothers. He told her they could write to each other and she could join him only when she had secured the consent of her family or when she came of age. In the spring of 1912, leaving behind his address with Ora Ray, Inayat set sail with his brothers once again, this time for England, where he had an invitation to play at a musical convention. His younger brother,

Musharraf Khan, joined him in New York before they left. After a mixed reception in England, the brothers moved to France in September 1912 in the belief that the French would be more inclined to appreciate their music.

Parisians were fascinated by all things oriental and soon the Royal Musicians of Hindustan were busy giving concerts, lessons and lectures. The famous dancer Mata Hari, the rage of the Paris nightclubs, engaged them as part of her troupe. She called them '*mon orchestre*' and had herself photographed with them in the garden of her house in Neuilly, with herself in the foreground striking a dance pose and the Royal Musicians of Hindustan standing behind her in all their finery, looking amused and slightly awkward. Ironically, many years later, Inayat Khan's daughter, Noor Inayat Khan, would also be a secret agent, though not quite in the Mata Hari mould. Like Mata Hari, who was executed by a firing squad in the Bois de Vincennes, Noor too would be executed.

In Paris, Inayat Khan was introduced to the leading French actor and director Lucien Guitry, who asked the group to take part in an Eastern-themed show called *Kismet*. Before long, the Royal Musicians of Hindustan were playing before the cream of French society. They met Edmond Bailly, the actress Sarah Bernhardt, the sculptor Auguste Rodin, the dancer Isadora Duncan and many other prominent people. During this time Inayat Khan also met the composer Claude Debussy, who encouraged the group by his understanding and appreciation of Indian music.

Meanwhile Ora Ray Baker had given up trying to persuade her brother to accept her relationship with Inayat Khan, and she wrote to tell Inayat that she was coming to France to join him. Her ship arrived in Antwerp where he met her and they left immediately for England. On the ferry they met another Indian who said he would perform a religious rite to solemnise the union.

On 20 March 1913, Inayat Khan married Ora Ray Baker at the civil register office at St Giles, London. They rented a place at 4 Torrington Square, Bloomsbury, and began a new life in England. Ora Ray Baker was given the new name Amina Sharada Begum. Inayat chose the name Sharada after Ma Sharada, wife of the Indian saint Ramakrishna Paramhans, in whose ashram in San Francisco Inayat Khan had first met his wife. Ora Ray's brother never forgave her and she severed all links with her family. She started wearing a golden sari to match her husband's golden robe and even wore a veil. Inayat himself had never asked her to wear Indian clothes but the Begum insisted she was doing it of her own free will. She said she had always envied the seclusion enjoyed by the women of the East.[3]

The couple received many social invitations and Amina Begum handled all her husband's correspondence, as well as organising his schedule and travels. In London they met the Indian poet Sarojini Naidu, a firm supporter of Indian independence, who was to accompany Gandhi on his famous Salt March of 1930. Inayat would practise the Indian stringed instrument known as the veena in the evenings and sing in the mornings. He often spent hours meditating at night.

In 1913 Inayat Khan and his group received an invitation to play in Russia. The invitation came from Maxim's, the Moscow nightclub, which wanted an Oriental night. The musicians did not like what they saw of Maxim's. The drunkenness and debauchery that prevailed there was alien to the men and they wanted to leave, but Inayat Khan persuaded them to stay and honour their commitment.

Moscow soon grew on Inayat Khan. He loved the intellectual atmosphere of the city and, despite the freezing climate, spent some of the happiest days of his career there. He realised that the people who went to Maxim's also frequented the concerts and salons and that Moscow was actually a deeply cultured city. He found in the people of Moscow the same sort of warmth that he experienced back home in India. In turn, Inayat Khan made an immediate impression and soon had among his friends Sergei Tolstoy, the son of Leo Tolstoy, who became the representative of the musical section of the Sufi Order in Moscow.

It was in Moscow that Inayat Khan made one of the first attempts to combine eastern and western music. He chose seventeen ragas and adapted them to a play based on an episode from Kalidasa's *Shakuntala*. Sergei Tolstoy and a friend, Vladimir Pohl, harmonised the Indian melodies and even scored them for a small orchestra. The theme was the liberation of the soul.[4]

Moscow, with its blue-green oriental domes, luxury and sophistication combined with poverty, reminded Inayat Khan of India. He rode in an open sleigh and met many priests and monks.

The city was seething with rebellion at that time as the Tsar was perceived as weak and under the influence of his wife and courtiers. Communists and anarchists fanned the people's discontent. The secret police spied on people everywhere. Even Inayat Khan and his brothers were followed to their concert one day. Later the person shadowing them became embarrassed and introduced himself as Henry Balakin. He confessed that he had been sent to watch over them. When Inayat Khan reassured him and said he understood why he did it, Balakin became his *mureed* or disciple.

At this time the family lived in a four- or five-bedroom house called the House of Obidin on the corner of Petrovka Street and Krapivenski. It was just opposite the Vusoko Petrovsky monastery and about 1.5 kilometres from the Kremlin. A modestly furnished place, it provided enough room for Inayat, his young wife and his three brothers.

The couple's first daughter, Noor, was born in Moscow at 10.15 p.m. on 1 January 1914. Noor was very special to Inayat Khan, being his firstborn. Like his father and grandfather before him, Inayat Khan reached out to his new baby through music. He would sing to her and carry her around as he gently lulled her to sleep.

Baby Noor's nurse had some rather unusual habits, however. She was a strong Tartar woman who horrified Amina Begum by giving her daughter black coffee to drink and scrubbing her with a brush made of stiff bristles as a sort of massage. She also started binding Noor's feet to keep them small as was the Chinese-Tartar custom. It was the nurse who gave Noor the name of Babuli (Turco-Tartar for 'father's child').[5]

Apart from her idiosyncratic ways, which were alien to Amina Begum, the widowed nurse nevertheless was a considerable support to the household. She had a 16-year-old girl, who Musharraf fell in love with and wanted to marry, proposing that both mother and daughter become part of the family and travel with them. Amina Begum strongly opposed the match, causing some conflict in the Inayat Khan household.[6]

When Noor was forty days old, Inayat Khan invited some friends and admirers to his house to attend a ceremony for Noor. The invitees included a group of Russian students who had met Inayat Khan at Maxim's. One of the students, Yevgenia Yurievna Spasskaya, later described the event in rapt tones:

> At last a velvet portiere opened and entering from the next room . . . I don't know what others saw, but I imagined that I saw Nesterov's Blue Madonna: against the background of the dark-red velvet portiere she stood slim, fair, in a blue scarf wrapped around her slender body, a young mother with a tiny tawny baby in her hands.[7]

The sight of the fragile Amina Begum in her blue sari with her head covered and flowing golden hair standing next to the tall stately figure of Inayat Khan had completely captivated Spasskaya. During the ceremony Amina Begum sat in an armchair holding baby Noor while the other brothers and musicians came up to her one by one, bowed low, sang a greeting and gave her a gift. Then the tabla player, Ramaswami, who had met Inayat Khan in New York and joined the group, sang a joyful song that he had composed especially for mother and baby, which amused everybody. This was followed by more music as all the brothers sang and a feast of Indian sweets and food prepared by an Indian cook was served.

Baby Noor sat quietly in her mother's lap through all the singing and a proud Inayat Khan told the students that she was already a theosophist.

Though Inayat Khan may have met Tsar Nicholas II through his friend Sergei Tolstoy, it is not certain whether Inayat Khan ever met the Russian mystic Rasputin. It is possible that he met him at St Petersburg, because Inayat Khan is known to have been in the city from 13 May till the end of the month.[8]

Meanwhile the political atmosphere in Moscow was becoming highly charged and one of the Tsar's officers advised Inayat Khan to leave the city. Sergei Tolstoy loaned them a sledge and they prepared to leave. But on the day they decided to go, riots broke out and the people put up a barricade, barring their path. As the excited crowds gathered around their sledge, Inayat Khan took baby Noor from his wife's arms and held her up. So impressive was the sight of Inayat Khan in his golden yellow robes holding up the tiny baby that the crowd immediately fell silent and drew back the barricade.

The family made its way to St Petersburg and then to France. The Royal Musicians of Hindustan had an invitation to play at the International Music Congress in Paris in June. Ramaswami decided to return to India but the other musicians played at the Music

Congress and stayed in Paris for a while, giving concerts and lectures. But soon war broke out in Europe. In August 1914, with German cannons pointing at Paris, Inayat Khan decided to take the family to London. Here he would be based for the next six years as Europe was torn by the First World War.

London in the war years was a hard environment for the family. Having drawn capacity audiences in Moscow and Paris, Inayat Khan now faced half-empty halls for the first few months. Everyone was preoccupied with the war. Noor was to spend the first few years of her life in considerable poverty and hardship. Yet her father's spirit, his calmness and meditative outlook, clearly imbued her with strength.

In London, Inayat Khan sang for Mohandas Karamchand Gandhi and brought tears to his eyes. He sang for Indian soldiers who lay injured in hospital and at charity concerts to raise funds for war widows. In June 1915 the Royal Musicians of Hindustan played in the opera *Lakme* and got good reviews.[9]

But though Indians backed the war effort, the British government was suspicious of Inayat Khan and kept a close watch on him. Once at a charity concert for Indian widows and orphans, Inayat Khan was overcome by emotion and started to sing patriotic Indian songs reminding his countrymen of their glorious heritage. He received thunderous applause, which made the British even more wary. The invitations to charity concerts died out and the family was left with hardly any income.

Musharraf Khan, in desperation, started looking for menial jobs as a road worker and Maheboob Khan started giving private lessons. Mohammed Khan accepted music hall engagements singing European arias and ballads. Amina Begum found it hard to run the large household. Coming from an affluent family herself it was particularly difficult for her. She also discovered to her dismay the prejudice against mixed marriages in British society and got rid of her veil as she felt it aroused unnecessary attention. The family survived on a meagre ration of plain rice and daal every day. There were days when there was only bread on the table.

Inayat Khan remained calm through these trying times. He practised his veena and sang to Noor every day. The family at this time moved to 86 Ladbroke Road in London and it was at this address that Inayat founded the Sufi Order in England in the autumn of 1915. The movement's symbol was a winged heart inscribed with the star and crescent. Soon there was more reason to celebrate. On 19 June 1916, a son was born to Inayat Khan and Amina Begum. They named him Vilayat, meaning Chief. He was given the title of Pirzade (son of the Pir). Noor called him *bhaijaan* (brother dear).

Little Noor adored her baby brother. He soon became her closest friend, and would remain so throughout her life. Though poor, the children were brought up in an atmosphere of loving warmth. Their earliest memories were of their father carrying them in his arms and singing them to sleep. Sometimes when they could not sleep at nights, he would sit down by their bed and sing to them. Often the children lay awake just to hear his songs. Inayat Khan believed that children of this age were so sensitive that they could feel the warmth of his music as he sang to them. He himself had been taught by Maula Baksh about the effect of music on the body and its role in maintaining health through resonance and rhythm.[10] He would never allow the children to be woken abruptly and often sang softly to wake them up.

Meanwhile, the war had a deep impact on Inayat Khan and he was very disturbed by the constant death and devastation. He tried to help people by simply talking about death and focusing their minds on prayer and brotherhood to make their suffering more bearable. In the difficult years in London, Inayat Khan became a *murshid* (teacher) himself, travelling and lecturing. Chapters of the Sufi Order were set up in 1916 in Brighton and in Harrogate in 1917. Gradually the halls started filling up as people sought spiritual answers during the war years.

In 1917 the family moved into a large house in 1 Gordon Square financed by the Sufis. Over the years two more children were born to Inayat Khan and Amina Begum: Hidayat, a boy, and Khair-un-nisa, a girl. Inayat called his second daughter Mamuli (mother's child). To Noor, Vilayat was *bhaijaan*, Hidayat was *bhaiyajaan*, and Khair was Mamuli or Mams. Noor, little more than a toddler herself, mothered them all.

The family spent happier times in Gordon Square. Though money was still scarce, the house was buzzing with activity and the four children kept Amina Begum's hands full. Noor was a delicate child, dreamy and sensitive. When she heard that children in Russia had nothing to eat she took it to heart, although she was only four. She began demanding chocolates from the adults, and as soon as she got one she would leave the room. Later her parents found she had a big box full of chocolates in her room, which she was collecting for the Russian children.

Noor would play with Vilayat in the Square and believed that she had seen fairies there. She even told her family that she talked to the little creatures who lived in the flowers and bushes. They did not question her, but the children in the neighbourhood did. They laughed at Noor's tales of fairies and it upset her so much that she stopped seeing fairies after that. Even when Noor grew up she loved fairies and would often sketch them in cards and write about them in stories.

The children lived in a somewhat unreal world. The house was full of visiting Sufis and they were often left to themselves. One day a child came and told Noor and Vilayat that Santa Claus did not exist. This upset both children and they rushed to their father and asked him for the truth. Inayat told them: 'When something exists in the imagination of anybody, you can be sure there is a plane on which it has real existence.'[11] All of which probably meant nothing to the two children, but both felt they had been told something very profound and left feeling quite elated.

As the guns of war were silenced in Europe, the family settled in to life in London. But the Home Office was still suspicious of Inayat Khan. The fact that Inayat Khan had met Mahatma Gandhi and nationalist leaders like Sarojini Naidu made them keep him under supervision. Nationalism was growing in the overseas Indian community at this time as the Jallianwala Bagh massacre[12] in Amritsar had had a strong impact on all Indians. Inayat Khan's friend, the poet Rabindranath Tagore, had returned his knighthood in protest.

Some Muslim friends of Inayat Khan invited him to preside over the Anjuman Islam, a committee to bring Muslims and non-Muslims together. But a member of the society sent out letters to collect money for a charity for Muslim orphans without registering the society and the Anjuman Islam became the subject of a police investigation. It was eventually cleared of shady dealings but the ill-feelings remained. Inayat Khan's house and movements were watched.

A faithful *mureed* in Southampton, Miss Dowland, advised him to leave England. She sent him money to tide over the financial crisis. Another *mureed* in South Africa also sent them money to relocate and a third devotee offered them his empty summer house in Tremblaye, a village in France.

In the spring of 1920, the family of Inayat Khan prepared to move once again. Vilayat was only four at the time. All he remembered was the small boat and how everyone was seasick.[13] Noor was just six, clinging to her mother and her younger brothers and sister as the family crossed the Channel again. Inayat held his veena and looked out at the sea. The war in Europe was over. He wondered what the future would hold for his young family.

TWO

Fazal Manzil

Noor and her family soon settled into their house in the small village of Tremblaye, north of Paris. Vilayat remembered it as a damp place with no heating and no food. Tremblaye was hardly a place to give Indian concerts and soon the family were once again in dire financial straits.

Inayat Khan left his wife and children behind and travelled to Geneva where some Sufi disciples helped him with generous donations. By now Hazrat Inayat Khan was an established *murshid* and everywhere he went, his *mureeds* helped him set up centres. The family struggled through the winter alone but early in 1921 Inayat Khan returned to Tremblaye and took them to Wissous, another small town to the south of Paris. The family enjoyed better days in Wissous. The house belonged to a naval officer and stood on the edge of the village overlooking fields. Inayat would meditate in the garden early in the morning while the children played around him. Later, he would play the veena and sing. At Wissous, Hazrat Inayat Khan held a summer camp for his close followers. In the evening the *mureeds* would gather in the large living room. The brothers played their instruments and there was an atmosphere of tranquillity.

In the spring of 1922, one of Hazrat Inayat Khan's devoted *mureeds*, a rich Dutch widow named Madame Egeling, offered to buy a house for the family. One day, as Inayat Khan and his disciples were walking in the Bois de Boulogne in Paris, they decided to cross the river and climb the hill at Suresnes. Suddenly, a large house surrounded by trees caught Inayat Khan's attention. 'It must be here!' he exclaimed.[1] The house, luckily, was for sale. Situated a few miles from the centre of Paris, near the Longchamps racecourse, it was perfect for the family. From the upper windows one could see the lights of the city and the Eiffel Tower in the distance, and on a clear day there was a view of Sacré Coeur and the Seine winding down towards the Cathedral of Notre Dame.

Inayat Khan called the house Fazal Manzil (the House of Blessing), and as far as Noor was concerned it would live up to its name, because she spent many happy years there. The house was surrounded by a walled garden and trees, and Noor specially loved sitting with her brothers and sister on the flight of stairs outside the house and gazing at the city spreading out below. Like Inayat when he had been young, Vilayat and Hidayat were naturally playful and loved climbing the trees around the house. If the *mureeds* expressed surprise at how naughty the boys were, Inayat Khan would say, 'I was worse,' remembering how he used to run wild in the house in Baroda.[2]

The four children, their parents and their three uncles settled comfortably into the large house. In summer it would overflow with visitors as the Sufi summer school was held there for three months. Inayat Khan invited the elderly Madame Egeling to come and stay with them and she helped educate the children and looked after the house. She remained a faithful *mureed* till the end.

Hidayat remembered on one occasion going to Paris with his father to buy yellow curtains for the living room. Inayat Khan would often buy an antique object that reminded him of the East: a lamp or a Moroccan rug. It was difficult for him to forget India and he filled the house with things that reminded him of the land of his birth. Though their mother was American, the children grew up very much in an Indian atmosphere. Noor would dress her brothers and sisters in Indian clothes and the four children would often perform short plays. She particularly enjoyed wearing a sari and dressing her brothers up in bright turbans. The children loved playing on the grounds of Fazal Manzil and the green in front of the house. At home the children spoke to each other in English. Since Inayat Khan and his brothers spoke to each other in Hindi, the children could follow some Hindi and Urdu as well.

It was at Fazal Manzil that Inayat Khan started the practice of Universal Worship, a ceremony where all the religions of the world would be honoured. Inayat Khan always believed in the oneness of religions; as a child he had an equal fascination for both Hinduism and Islam and studied both. Now he formalised the belief. The service was held in the large living room of Fazal Manzil where candles and incense sticks would be lit. The children would sometimes listen to the service with fascination. The idea of tolerance of all religions would stay with Noor all her life and motivate her actions in the future.

On Saturday, Inayat Khan would sit on the roof of Fazal Manzil and meditate all day. He would go into a trance and two men would have to support him to help him down. As a child Noor would watch, captivated. 'Have you seen Abba's eyes?' she asked Vilayat one day.[3] Her brother noticed that she would have tears in her eyes when she saw her father in a trance.

Inayat Khan remained at heart a musician. He taught his children Indian music and often questioned them about the ragas. Noor always listened attentively and answered his questions. She also wrote down the words of the songs in both English and Urdu (she wrote the Urdu words in Roman script as she was not familiar with the Urdu script).

Inayat found it difficult to scold his children, so he had his own way of disciplining them if they were naughty. He would hold court on the steps and would never allow the children to denounce each other.[4] He would ask why they had been naughty and if they agreed that they had done wrong. He would then ask them if they thought they should be punished. The punishments involved running around the garden ten times or sitting in a corner, or not speaking for a few hours. Once a Dutch disciple related an amusing incident about the children. Some of them had been naughty and Inayat Khan called Noor to him and asked if she had been naughty too. She replied, 'I wanted to, but my goodness prevented me'.[5]

The family ate together at mealtimes but the children were expected to sit in silence. They felt the discipline was part of their father's love for them and did not mind. After finishing work Inayat Khan would call the children to him, and they looked forward to these precious moments with their father.

The children knew they had to share their father with the world. As Inayat Khan's lecture schedules and engagements became more pressing, he hardly spent any time in Fazal Manzil except in the summer months when he was surrounded by his *mureeds*. He was a majestic figure with his golden robes and flowing beard, probably looking much older than his forty-odd years. The children would lie on the grass and watch him walk to the lecture hall. Vilayat said they could feel his presence reaching out to them.[6]

Noor loved going to her father's lectures. She remembered one at the Musée Guimet in Paris which impressed her very much, even though she was very young at the time. After the event, she threaded her way through the crowds to hear what people were saying about the lecture and then breathlessly recounted all that she had heard to her amused father.[7] Her happiest moments were the ones she shared with him, listening to him talk or learning to sing from him. Then she would sit cross-legged in front of him, singing the notes after him as her father took her through the intricacies of Indian ragas.

When he was not around, the children missed him a lot, but learned to live with it. Vilayat often wished he had a father like the other children in the school, but would soon dismiss the thought. Noor, on her part, would lock herself away in her own world, playing fantasy games and writing poems.

When she was eight, Noor started school in the local Collège Moderne de Filles at Suresnes. School was not easy for Noor. The children did not know any French at this time (they spoke English at home). Now they had to take their lessons in French and converse with the other students. Hidayat remembers that it took a lot of courage to adapt to a French-speaking school.[8] Some of the French students were not used to foreigners and the children faced problems on that score as well. Slowly they learnt the language and gradually became fluent in it, but even so the Inayat Khan family was always fairly conspicuous in the Paris suburb of Suresnes.

Noor stood out from the other students because of her dark skin and hair. Slowly, she fought the isolation and made friends. She was always a quiet, dreamy child and soon endeared herself to the other girls. They even gave her a Good Comradeship award.[9] However, coming from the background that she did, it was inevitable that she would be different from the other girls in both looks and manner. Though she played and chatted with them, she was in some ways more grown up and serious than they were.

Later Noor's younger sister, Khair, joined the same school and faced the same problems. She changed her name from Khair-un-nisa to Claire and preferred to be called this all her life. She was the quietest of the four siblings and, as the youngest, the most protected, so she suffered a lot in school when she was on her own.[10] Noor, on the other hand, dealt with problems at school by living in her own world and creating a shell for herself.

Despite her own troubles settling into school, Noor gradually made some good friends there. Her best friend at school was Raymonde Prénat, who remained close to Noor all her life. Raymonde was the second of three sisters, with a French father and a Spanish mother. Her family were neighbours of the Inayat Khans, and she and Noor spent a lot of time at each other's houses. Madame Prénat developed a great deal of admiration for Noor, perceiving that she had enormous courage and determination despite her youth. On their birthdays the girls would give each other cakes decorated with candles. Their birthdays were just six weeks apart and this made them closer still. Noor would always make a birthday card for Raymonde as well, and often wrote a little verse specially for her.

As a child, Noor wrote poems and stories and made up little pieces of music which she would play on the piano to the amusement of her family. She had a high-pitched voice, which would become even higher when she was excited. Noor had learnt to read music from her father and started writing down Indian Sufi songs with western-style notation.

She had always been creative. For their birthdays, her friends and family would get a card hand-painted by her with a little poem inside. She would write in both French and English (in French to friends like Raymonde and in English to her parents and siblings). At the age of eleven she wrote a poem in French called 'La Violette', which shows that at a young age she was already developing a certain style. The poem begins:

Modeste et honnête
Jolie petite violette
Qui jette son beau parfum
Dans mon petit jardin

(Modest and honest
Pretty little violet
Who casts her lovely perfume
In my small garden)

Noor was a happy child, always smiling and ready to help others. Even at an early age, she always thought about those less privileged than her. In a Christmas poem written to Santa Claus, she wrote:

Come bring bright shiny sunbeams
To rejoice our happy home
Give each child their sweetest dreams
Then amidst sweet fairies roam
Then go to the poor shanty
To gladden each weary heart
Where everyone is hungry
Put on the table a tart.

When she was twelve, Noor fell in love for the first time. The object of her affections was Floris van Baron van Pallandt, the seventeen-year-old son of Dutch Sufi disciples who lived in Suresnes. The boy's family were very close to Inayat Khan, and Noor's father soon noticed that she would rush down the stairs to open the door whenever they came calling.[11] Then the two youngsters would stand in the hall and talk. Floris was equally attracted to Noor but the relationship was not to last. The Inayat Khan family was a very conservative one and disapproved of Noor running down to open the door for guests. This job should properly be done by the staff in the house, and Inayat Khan reminded Noor about these formalities. Floris overheard him scolding Noor and took it to mean that Inayat Khan disapproved of the relationship. Following this misunderstanding, Floris withdrew his affections and the romance was soon over.

After the break-up with Floris, Inayat Khan started planning a match for Noor. Arranged marriages were the norm in Indian families. Inayat Khan wanted Noor to marry Alladutt Khan, the son of Ali Khan and grandson of Maula Baksh, who lived in Baroda.[12] Though a cousin of Inayat Khan's, Alladutt was much younger than him. Inayat Khan now encouraged Noor to write letters to his family. It would be improper for her to write directly to Alladutt, so she wrote to his parents. Slowly Noor began to accept the idea of marrying Alladutt when she came of age. The match was important for Inayat Khan in more than one way. Alladutt Khan, being the sole male heir of Maula Baksh, was very wealthy. His finances would have helped the Sufi movement and made Inayat Khan less dependent on his western *mureeds*. Also, it would give him the satisfaction of bringing all his brothers and cousins to the West, since Alladutt was the only one still residing in India.

Meanwhile Inayat Khan was still heavily involved in building the Sufi movement. While the children settled down to life in Paris, he travelled widely, establishing groups of disciples in England, Germany, Switzerland, Belgium, Holland, Scandinavia and the United States. In 1925 Inayat Khan fell seriously ill on a trip to England. Though he was only forty-three, the strenuous travelling was taking its toll on him. After a trip to the USA in 1926, he felt that Sufi centres had been established successfully all over the West from Britain to the US and in many countries in Western Europe. Though he was detached from most things, Inayat Khan's only worldly attachment was to the land of his birth. He had always missed India and now he decided to go back to the country he had left over a decade previously, even if it meant leaving behind his wife and children whom he loved deeply.

Noor was just twelve when Inayat Khan began his preparations to go to India. There was an air of finality in the preparations and somehow everyone knew he would not come back. Vilayat recalled later how he had a dream that he had to take his father to the train, but he lost him. He screamed in his sleep and woke up, and Inayat Khan rushed in to console him. 'It's all right,' Inayat told his son.[13] Vilayat begged him not to go. An astrologer had told Inayat Khan that the end of January 1927 would be a very dangerous period. Vilayat again pleaded with him to postpone his journey for a year. Inayat Khan took his son for a quiet walk in the garden, and told Vilayat that he would like him to follow in his footsteps.

That summer Fazal Manzil seemed to be shrouded in an atmosphere of gloom and foreboding. Noor watched as her father paced up and down in the garden alone. Noor too had a dream at this time. She dreamt that their baker was flying away in an aeroplane. She tried to call him back but he didn't return. The next day she related the dream to her father and he looked at her and said, 'Yes Babuli, the bringer of bread will not return.'[14]

On 13 September 1926 a small ceremony was held in the garden of Fazal Manzil. The foundation stone of a temple to be called L'Universelle was laid, and manuscripts and coins from all the countries with Sufi centres were buried beneath it. Inayat Khan then put a ribbon around the neck of ten-year-old Vilayat (dressed in a sailor suit) and asked him to lead a procession of his disciples. The significance of the ceremony was not lost on anyone. Vilayat was designated as the head of the Confraternity of the Message. Inayat laid the foundation stone and walked slowly down the long path back to the house, lifting his hand as if in blessing and in farewell.

The next morning Inayat said goodbye to his family and left Fazal Manzil. Amina Begum and the children were heartbroken but they felt they had to let him go. Inayat went to India, travelling to Varanasi, Agra and Jaipur. He then went to Delhi and visited the mosque of the Sufi saint, Hazrat Nizamuddin Aulia. The Pir of the mosque, Khwaja Hassan Nizami, showed him around the area. He took him to a watchtower on the roof of his own house. From there Inayat Khan looked out at the village of Nizamuddin in the heart of Delhi and saw the small alleys and crowded lanes where Hindus and Muslims had lived peacefully for 600 years. Close by were the gardens and domes of Delhi's elegant Mughal monuments. It filled him with peace and he told Hassan Nizami, 'Here I would like to stay.'[15]

Inayat had to make a final pilgrimage. He returned to Baroda to the house of his grandfather, Maula Baksh. But his uncle Pathan was away and he was saddened to see the ruined state of his childhood home. He fell ill on his return to Delhi and on the night of 4 February 1927 lost consciousness. On the morning of 5 February Hazrat Inayat Khan died. He was buried the same day in a plot of land opposite the watchtower from where he had looked out over Nizamuddin village.

Back in Suresnes the same day, Hidayat heard his father's voice calling out, 'Babuli, look after the little ones.'[16] The next day they got the news of their father's death.

Amina Begum collapsed in grief. The burden of looking after the family now fell on Noor's tender shoulders. She was just thirteen.

Three months later, the family went to India to visit Inayat Khan's tomb. It was Noor's first trip to the land of her father's ancestors and it had a profound effect on her. For the first time she saw the colours of India, the early morning mist over the Ganges and felt the warmth and affection of the people. They went to the Dargah of Moinuddin Chisti in Ajmer, one of the holiest Sufi sites, and then to the house of Maula Baksh in Baroda.

The state of neglect of the ancestral home affected them as it had Inayat Khan. Noor was moved to see the affection shown to her by the children of the retainers who had smuggled Tipu Sultan's granddaughter Casimebi. One of the sons of the retainers, Shabaz

Khan, was in charge of Maula Baksh's vast library and showed Noor around. Another old lady told her she reminded her of Inayat Khan. For Noor, the trip to India reconfirmed her roots and her royal ancestry. In Baroda she also met Alladutt Khan, who Inayat Khan had hoped she would marry. The two youngsters took an immediate liking to each other and spent a lot of time together listening to music and old records.[17]

Inayat's uncle Pathan, who was now established at the court of the King of Nepal, suggested that the children stay behind with him and continue their education in a good school in Kathmandu. But Amina Begum objected, not wanting to relocate the family, and after a brief fall-out the family decided to return to France. They left India in June 1927. Noor was only thirteen and heartbroken for the second time as her planned marriage to Alladutt was called off.

It was a difficult time for Noor. In the space of a few months, her life seemed to have changed completely. Her mother was still frail and unable to look after the affairs of the house. Amina Begum retired to the upper floor of Fazal Manzil, darkened the room, and remained in mourning – seldom seeing anybody apart from her immediate family. Sometimes Noor would take her friend Raymonde up to see her mother. The day-to-day running of the house fell entirely to Noor. If her brothers or sisters fell ill, she would nurse them and give them their medicine. She would order the provisions for the large house and supervise the housework. Visitors were touched by her dedication to her family.[18]

In October that year, Noor transferred to secondary school at the Lycée de Jeunes Filles in St Cloud. Her favourite subjects at the time were literature, French and English. She also studied German and Spanish and enjoyed sports.[19]

Noor now had to balance her life between her household chores, looking after the family and coursework. Madame Egeling started taking the service at Fazal Manzil every day and the uncles presided over the summer school. But the children could not help noticing that the apricot tree under which Inayat Khan used to sit had died. They believed this was an omen, but they kept their pain to themselves because they did not want to upset their mother. Fazal Manzil was still a busy and open house and Noor, now a teenager, found solace in her room. Here she buried herself in books and wrote several poems and stories. The death of her father had a profound influence on Noor and she entered a new phase in her life. On one hand was the despondency brought on by the death of her father. On the other hand she wanted to cheer up her mother and draw her out into the world again. One way in which she tried to do this was through her poems, which demonstrate a selflessness rare in a teenager. In 1929, two years after Inayat Khan's death, the fifteen-year-old Noor wrote this poem for her mother:

TO OUR AMMA

Beloved! Ah! Beloved Amma,
A treasure stored deep in our heart,
'Tis flowers of our gratitude,
A treasure that n'er will depart.

Behold! For their petals are carved
With Allah's own heavenly art,
Their beauty on this longed for day,
To you and Abba we impart

Through life's struggle and through life's strife,
May we treasure as our life's gem
The seed in our heart, you have sown,
Ah! quote in the sacred Nirtan,
And always remember this:
The path of the heart is thorny,
Which leads in the end to bliss.

Noor would never forget to include her father, Abba, in her poems to her mother at this stage. In 1930, she wrote:

Lo! His thought so deep
In sparks are manifest,
To console your heart,
Throughout life's painful test.

Noor wrote the poems on behalf of all the four children, trying to cheer up her mother and letting her know that their father was always with them. Amina Begum would often feel that she had somehow been abandoned by Inayat Khan. She had given up a wealthy lifestyle and cut off all links with her family to come and live with him, but Inayat had left her and the children and returned to India.

Amina Begum's self-imposed isolation made life harder for the children. Though she took an interest in her children's education, Amina could not be persuaded to leave the house. Noor and her brothers were particularly upset that their mother would not even attend prize-giving day at the school. In the end Maheboob Khan's mother-in-law, Madame van Goens, who lived in Suresnes, felt sorry for the children and went with them to this important event.[20]

Noor, however, felt no bitterness towards her mother. She simply accepted the fact that she had to take care of the children and manage the house. In 1931, at the age of sixteen, she wrote:

> This poem Abba has written,
> To console your heart,
> His thoughts through his dear children,
> To you he doth impart.

Each card was beautifully illustrated by her and has been carefully preserved by the family. Always the dreamy child, Noor wrote stories and poems about fairies and flowers and little creatures in the woods. An avid reader, she had access to the vast library of Inayat Khan and read books on subjects ranging from philosophy and religion to adventure and gallantry. Her favourite heroine was Joan of Arc and she loved stories of chivalry and sacrifice.[21]

At seventeen, Noor got her Baccalauréat certificate from the Lycée de Jeunes Filles. Throughout secondary school she had been rather lonely and had made few new friends.

Music always had a special place in the Inayat Khan household. Noor had learnt the basic Indian ragas from her father. She had taken piano lessons and composed her own pieces while at school. Now she decided to learn the harp. It seems she was attracted to this instrument because she had seen medieval paintings of angels playing the harp and it appealed to her feminine side.[22]

Noor's inherited love for music took her to the Ecole Normale de Musique de Paris in April 1931 where her teachers included the famous Nadia Boulanger. For six years Noor studied the harp, piano, solfeggio, harmonic analysis and harmony. At the same time she took private harp lessons from Henriette Rénie for two years and even played in a matinee performance at the Salle Erard during her second year, which was very well received.

All four of Inayat's children played at least one or two instruments. Noor played the harp and piano, Vilayat the cello and piano, Hidayat the violin and piano and Claire the piano. Vilayat learnt under Stravinsky and Maurice Eisenberg, and Claire and Noor under Boulanger. Hidayat would become a composer basing his work on Indian ragas written for western orchestras. His moving composition for Noor after her death, 'La Monotonia', has been played in Paris, Munich, Amsterdam and other European cities bringing tears to the eyes of concert-goers. He also did the orchestration for one of Noor's poems, 'Song For the Madzub'.

Not content with just studying music, Noor registered at the Sorbonne, University of Paris, in 1932 to study child psychology. She was always interested in children and thought the course would help her to understand them better.

Her family and home life was in many ways conservative and traditional. After the death of Inayat Khan (who had always been very liberal), the uncles were in charge of the house. They concentrated more on Vilayat and Hidayat, the men in the family. It was widely thought that Noor and Claire would marry rich Indian men and live the life of high-society Indians. Both girls were encouraged to develop their musical abilities rather than their intellectual or academic ones. The emphasis was on preparing them for their future place in society and it was not even considered that they would have to go out and fend for themselves in the world. Praise and encouragement went to the boys and the girls were not taken seriously.[23]

The male-dominated Indian atmosphere of the house probably prompted an overwhelming determination in Noor to do more than her share for a cause she believed in.[24] By her twenties she was already forging a stronger identity for herself within her circle of friends and activities in Paris, going to university and studying music.

It was while studying at the Ecole Normale de Musique that Noor fell in love again. This relationship was to last for six years.

His name was Goldberg[25] and he was a fellow music student, and although the family did not approve they became engaged. Goldberg was a Turkish Jew who lived with his mother in Paris. The family came from a working-class background and his mother worked in a laundry. Goldberg struggled to pay his fees at the exclusive École Normal de Musique.[26] The family felt Noor's attachment to him stemmed initially from sympathy because of his deprived background. But the relationship lasted for years, despite the disapproval of the family and the Sufi fraternity. Between the Inayat Khans and the Goldbergs was a class divide. The Khans were of royal descent, even though they did not live an extravagant life. They were surrounded by western Sufi disciples, who were inevitably theosophists from the wealthy, leisured class. Goldberg was a rank outsider in this circle. Noor's mother, Amina Begum, objected to her relationship with him, as did her brothers and uncles.

Goldberg visited Fazal Manzil regularly and was even initiated into the Sufi fold and given the name of Huzoor Nawaz. It was then that the larger Sufi fraternity learnt about his relationship with Noor and expressed their disapproval. To them Pirzadi Noor could not marry beneath her class.

The brothers had other reasons for objecting to the relationship. According to Vilayat, Noor's fiancé was too overbearing and that distressed Noor.[27] Goldberg would threaten to commit suicide if she left him and Noor never dared to test this threat. She believed he might actually try to end his life and that she could never forgive herself if he did so. Noor's family felt that her relationship with Goldberg was putting too much pressure on her, while she felt they did not have any understanding of her situation.

It was true that Noor was under great strain, trying to balance her love for her family and love for her fiancé. For six years she struggled with her emotions, sometimes falling quite ill with the stress of it all.

Noor felt that her family underestimated her fiancé and never appreciated the fact that he was a fine pianist. She confided in her friend Raymonde's mother, Madame Prénat, and told her: 'He is a man in a thousand.'[28] Strangely, Noor never told Raymonde, her closest friend, about her fiancé. Noor felt Raymonde was too young and innocent to understand the complexity of her relationship.

Noor's emotional ups and downs are reflected in her poems from this time. In this one, to her mother, she apologises for her faults and the pain they may have caused.

> How oft throughout life's puzzling path,
> Our feet have gone astray,
> Ah! Dear Amma you will forgive,
> Our endless faults this day.

Two other poems of the period, 'The Song of the Ocean' and 'The Song of the Night', are also very melancholy in tone. In the latter poem Noor wrote 'Who has heard my painful cry, who has heard my sigh. . .' reflecting all the emotions she was going through.

Musically, Noor was making good progress. She was particularly influenced by the guidance she received from Nadia Boulanger. Between 1930 and 1934, all four of the Inayat Khan children played in concerts at Fazal Manzil when the summer school was on. The audience consisted of visiting Sufis from all over the world, many of whom were also trained musicians. The instruments used by the Inayat Khan family quartet were the violin, cello, piano and harp.

The four siblings would often go to concerts at the Music School and the large Paris concert halls. The students received free tickets to these concerts and were encouraged to attend them. After the performance they would go and talk to the musicians and Noor, Vilayat, Hidayat and Claire had the privilege of personally meeting the great violinist Joseph Zigetti and the members of the Lener Quartet, besides others who had a great influence on them. The four Inayat Khan youngsters enjoyed these outings, and would often return late at night from the concerts animatedly discussing the merits of the performance. The four were totally immersed in their music studies and Sufi background and had few friends outside the family circle. It is not surprising that they were rather insular and other-worldly.

One of Noor's early compositions during her École Normale days was 'Song to the Butterfly'. Piano music for the piece was given by a Sufi disciple of Inayat Khan. She also composed 'Prelude for Harp' and 'Elegy for Harp and Piano' which were played at concerts in Fazal Manzil during the summer school to a very good reception.

When she was in her twenties, Noor took to a more European style of dressing and started using light make-up. She presented an image of a beautiful young lady, elegantly dressed, well mannered and gentle. Vilayat wore a black robe while in Fazal Manzil but in Paris he changed into normal western clothes. Claire, the quiet sister, had always preferred western clothes. The influence of the uncles in Fazal Manzil was now diminishing. Only one of them, Mohammed Khan, still lived there. Maheboob Khan had married the daughter of a leading Dutch family, the van Goens. Musharraf Khan too married a Dutch lady. The Sufi branch grew strong in Holland. The uncles disapproved of Noor going alone to attend classes and returning home late from concerts. But Noor, though always respectful of her elders, was determined to carry on and do exactly what she wanted to do.

Along with her music, Noor's interest in creative writing continued. She always loved children and would invite the children of the neighbourhood to Fazal Manzil and tell them fantastic stories from the Indian epics the Ramayana, the Mahabharata and the Jataka. To the children she was an exotic creature – gentle and lovely – with magical stories to tell of adventures in faraway lands.

She continued to write poetry and never forgot to write her family a poem on their birthdays. For Vilayat, when he turned twenty-one, she wrote:

May every wish of yours come true
And every day be clear and blue
O! My brother dear, a man this day,
May joy come all along your way

On Amina Begum's birthday, Noor would always try to bring a smile to her mother's face. Her poem 'The Birthday Man' was typical of Noor's childlike exuberance:

I saw the little birthday man,
Skipping 'long the way,
I stopped awhile and listened,
To hear what he would say.

He put his little finger
Upon his little head.
He blew the dandelions, and
Danced around and said:

'Why, this is my best birthday,
For on this very day,
The storks brought down a girly
Whose name is Ora Ray.

'I must put on my sweetest
And wear my golden crown.
I'll take my happy knapsack,
And wear my grand new gown.

'She has had cloudy hours
And many cloudy years,
And many hard adventures,
And many many tears.

'Life has been very naughty
But I shall fight the wrong,
And make her whole life happy,
Just with my little song.'

The bond between mother and daughter grew over the years. Amina Begum herself penned some poems for Noor in which she said: 'Thro' all the stress and storms of life, She moves in quiet dignity . . . She has a gift that few possess, the gift of love's sublimity.'

Once when Noor was in her early twenties, two of her father's disciples, Baron and Baroness van Tuyll, invited her to spend some time with them at the Hague. Noor was reluctant to leave her mother alone but was eventually persuaded. The holiday (her first) was a fresh change for her. She toured the city's art museums, read in the extensive library and even learnt to ride. The van Tuylls had their own stables and they found that Noor had no physical fear. She was not afraid of falling off her horse and simply carried on even if she did.

While she was at the Hague, she was told to give some piano lessons to her younger cousin Mahmood, son of her uncle Maheboob Khan. Mahmood (then nine years old) remembered Noor as a 'very pretty, delicate young lady'.[29] Noor started teaching him the piano with a difficult Mozart piece. Since Mahmood was quite overwhelmed by the piece, she helped him along telling him stories about rabbits and hares and fairies and making sketches for him. He began to love her visits, which to him meant entering an imaginary world. He remembered with amusement that the next summer Claire, or Mamuli as they called her, came visiting and was supposed to give him lessons. But Claire was silent and withdrawn and suddenly there were no dancing rabbits for him. To the young Mahmood, Noor was a fairy-tale character, delicate and charming, with a determination and strength of character that he could sense even then.

Back home from the Hague, Noor had to take charge of Fazal Manzil again, a task that was never easy. Madame Egeling gave Noor 3,000 francs a month on which she had to run the household. It was not a large sum, as Madame Egeling, though very wealthy, was not one to indulge in luxuries. Every job – from making the beds to calling the plumber – was Noor's responsibility. Claire began to help her with the washing and darning, following her about devotedly. Noor was apparently quite dreadful at sewing and Claire happily took on these tasks.

Adding to the pressures of domestic life at Fazal Manzil was Noor's troubled relationship with her fiancé and she was often quite weepy at this stage.[30] At one time Vilayat felt she was heading for a breakdown, but she pulled through. After years of mourning, her mother, however, was finally beginning to take some interest in worldly things. Her health improved and she even started going for little walks dressed in European clothes. It was a huge relief to the children.

Thinking an outing would be good for her, Vilayat encouraged the family in the summer of 1933 to go to the south of France where the weather was warmer. 'We explored the Massif Central, the Alps and the Cote d'Azur from Monte Carlo to Marseilles – Royan – Rochefort, Deauville, Trouville, le Havre, Dieppe. All these travels in a sports car,' wrote Noor.[31]

With Vilayat she travelled further to Spain. In 1934 they went to Barcelona and visited Pablo Casals in San Salvador. Noor was always closest to Vilayat and the two of them loved doing things together. The next year they went to Italy and toured Padua, Venice and Milan, attended operas and concerts, and Noor sent ecstatic letters home.

In one of her letters she wrote about the operas she had seen – *Aida*, *Rigoletto*, *Trovatore* and Puccini's *La Bohème*. She wrote how in the middle of a performance of *Rigoletto*, someone recognised the Duce (Mussolini) and cried out 'Il Duce!' This led to pandemonium in the auditorium and on stage, with the actors swooning with emotion and the musicians almost dropping their instruments. Absolute silence fell, then a profound sigh of joy rose from the crowd and the opera was resumed. Noor and her brother were witnessing the early years of Fascism, but at this time Noor was clearly not politically conscious. The Duce, to her, was just a popular leader.

In the summer of 1937, when Noor was going through a particularly difficult period with her fiancé, Vilayat took her to Switzerland in the hope that a holiday would take her mind off her problems. In Switzerland, as with all parts of Europe, there were Sufi families they could stay with. They travelled to Geneva and Zurich, toured the Swiss lakes and mountains, went climbing and skiing and thoroughly enjoyed themselves. Vilayat was pleased to see Noor having such an enjoyable holiday, and later recalled that it was probably the happiest time they had ever spent together.[32] Brother and sister rented bicycles to explore the countryside. They would pause, lie on a mountainside, watch the clouds go by and talk about the future. Vilayat told Noor that he hoped she would finally break off her engagement and put the past behind her. He felt the relationship was draining her. Noor had come close to a breakdown – she was often tearful and could not cope with any stress or criticism. Vilayat tried to get his sister to take life a little easier, and warned her not to carry the burdens of the world on her shoulders. He felt this was sapping her of her vitality and creativity.

In Switzerland, Noor went rowing on the lake in Geneva. It brought back memories of her father. She understood how the peace and quiet of the lake must have inspired him to start a Sufi centre there. She met many of her father's disciples and thought of his work and teachings a great deal. She even sang some of his songs to the children of other *mureeds* and was delighted to see how much it calmed them and put them to sleep. In the tranquil lakes and mountains of Switzerland she felt close to her father. She remembered how he would put her on his knees and say: 'When Abba's love is there, what fear is there?'[33] She felt these words were like a consolation to her from him. Many years later, when she was incarcerated in a German cell, her father's words would console her again.

The Swiss trip certainly helped cheer Noor up. Back home in Paris, she felt energised once again and now decided to take on another venture. She felt she was forgetting her Hindi and decided to relearn it. Vilayat and Noor began taking lessons at the Berlitz school and Noor also joined the Ecole des Langues Orientales of thc University of Paris, where she studied Hindi for two years. In the summer of 1938 she sat her exams at the university and got her *licence* (degree) in child psychology.

With university behind her, Noor had to decide what to do next. The decision was not as straightforward for her as it might have been for the typical student. The Inayat Khan family had not been brought up in the expectation that they would take up traditional jobs. So despite her qualifications, Noor did not apply for a teaching post or try to become a professional musician. She was still engaged to Goldberg, despite Vilayat's attempts to get her to break off her relationship with him. Noor had a stubborn streak, in that she would only do what she wanted to do, and she still hoped that her family would come round to accepting her fiancé.

To visitors who flooded through the gates of Fazal Manzil for the summer school, Noor gave the impression of being a shy, reclusive girl. She never spoke at the meetings which were often chaired by Vilayat and sometimes went for walks by herself in the evenings. Often she could be heard playing the harp by herself.

The family friend Baroness van Tuyll, who had invited her for her first holiday, now made her a proposal. Baroness van Tuyll was an illustrator of children's books and worked under the professional name of Henriette Willebeek le Mair. She suggested to Noor that she work on an English translation of the Jataka Tales, a collection of about 500 stories and fables about the previous incarnations of the Buddha, which had always fascinated Noor as a child. Noor got to work immediately and chose twenty stories from the book.

She began waking up at six in the morning and writing continuously till around nine. Producing the book gave her a new purpose in life and she immersed herself in the stories of bravery, loyalty and sacrifice that she was translating. Afterwards she would come downstairs and tackle the mundane household tasks with renewed energy. Once she had submitted the manuscript she went for a holiday to the van Tuylls again and spent the winter with them.

She studied the Koran and the Bible. She also continued her Hindi lessons and wanted to learn the Devanagari script saying it would help her in learning Sanskrit. The baroness taught her to play the veena, the instrument that Inayat Khan had played, and Noor spent a few happy months practising it.[34]

Noor was becoming established as a writer. In 1938 she wrote for the children's page of the *Sunday Figaro* and soon became one of their regular contributors. Her stories – usually about magical creatures and nature – were greatly appreciated by the paper. Noor had an endearing style that immediately drew in young readers.

'Amongst the nymphs who lived on a high mountain slope was a little one who talked and talked and jabbered and chattered, even more than the crickets in the grass, and more than the sparrows in the trees. Her name was Echo,' wrote Noor in her short story 'Echo'. In another short story called 'Perce-neige' (Snowdrop) her protagonist was the daughter of 'Great Sun', a pretty little thing with 'sun-ray hair and sky blue eyes' who came down to earth to explore the big world. In both the stories, the bubbly characters spread joy all around, but were later called upon to make a sacrifice – a theme that seemed to run through many of Noor's works.

Noor wrote prolifically, filling page after page with stories. She would always write in both English and French and often sketch as she went along. She wrote alone in her room, late into the night, and it seems that the fantasy world of her stories took her away from the troubles of Fazal Manzil and her unhappy engagement.

Noor's stories and poems started taking on a happier tone, perhaps reflecting her pleasure in her newfound success as a writer. On the home front things began to improve as Amina Begum emerged from her phase of depression and the family began to settle down into a more regular routine.

In 1938, the poem Noor wrote for her mother's birthday reflected her own sunny mood at the time. The poems also show her own childlike innocence, even though she was twenty-four by this stage.

A little fairy told me why the flowers wake in May
She said: 'It's for the birthday of a little Ora Ray
The sun, they say, is jealous of her lovely golden hair
The flowers look their sweetest just to try and be as fair.'

By the middle of 1939, Noor was at last beginning to realise that her relationship with Goldberg was going nowhere. A wealthy Dutch Sufi aristocrat, Peter Yohannes Eekhout Jonheer, had been showing an interest in Noor for some time. But Noor had rejected his advances because of her relationship with Goldberg. Peter Yohannes then entered the diplomatic service and left for India where he was based in Calcutta. Persuaded by Vilayat, Noor now decided to give the relationship with Peter Yohannes a chance. But they had no money to pay the fare to India.

Noor and Vilayat paid a visit to Mahmood's grandmother, who was related to Peter Yohannes, and told her they would like to visit Calcutta. Madam van Goens was delighted at the prospect of them going to India and meeting her nephew, but did not realise that the brother and sister had actually come to suggest that she finance the trip as well. Vilayat and Noor were too shy to ask for money outright, so the matter was dropped, along with the chance of Noor accepting the proposal of Peter Yohannes, which may have changed the course of her life.[35]

Noor's career as a children's writer was flourishing by now. Her beautifully illustrated story 'Ce qu'on entend quelquefois dans les bois . . .' (What One Hears Sometimes in the Woods) received pride of place on the children's page of *Le Figaro* on 13 August 1939. Noor's stories were also broadcast on the Children's Hour of Radio Paris, and received good reviews.

She wrote articles based on Indian and Greek legends, and articles about women singers like the Indian poet and singer Mira Bai and Emma Nevada and her daughter Mignon Nevada. Both the articles on Mira Bai and Emma Nevada were inspirational stories about devotion, love and sacrifice, themes close to Noor's heart. She began adapting French and Nordic folklore and wrote stories about Emperor Akbar and Charlemagne, adding history, myth and legend to her repertoire.

Just as Noor was establishing herself as a writer, the threat of war was hanging over Europe. On 15 March 1939 Germany invaded Czechoslovakia. By May, Germany and Italy had announced their formal alliance and German designs over Western Europe were becoming uncomfortably clear. Noor's book *Twenty Jataka Tales*, with illustrations by Henriette Willebeek le Mair, was published in England by George G. Harrap in 1939. Noor's reaction to the publication of her first book was unexpectedly understated.[36] She was probably thinking about her father at the time. Ever since his death, no parties or joyful celebrations had been held at the family home.

At the same time, Noor was enthused by her first publishing success. She came up with the idea of publishing a children's newspaper, and worked on it with the famous journalist Alexis Danan of *Paris Soir*. She wanted to call it *Bel Age* (The Beautiful Age), and had collected some material for it including illustrations by her neighbour Madame Pinchon. Danan was fascinated by the dazzling engravings of trees and fairies and the accompanying text, which he described as a 'genius of narration'. Noor's story was an oriental legend for children with fairies and creatures of the forest.[37]

But events in Europe were soon to overtake the budding writer. On 1 September 1939 Germany invaded Poland and on 3 September, Great Britain, France, New Zealand and Australia declared war on Germany (France did so rather reluctantly, being more or less dragged into it by Britain). The reaction at Fazal Manzil was one of complete panic. Noor was so involved with her writing and her brothers and sister so immersed in their studies and music school that they had not really been following the events in Europe. They never listened to the news on the radio and the political developments had passed them by. The thought of another war in Europe now filled them with gloom and anxiety.

The first few months of the war saw little change in Paris, hence it was dubbed the 'phoney war' or the *Sitzkrieg* (the sitting war) as opposed to the *Blitzkrieg* (the lightning war). Alexis Danan told Noor it would be impossible to go ahead with the children's newspaper at this time. It was unlikely that there would be any interest in such a thing in the middle of the war. He was also concerned that the project she had in mind was so beautiful that it would be very expensive to produce and hence quite unaffordable by youngsters. All plans for *Bel Age* were stalled. Noor's radio and newspaper work also suffered because of the war as there was less space for children's stories.

To Noor, the ideology of the Nazis and their pogrom against the Jews was fundamentally repulsive and opposed to all the principles of religious harmony that she had been brought up with by her father. She was Muslim by birth but she had loved a Jewish man, and Noor felt the urge to do something to help the war effort. Her first thought was nursing, and she and Claire signed up for a training course in Nursing and First Aid with the Union des Femmes de France (the French Red Cross). Here the sisters learnt the basics of nursing and first aid so as to be able to help when the time came. When the war began, Noor and Claire remained at work till the hospital was evacuated and they were cut off from the unit.

At this time, Noor also made a significant decision about her personal life. After years of emotional conflict, she finally broke off her engagement with Goldberg. She told Madame Prénat, her closest confidante, that she did so because she wanted to be free to go into action or serve as a nurse on the front line if the need arose.[38]

On the afternoon of 4 June 1940, as the German guns pointed towards France, Noor and Vilayat sat down on a sofa near the big window in the living room of Fazal Manzil. Outside they could see Paris stretching out below them. They had to take an important decision.

They had been brought up as Sufis, with the principle of non-violence firmly entrenched in them. Inayat Khan had taught them about Gandhi and his methods of peaceful protest in the freedom struggle. Many of the *mureeds* thought their first responsibility lay towards the movement. But brother and sister were confused. On the one hand they knew that war meant death and destruction, on the other they had seen the Germans' activities at first hand.

'If an armed Nazi comes to your house and takes twenty hostages and wants to exterminate them, would you not be an accomplice in these deaths, if you had the opportunity to kill him (and thereby prevent these deaths) but did not do so because of your belief in non-violence?' Vilayat asked Noor. 'How can we preach spiritual morality without participating in preventive action? Can we stand by and just watch what the Nazis are doing?[39]

They knew that they could not stand by, and so they decided to act to 'thwart the aggression of the tyrant'.[40] Noor and Vilayat decided they would go to England and join the war effort. Vilayat would join the services and Noor would volunteer to help in whatever way she could, nursing or services. They went up to tell the rest of the family of their plans, feeling immensely relieved that they had come to a decision at last.

Hidayat was the only one who was married and he said he would take his wife and children to the south of France where he would help the Resistance. The uncles would also stay behind. Noor and Vilayat would take Claire and their mother with them to England. Hidayat would drive them as far as Tours. They decided they would have to leave at once since the roads would be thronging with other people getting out of the city.

Noor ran to her friends and neighbours around Fazal Manzil and said goodbye. She asked them to look after the house and remove and keep anything of value that they found there. On 5 June 1940 they packed a few essentials, took one last look at the house that had been their home for nearly twenty years and began their long journey. The family of Inayat Khan was on the move again. Noor hugged her mother and held on to her. She was fighting back her own tears.

THREE

Flight and Fight

As Noor and her family left Paris on 5 June they found that masses of other people were also fleeing the advancing Germans. The streets were thronged with people, all on the move – with whatever possessions they could take with them and on any form of transport they could get. Cars, vans, trucks, cycles, push carts crawled slowly down the road as entire families scrambled to get out of Paris. The crying children, the anxious parents, the terrified expressions on the faces of the elderly told their own story. Noor held on to her mother. Vilayat drove in tense silence.

More than two-thirds of the whole population of Paris went on the road to escape the city before the Germans arrived. The city's population of three million had dwindled to 800,000 by the time the enemy reached Paris: in affluent areas only a quarter of the population remained behind.[1] In poorer areas about a half stayed back. By June 1940, between six and ten million people in France are said to have left their homes.

The countryside outside Paris was beautiful with flowers in the hedges and summer in the air. But the convoy of vehicles crawling out of the city presented a stark contrast with the natural beauty of the surroundings. All along the road there were abandoned cars which had run out of petrol or broken down. It led to more traffic jams and pile-ups. Rich, poor, old, young – every type and class of person seemed to be on the road. The full impact of the war had suddenly hit the civilians of France. But worse was to come.

The roar of German jets sent the refugees diving for cover. The low-flying planes dropped bombs indiscriminately over the convoy. Within minutes cars were ablaze and the green country roads smelt of burnt flesh and tyres instead of fragrant hedgerows. The sound of the jets would fade and then almost immediately it would return as the German bombers came to finish off what they had left undone. Vilayat swore he would join the RAF. Noor was devastated by this bombing of innocents. What sort of regime would bomb refugees, women and children? she wondered. It strengthened her resolve to fight such a force.

After a harrowing day on the road, the family reached Tours at nightfall. Here they found shelter in an outhouse near the station, along with many other families. The next morning the family said goodbye to Hidayat and his family, and their uncles, and went to the station. They planned to catch the train to Bordeaux from where they could get a boat to England.

When the train arrived it was already packed and the four of them struggled to get on it. When it reached Bordeaux, however, the station staff refused to let the passengers alight, saying the town was full and there was no room for any more refugees. Sheer panic followed as frantic passengers fell on the door trying to get out. But the doors were slammed on them and the train began to move. Finally at Le Verdon, fifty miles from Bordeaux, the train stopped and the passengers were allowed to get out. The little town was already heaving with people and the family made their way to the town hall. The British government was evacuating its citizens and Vilayat (who was born in London) asked if his family could get a place on the boat going to England. They were given permission, but told that the queue was long and they would have to wait a few days. The family rented a room to stay in while waiting for the boat.

Noor's account of how the family left France survives in her personal files. When the family found they had to wait in Le Verdon, Noor and Claire started searching for their evacuated hospital unit, which had been shut down when the Germans approached Paris. The British consul told them that the staff had left for St Nazaire. The girls desperately wanted to carry on working for the Red Cross, but their certificates were with the evacuated staff. On a whim, the sisters decided to dash to St Nazaire and try to track down the Red Cross boat. Despite the pleas of Amina Begum and Vilayat, they insisted on making the 200-mile trip; it was a measure of Noor's stubbornness that she was prepared to take such risks just to get the certificates.

The girls travelled through the night through the mass of traffic and finally made it to the docks of St Nazaire, looking for the boat carrying the Red Cross staff and documents. As they were searching the docks a suspicious policeman arrested them on charges of spying. Noor's passport showed she was born in Moscow and the policeman was taking no chances in wartime. After a night spent in a cell the girls finally convinced the officer that they were innocent and he helped them make enquiries about the ship. Sadly, it had sailed the night before. The ship was contacted by radio and the crew agreed to take the two women on board as Red Cross staff if they could get a boat to drop them off, but Vilayat and their mother were in Le Verdon and so Claire and Noor simply had to go back.

It was while Noor and Claire were on their mad dash for the Red Cross certificates that they heard the dreaded news of the fall of Paris. The Germans had arrived there on 14 June to find a deserted city with empty streets, closed shops and shuttered houses. Tanks, armoured vehicles and German motorcyclists in heavy leather coats now drove through its grand boulevards. The swastika had swiftly replaced the tricolour. On 16 June the French Prime Minister, Paul Reynaud, resigned and was succeeded by Marshal Henri Pétain, hero of Verdun in the First World War. France had fallen to the Germans. The next day Pétain broadcast from Bordeaux that he intended to ask Hitler for an armistice. The girls heard the news in silence.

By the terms of the armistice, Paris and the north of France and the entire Atlantic coast was to be administered by the German military command. A so called 'free-zone' south of the Loire would be administered by the French under Marshal Pétain. His headquarters would be set up in Vichy in the Auvergne. The Vichy regime, sympathetic to the Germans, would administer this area.

Unsuccessful at tracing their certificates, Claire and Noor headed back for Le Verdon. Meanwhile Vilayat was in a panic because he had been told that the last boat for British subjects was leaving the port in half an hour, yet Noor and Claire had not returned. He knew it would be a scramble to get to the port area from their lodgings at the town centre, and he bought a motorbike to ferry the family to and fro. Just at the point when Vilayat and his mother were giving up and thought they would miss the boat, Noor and Claire returned. They had taken a week to get to St Nazaire and back. Vilayat dashed on his bike to the harbour where the boat – a tiny Belgian vessel called *Kasongo* – was ready to leave. He explained his desperate situation and the captain agreed to wait till he fetched his family. There was no place for any luggage, however. Vilayat made three trips from the town centre to the boat carrying Noor, Claire and his mother one at a time on the pillion.

Noor, as usual, was saying her goodbyes. To the people in town who watched them leave she shouted: 'We shall come back.'[2]

Barely had they managed to scramble aboard when the ship set sail. A breathless Vilayat looked out on the coast of France. On the harbour stood the abandoned motorbike that he had used to ferry the family back and forth. It was 19 June, his birthday, but there was nothing to celebrate. France, the country they loved so much, was occupied. Vilayat felt they had managed to leave just on time. Noor was determined to return.

* * *

After an uncomfortable journey in the cargo boat, which was infested with beetles, the family landed at Falmouth. Noor and Vilayat breathed a sigh of relief, as their mother was clearly exhausted and desperately needed to rest. They headed for the home of Basil Mitchell, an old family friend who lived in Southampton.

They travelled all night and arrived early in the morning, exhausted, and were quickly taken in by the surprised Mitchells. But Southampton was not safe from bombs either and so Mrs Mitchell decided to take Amina Begum and her daughters with her to a friend's house in Oxford. Basil Mitchell took Vilayat to London. Vilayat applied immediately for the RAF, but he came down with paratyphoid fever and had to return to Oxford where he was admitted to the Headington Isolation Hospital. The girls and their mother remained in Oxford, and Noor and Claire went to the hospital every day to enquire about Vilayat. Slowly they began to come to grips with their new life.

Noor was cheered to learn that General De Gaulle had managed to escape from France and had reached Britain. De Gaulle was immediately allowed to broadcast from London and he called for a continuation of the struggle and rallied the Free French Forces to his side. They set up offices in Duke Street in London.

On a trip to London the Mitchells introduced Noor to Jean Overton Fuller, who later became a close friend and wrote her biography after the war. Fuller describes Noor at that time as small in build, with brown hair and hazel-brown eyes. She had a gentle voice which was also high pitched and faint. She remembered that

Noor had a most peculiar accent: a mix of Indian, English, French and American.[3] Though the young woman didn't say much, Fuller was immediately drawn to her.

Noor was wearing the new emblem of the Free French, a double-barred cross in silver. It was clear she was impatient to do something to help. She even mentioned to Fuller that she felt it was wrong to flee France and she wished she could be used as a liaison agent. She was clearly pleased that the Free French had begun to organise under General De Gaulle.

Already in August 1940, London was burning. The Battle of Britain had begun and in the skies people could see the German Luftwaffe take on the British Spitfires. In London, Noor experienced the true horror of the bombing. Every night the planes could be heard and the bombing continued till dawn. Offices and residential buildings were hit and people spent all night putting out fires. Many were homeless. It was a time of blackout paper, air-raid sirens and ration cards. Posters everywhere urged women to 'Serve in the WAAF with the men who fly', 'Join the ATS', or to 'Come and Help with the Victory Harvest' by joining the Land Army. Noor was desperate to do her bit to help.

By autumn that year, after finally having managed to secure her Red Cross certificate, Noor joined the Fulmer Chase Maternity Home for Officers' Wives near Slough. The family at this time was living on a very meagre allowance as the little money they had brought from Paris was running out. Noor's job at the maternity home involved no serious nursing and mainly consisted of domestic chores. She longed to be of real use and volunteered to join the Women's Auxiliary Air Force (WAAF), much against her mother's wishes. Her decision to do so was clearly influenced by Vilayat, who had joined the RAF. But to her dismay her initial application was rejected on the grounds that she had been born in Moscow. This infuriated her and she shot off a letter to the ministry saying that as a person holding a 'British Protected Person' passport she should be allowed to serve her country. Almost immediately she was sent a reply – an apology and an appointment letter welcoming her to the WAAF.[4]

The WAAF was created in June 1939 to help out the RAF and train women to take up jobs so that men could go into the field. Thousands of women were recruited as telephonists, teleprinter operators, plotters and radar operators for RAF stations. By 1940 recruitment increased so as to release more men for flying duties. The Air Ministry Committee agreed that 'no work should be done by a man if a woman could do it or be trained to do it'. The WAAF Commandant in Chief was the Queen and thousands of volunteers poured in.

On 19 November 1940, Noor Inayat Khan joined the WAAF as 424598 ACW2 (Aircraftswoman 2nd Class). She was registered as Nora Inayat Khan with her religion given as C. of E. (Church of England). She chose the name Nora because it sounded closest to Noor. She gave her religion as Church of England to avoid complications. It was Vilayat's experience while trying to register his name that led her to take this option. (The clerk had got so exasperated at trying to register Vilayat's full name that he simply called him Vic. He made no attempt to find out the young man's religion, simply entering him as Church of England.) Noor thought it best to follow suit. Her civil occupation was entered as a 'writer' and her other qualifications were given as 'Fluent French'[5].

She was now sent to Harrogate for training in wireless operation, along with forty other young women: the first batch of WAAFs to be trained as radio operators. Noor's character was described as 'V.G.' (Very Good) and her progress was marked with an A. It was a new world for Noor. For the first time she became part of a group, wearing a uniform and marching with the other women for meals, lectures and training. Physical training and sports were compulsory and she found she had to run in races and do regular drill. The recruits slept in huts on straw-filled mattresses and had to assemble their kit for a monthly inspection. It was cold and uncomfortable and unlike anything she was used to, but she was determined to get used to it.

A month later, on 23 December 1940, Noor was sent to Number 34 (Balloon Barrage) Group, RAF Balloon Command in Edinburgh where she was to spend the next six months training as a wireless telegraphist. Once again, Noor got an A in her signals training. Her character was always marked with a 'V.G.'. Begum Amina now moved to Edinburgh to be near her.

After some initial hesitation, Noor soon settled down with the other young women and began to enjoy the camaraderie of the services. Eager to do her best, she worked hard at her radio training, memorising her Morse code and trying to build up her speed. Irene Salter, a fellow trainee, knew her as 'a gentle girl who suffered badly from chilblains. For this reason she had to wear shoes two sizes larger than normal, and was unable to grasp the Morse key because of her swollen fingers.'[6] The girls had to learn Scottish folk dances and Noor wasn't particularly good at them because of her feet. Moreover the hard, flat, black leather shoes supplied by the WAAF usually took a while to break in and gave her blisters. But though the other girls teased Noor about her dancing, she never dropped out and completed all the sessions, taking it all in good humour. Her gentle personality and sportsmanship earned her the respect of her colleagues and she made a number of friends.

Another colleague at the time, Dorothy Ryman, remembered Noor as someone who always had a smile or a pleasant word for others, despite the hard knocks they had to take while training and the tedious nature of the job. Once a week the women had to stay in their huts for special cleaning sessions, darning their grey cotton socks and bringing their uniforms up to scratch for the kit inspection. It was usually accompanied by a chat around the stove and a cup of hot cocoa before lights out at 10.30 p.m.

In April 1941 Noor was sent to No. 929, Balloon Squadron, Forth and Medhill, for further signal training. One of her close friends was Joan Clifton and on 10 June 1941 the two women were posted together to HQ No. 6 Group, RAF Bomber Command at Abingdon. Noor was now promoted to Aircraftswoman 1st Class. The station at Abingdon was an advanced training centre for bombers and Noor and Joan were often on duty together working side by side with the men transmitting and receiving messages. The work was very technical but Noor soon mastered it, proving herself far better than many of the men. She was always ready to help others and most people liked the shy young Indian woman.

Another colleague, Nora Wenman, remembered Noor as an efficient operator. She remembered that her Morse key seemed to have a wide gap and there was a loud 'clackety-clack' sound as she used it. Her colleagues used to call her 'Bang Away Lulu' because of the sound, but Noor would simply smile at their teasing.[7]

After nearly ten months with the WAAF, Noor had adjusted to the working environment. The fact that the people around her knew nothing about her and her family background came as something of a welcome break. Noor did not want to appear exotic to them and was determined to find her own identity. She never spoke to her colleagues about her father, or her ancestry, or the Sufi faith. She remained Nora Inayat Khan to them and attended regular church service, since her religion was registered as Church of England. In Suresnes and in the Sufi circle, she had always been known as Hazrat Inayat Khan's daughter. She had made small beginnings in Paris in establishing her own identity as a writer. Now Noor had to reinvent herself among people who did not know her at all.

In many ways the anonymity of being a number was welcome to her. Back in Paris, the Sufi brotherhood could be oppressive. They constantly supervised the lives of Hazrat Inayat Khan's children and set the code of conduct for them. Noor's friend Jean Overton Fuller got the feeling that when it came to the Inayat Khan children and the Sufis 'there was a lot to look up to, but a lot to get away from.'[8] In the cramped Nissen huts of the WAAF, Noor felt a sense of freedom and purpose and felt she could breathe again.

Noor's friendship with Joan sustained her when the regimental life began to tire her. For some time Joan and Noor shared a room in a large house outside Oxford at Boar's Hill, which had been taken over by the WAAF. They made the most of their posting and decorated their tiny room with posters and knick-knacks. The women also rented a radio as both enjoyed listening to music. They bought old bicycles to ride to work and cycled through the countryside, sometimes singing together on the way back. Often they would cycle to Oxford, where Amina Begum lived and worked in a hospital. When they had a thirty-hour break, they would hitch-hike to London and enjoy a day out. Joan remembered Noor as a happy young woman who was always smiling, but she was acutely aware that Noor missed her home and her life in France.[9] It was obvious to Joan that she was very attached to her family and spent most of her time fretting about her mother and her sister and brothers.

Neither of the young women particularly enjoyed the regimental aspect of service life, but they made the most of it. Noor would tell Joan that once the war was over she would get married and have lots of children and resume her writing career. While the training at Abingdon threw up new experiences for Noor, the everyday aspect of service life did not appeal to her. She was no good at drill, had no coordination between her hands and feet and was often clumsy.

At Abingdon her colleagues remembered her for being completely selfless and always willing to help. The hours at Abingdon were long. They worked in shifts – maintaining contact with the planes which were on training flights – from 4.30 p.m. to midnight, then again from 8.00 a.m. next day to 4.30 in the afternoon and then again the next day from midnight to 8.00 a.m. The shifts were done by two pairs of operators, one pair sleeping while the other pair kept watch. Noor, who was already an accomplished operator and far ahead of the others, would help them. F.R. Archer, a young aircraftsman, remembered how Noor would often volunteer to forgo her sleep to help others even though she was exhausted herself.[10]

Meanwhile back in London, Vilayat had discovered to his dismay that his eyesight was weak and did not fit the requirements for the RAF. He applied now to the Navy instead and was asked to study for an examination in navigation. He continued to live in London in a small room in Premier House, 150 Southampton Row in Bloomsbury and barely managed to make ends meet. Noor would come to see him whenever she managed to get an overnight pass. She would sleep on the bed while Vilayat slept on the balcony. Noor would inevitably try to tidy up Vilayat's tiny room when she was there. Brother and sister remained very close. Sometimes they would go to see a film in London or visit the zoo. Here Vilayat compared Noor to a deer, saying, 'Tipu Sultan was a tiger, my father was a lion, I am a gargoyle and Noor – Noor is a deer.'[11]

Claire had begun to study medicine in Edinburgh, and the family scrimped and scraped to pay her fees. Noor was always concerned about her mother and worried about her health. She felt that hospital work was far too strenuous for someone as frail as Amina Begum.

On 19 June 1941, a year after they had left France, Noor saved up and bought a copy of Nehru's *An Autobiography* and presented it to Vilayat for his birthday along with a score of Bach's Toccata and Fugue in D Minor. *An Autobiography* had been published in 1937 and had attracted considerable publicity. Since they had come to England, both Noor and Vilayat had become more aware of the Indian Independence movement.

In London and Oxford, Noor had met many Indians involved with the freedom struggle and had become acutely aware of political developments back home. Led by the flamboyant Krishna Menon, the India League in London had come to play a significant role in mobilising Indians abroad. It also had the support of Indophiles and theosophists such as Horace Alexander, Agatha Harrison, Fenner Brockway, Wedgwood Benn, Marie Seton and others. Young Indian barristers like P.N. Haksar regularly attended the meetings as did Indira Nehru's fiancé, Feroze Gandhi. From its offices in the Strand, the India League brought out a weekly newspaper keeping people in Britain up to date with developments in India and promoting Indian independence. London was buzzing with young Indians, many studying law or economics at the London School of Economics while doing their bit for the freedom struggle, and Noor and Vilayat were very aware of this work.

The war in Europe had seen the Indian push for independence enter a new phase. Most leaders of the nationalist Congress party were in favour of the war against Fascism, but they wanted some concessions and reassurances in return for backing England. Other leaders, such as Subhas Chandra Bose, favoured an alliance with Germany to get rid of imperialism. Noor admired Bose's patriotism but did not agree with his politics. She favoured those of Nehru and Gandhi, but she also had strong views of her own.[12]

Though she firmly believed that Britain should give Indians their freedom, Noor was convinced that Indian leaders should not press for independence when Britain had its hands full fighting the war. She felt that if the Indians backed Britain and won many gallantry medals it would create a sense of confidence in them, and the British would readily grant independence to India after the war. On a personal level Noor always felt that, as an Indian, her part in the effort from her post in Abingdon would in its own small way have a positive effect for Indians as a whole. She once told Jean Overton Fuller: 'I wish some Indians would win high military distinctions in this war. If one or two could do something in the Allied services which was very brave and which everybody admired it would help to make a bridge between English people and Indians.'

Her brother Hidayat was convinced that if Noor had survived the war, her next cause would have been Indian independence. She was passionately opposed to forces of occupation and she often discussed the future of India with Vilayat. She would sometimes talk about going to India after the war, and worried about the fate of the Congress leaders.

The spit and polish of service life at Abingdon began to tire Noor out, and she became restless, feeling that she was too far away from the real action. Towards the end of 1941 Joan and Noor applied for commissions. Joan was recommended for Code and Cypher and Noor for Intelligence. Joan's interview came up earlier and she was sent on a Commission Course in April 1942.

Noor, still waiting for her interview, was posted to No. 3 Signals School at Compton Basset in Wiltshire on 11 May 1942, for a further seven-week Advanced Signals and Wireless course. Again her proficiency was marked with an A and she was clearly making very good progress. Noor was now selected to be part of a small group that would receive training in a secret course of signals and instructions. The intensive course involved a lot of mathematics and Noor soon found herself studying geometry and trigonometry, and having to pore over technical wireless books. She kept up conscientiously and found that she was far ahead of many of the men who had trained in these earlier, and had quick and appropriate answers to many of the problems that came up.

Throughout her training period Noor made sure that her mother never felt too isolated, and visited her whenever she had the time. On Amina Begum's birthday she always received the customary poem and handmade card from her daughter. Though busy with her signals training at Wiltshire, Noor wrote cheerily to her mother:

> So dearest, chin up, it's your birthday,
> And all that we wished shall come true,
> We're on duty but its play-day,
> And life is just all pink and blue.
>
> And our cheers are going all over England,
> Three cheers from the Bodleian lanes!
> Three cheers by wireless from Scotland!
> Three cheers from the RAF planes!

Looking after her mother was always Noor's top priority. She had taken on the responsibility at the age of thirteen and it sat heavily on her shoulders well into adulthood. She gave her WAAF earnings to Amina Begum and strove to make her life a little more comfortable. Her colleagues admired her devotion to her mother. While they used their days off to meet their boyfriends or go dancing, Noor would inevitably spend hers with her mother.

Noor was posted back to Bomber Command, Abingdon, on 12 August. After what seemed to her like an endless wait, her interview date for the commission finally came up. It was to be at the end of August 1942. A few days before the interview she wrote to her brother asking him to lend her a pound so that she could get a perm and look smart on the day. The letter was apologetic as she knew that Vilayat was living a hand-to-mouth existence and had hardly any spare cash. Yet it was clear she was very keen to get the commission and felt her appearance would matter. Vilayat borrowed the money from Jean Overton Fuller and sent it to Noor, who was delighted and thanked him profusely.

She splurged on a 'Eugene' perm and went for the interview on 28 August 1942. But things took a very unexpected direction when Noor was asked about her attitude to Indian independence. Never one to lie about her beliefs, Noor was forthright with her answer. She told the board that she believed Indians should be allowed to organise their own defence and form a sort of Home Guard which would be armed so they could defend themselves against the Japanese. She knew that this idea was not popular with the British, who were reluctant to allow Indians to possess arms in case these weapons should be used against them.

Although she sensed the disapproval of the board, Noor carried on passionately explaining her views. One of the officers then asked her if she would back Indian leaders who took steps against Britain. She said she would support any responsible Indian leader in a step they thought necessary. Asked then whether this was not contradictory to her oath of allegiance to the Crown, Noor was equally forthright. She told the board that as long as the war with Germany was on, she would be loyal to the British government and the Crown. But after the war she may reconsider her position and might find that she had to support India against Britain in the fight for independence. It was the voice of Tipu Sultan's great-great-great-granddaughter speaking.

Noor was very aware that the situation in India was highly volatile at the time. In 1941, India's eastern flank lay open to invasion from Japan. In March 1942, worried about getting Congress support for the war, Churchill sent Sir Stafford Cripps to

India to meet with Congress leaders and address the 'India question'. Churchill promised India full dominion status *after* the war if the Congress cooperated during the conflict. But the Cripps mission failed. Gandhi described it as a 'post-dated cheque on a failing bank' and called on Indians to 'Do or Die'.

In London the War Cabinet watched the crisis in alarm and authorised Lord Linlithgow, the Viceroy, to make widespread arrests including the entire Congress leadership if he needed to.

On 8 August 1942 Nehru called on the British to 'Quit India', launching a major movement, and overnight the top Congress leadership was jailed. They remained in jail for over two years (Nehru himself for two years, ten months) as the war raged in Europe. By the end of 1942, over 60,000 people had been arrested in India.

Churchill was remorseless. 'I have not become the King's first minister in order to preside over the liquidation of the British Empire,' he declared.[13] The British were using the resources of Empire to fight the war and hundreds of thousands of Indians were being recruited to the services to fight in Africa, Italy and in the jungles of Eastern India and Burma. Noor was well aware of these developments, as her passionate address to the board made clear.

Unknown to her, even as she was speaking her mind on Indian independence, Indian leaders were being watched by Indian Political Intelligence, the British internal intelligence service MI5 and the Secret Intelligence Service (SIS) which dealt with external intelligence. A section of MI5 running deception, headed in Delhi by the flamboyant Peter Fleming, brother of James Bond creator Ian Fleming, was planting agents and double agents on Indian soil. One of these double agents[14] was to watch over Nationalist Indian leader Subhas Bose, who had escaped from house arrest in India in 1941 and travelled to Germany where he was trying to get German support for Indian independence.

Against this background of Indian unrest, Noor's brutally frank answers must have stunned the board. Noor thought she had blown her chances and was upset that she had allowed herself to become emotional. But at the same time she was not one to lie about her beliefs. Vilayat told her the British may like her straightforwardness but Noor was not hopeful that she would get the commission.

On 2 September Vilayat passed his exams for the Navy and received a letter asking him to join HMS *Collingwood* in two weeks.

Noor helped him pack and took away all his remaining possessions to Oxford. Around the same time, her friend Joan got engaged, left the post at Abingdon, and went off to Ireland where she settled down with her husband. Noor began to feel lonely. With Vilayat and Joan both gone, she felt she was the only one stuck in a rut in Abingdon. She did not get her commission till several months later but was promoted to Leading Aircraftswoman (LACW) on 1 December 1942.

But things were moving very quickly in another direction for Noor. Unknown to her, while she was working diligently at her Morse, the authorities at Military Intelligence were carefully following her progress.

On 21 October 1942, an internal memo of the Special Operations Executive (SOE) suggested that Noor Inayat Khan, WAAF No. 424598, be called for an interview at 1600 hours on 10/11/42 at Room 238, Hotel Victoria. The brief entry simply said: 'Has interesting linguistic qualifications which might make her of value for operational purposes.'[15]

The fact that Noor was bilingual, equally at home in French as in English, was of interest to the SOE. They had their own plans for the dreamy writer of children's stories. Soon Noor received the formal letter inviting her for an interview at the War Office in London. She was to meet a Captain Selwyn Jepson at the Hotel Victoria in Northumberland Avenue on 10 November 1942.

Despite her disagreement with Churchill's stand on Indian independence, Noor was now heading for a job in a department that had been specially created by Churchill. She was to be recruited as his secret agent in the war against Fascism.

FOUR

Setting Europe Ablaze

After a year with the WAAF, the shadowy world of the Special Operations Executive (SOE) would be a totally new experience for Noor. The shabby rooms of the Victoria Hotel, where she had to report, belied their importance. In one of the bedrooms on the third floor, the SOE had set up an interview room. It was here that they vetted potential recruits. The stark room consisted of a kitchen table, two hard chairs (one, according to SOE (F-section) chief Maurice Buckmaster, in a 'permanent state of collapse'), and a naked light bulb. There was the faint smell of disinfectant and very stale shaving soap.

The SOE was born in the summer of 1940 when the Battle of Britain was in full flow. As the RAF clashed daily over the skies of London with the German Luftwaffe, Winston Churchill presided over his War Cabinet in the bunkers below Whitehall, making plans to fight the Germans on the beaches and in the air. But already a small group were plotting a different sort of battle, one that would be unconventional and one that was conceived out of the need to fight the very core of the Nazi regime. Britain was the last country in Europe still facing up to the German military machine. Hitler and the Third Reich had already overrun Austria, Czechoslovakia, Poland, Denmark, Norway, Holland, Belgium and finally, in June 1940, France. The war had now come to Britain's door. On 16 July 1940, Hitler signed the Führer's Directive No. 16, Operation Sealion, for the invasion of Britain.

That same night Churchill summoned his Minister for Economic Warfare, Hugh Dalton, and told him to 'set Europe ablaze'. This was to be done by building a new secret service that would sabotage the German war effort and help the resistance fighters in the conquered countries. Dalton defined the mission as: 'the corrosion of the Nazi and Fascist powers by action from within to be achieved by careful recruitment and training of agents and meticulous planning during a long preliminary period.'[1] After the fall of France, the government realised that potential allies lay behind enemy lines and could contribute to staving off the invasion and, by general subversion, undermine and destroy the German New Order. Dalton thought this force could be a like a 'fourth arm'.

Ironically, it was the very person accused of appeasing Hitler, former Prime Minister Neville Chamberlain, who in his role as Lord President of the Privy Council, organised the details. On 19 July 1940 he signed the secret paper which became the founding charter of the SOE. It was Chamberlain's last important act as he died a few months later on 9 November. The document said: 'The Prime Minister has further decided . . . a new organisation shall be established forthwith to co-ordinate all action, by way of subversion and sabotage, against the enemy overseas . . . This organisation will be known as the Special Operations Executive.'[2] And with that the SOE came into existence. From now on sabotage and subversion would take their place alongside sea blockade and air bombardment as the main devices for bringing Germany down.

The SOE started out in three gloomy rooms on the third floor of St Ermin's hotel on Caxton Street in the heart of Westminster. Nobody knew quite who the men in the rooms were. Sometimes they said they were from the Admiralty, sometimes the Army or the Air Ministry. Occasionally they described themselves as the Inter-Services Research Bureau or the Joint Technical Board, or Special Training Schools Headquarters, all of which were their cover descriptions.

Soon they took over the three top floors of the hotel. The SOE was answerable only to the Prime Minister and the Minister of Economic Warfare. Its work would be distinct from MI5, which dealt with security at home, and MI6, also known as the Secret Intelligence Service (SIS), which gathered intelligence from sources abroad. The SOE was to support the resistance movements in the various occupied countries. Churchill called it the 'Ministry of Ungentlemanly Warfare' and gave Dalton two directives. First, the SOE was to create and foster the spirit of resistance in Nazi-occupied countries. Second, it was to establish a nucleus of trained men who would be able to assist as a Fifth Column in the liberation of the country. The SOE was an unorthodox organisation created to carry out war by unorthodox means in unorthodox places.

According to SOE historian Michael Foot: 'Nothing quite like it had been seen before and nothing quite like it would be seen again, for the circumstances of Hitler's war were unique and called out this among other unique responses.'[3]

Hugh Dalton, Minister of Economic Warfare, was a man of tremendous energy. He was determined to beat the Nazis at their own game and wanted to organise movements in every occupied country along the lines of the Sinn Fein in Ireland, the Chinese guerrillas fighting the Japanese and the Spanish irregulars who had defeated Napoleon in Spain. His modus operandi were to be industrial and military sabotage, labour agitations and strikes, continuous propaganda, terrorist acts against the German military and leaders, boycotts and riots.

Establishing the new organisation was not without its difficulties. The SOE was not popular with other intelligence services and there were clashes with the SIS. The SIS had reservations about the SOE methods of sabotage and terrorism, as activities like blowing up bridges attracted the attention of the Germans. The SIS preferred to work quietly, blending in with the local population. Stewart Menzies, head of the SIS, thought the SOE consisted of upstarts and amateurs and he recorded his opinion that difficulties would follow if two sets of agents worked independently in the same territory.[4] Even RAF Bomber Command and its head, Arthur 'Bomber' Harris, is said to have disapproved of the SOE. Harris's preferred method in the war was bombing the Germans into submission and he did not like to spare his aircraft for clandestine activity. The problem was that the SOE was heavily dependent on the other services. It needed boats from the Admiralty to ferry agents across to the Continent, weapons and ammunition from the Army and aircraft from the RAF to drop agents and supplies. In the early years, most requests were turned down and the SOE had fewer planes, less finance and little equipment with which to 'set Europe ablaze'. The SOE also had to share the same wireless operators as the SIS and this led to considerable confusion in the early years as messages were sometimes delayed. It was only in 1942 that the SOE acquired the right to build its own sets, use its own codes and run its own network.

These were not problems that would daunt Dalton. He set to work building the core team. The SIS had a dirty-tricks department called Section D (D for destruction) which had thought of imaginative schemes like destroying Romanian oil fields, blocking the Danube and sabotaging iron ore exports from Germany. But these had not yielded results. In the autumn of 1940, D-section was formed into a new department known as SO2 and placed under Dalton. This was done without consulting the SIS chief, Stewart Menzies, which angered him further. There was also a small subdivision of Military Intelligence called MI (R) which was planning paramilitary action. This was transferred to the Ministry of Economic Warfare. A third group attached to the Foreign Office called Electra House, which dabbled in subversive propaganda, was also handed over to Dalton. In the initial years, the SOE fused the work of all three departments and used their resources to get their plans on the road. Interdepartmental rivalry with the SIS remained high.

Dalton, an old Etonian, worked on the old-boy network and recruited many bankers and influential lawyers from Section D. These included Charles Hambro of the banking family, who had powerful connections in Sweden, George Taylor, a ruthless Australian with business interests around the globe, and a banker from Courtaulds. In the early years of SOE it looked very much like a gentleman's club from the city and legal world. The SOE was divided into three sections – SO1 for propaganda, SO2 for active operations and SO3 for planning.[5]

By October 1940 it had extended its offices from the grubby St Ermin's hotel. Although it retained the first three floors of the hotel it now moved its main base to 64 Baker Street, further down the road from 221B, home of the fictional sleuth Sherlock Holmes. Later it took over Norgeby House, 83 Baker Street, and then the top floor of Michael House, the corporate headquarters of Marks & Spencer at 82 Baker Street, which housed the cipher and signals branches. SOE officials from now on came to be known as the 'Baker Street Irregulars', borrowing the phrase from Arthur Conan Doyle who used it in his detective stories.[6] The SOE had different sections dealing with the occupied countries. It soon established offices around the world from Istanbul and Cairo to Delhi, Algiers, Kandy, Brisbane and New York.

All branches of the SOE had the same aim: aiding resistance movements in occupied countries through acts of sabotage. From

Delhi, the SOE sent agents into Burma to counter the Japanese, from Cairo they armed resistance groups in North Africa and Italy. The Balkan theatre covered Yugoslavia, Poland and Romania, the Western European section covered France, Netherlands and Belgium and the Mediterranean theatre covered Greece, Italy and Spain. The SOE in the Far East covered Burma, Malaya, Thailand, French Indo-China, China and Sumatra. In Ceylon, it had a base in Kandy. When the Soviet Union was drawn into the war in July 1941,[7] followed by the United States in December of that year, it gave Britain crucial allies and made it possible for it to plan to build up large bodies of armed men behind the enemy lines ready for the day when the Allied armies entered Europe.

The SOE had six sections working in France. The two main ones were F-section and RF section. F-section sent agents trained in London to France to help the Resistance in sabotage activities. Recruits consisted of French-speaking Englishmen and women and people from British protected areas and French-speaking colonies. F-section was entirely British-run. Apart from a few exceptions in the early years, French exiles were recruited not to F-section but to RF section, which backed de Gaulle and worked closely with the Gaullist Free French headquarters in Duke Street. The Gaullist-run RF section consisted almost entirely of French agents and was based at 1 Dorset Square. RF section took their orders jointly from De Gaulle's staff and from the SOE. Their aim was to disrupt both the Germans and the Vichy regime. There was some rivalry between the F-section and the RF section, as there was between the SOE and MI6. Other branches of the SOE in France consisted of the DF which ran escape routes, EU/P which worked in Polish settlements mostly in France, AMF which operated from Algiers, and the Jedburgh teams. The last were not meant to reach France till the main invasion, Operation Overlord (the Normandy landings), began in June 1944. The main aim of the French section was to prepare the ground for the invasion of France.

In February 1942 Dalton was replaced by Lord Selborne, a friend of Churchill, who had backed him over his India policy in the 1930s. He was the grandson of Lord Salisbury and had greater access to the Prime Minister. From this period, the SOE started coming into its own, the groundwork having been done. The first agents had entered occupied territory and the organisation now grew in strength. At the height of its operations in 1944, about 15,000 people passed through the SOE. It employed 1,500 wireless operators and cipher clerks at four receiving stations in Britain and worked round the clock looking out for messages coming in from several hundred agents behind enemy lines. Some 10,000 men and 3,000 women worked for it around the globe in various headquarters, missions and sub-stations; about 5,000 of these were agents in the field, almost all of them men. They worked with an estimated two to three million active resisters in Europe alone.[8]

Most SOE recruits were receiving messages from the agents in the field and working as coding clerks and wireless operators. Others worked in planning, administration, intelligence operations, supply, research, security and transport. Some were employed in the 'dirty tricks' department covering explosives, forgeries and disguises. The switchboard began with 12 lines and grew to 200 at the peak of operations. In London, close to the Baker Street headquarters, nearby streets like Dorset Square and Portman Square housed various country and technical sections of the SOE at Orchard Court, Montague Mansions and Chiltern Court. Interview rooms were at the Victoria Hotel. Orchard Court at Portman Square had the offices of the F-section, where Noor would work.

Recruitment for the SOE had to be done in secret. As with any intelligence organisation most of the recruits came from recommendations and personal contacts, and were family or friends or simply part of the old-school network. Later, as the need for recruits grew, a general instruction was informally put out to all services department to look out for people with language skills.

Language was crucial to recruitment in the SOE. Maurice Buckmaster, head of F-section of the SOE, wrote in his book *Specially Employed* that the vetting process was elaborate. First the MI (Military Intelligence) sent in a list of people with language skills. However, 'fluent French' was not enough. Applicants could not have the slightest trace of a British accent and had to speak French like a native. Their appearance, too, had to be just right. They would have to be taken as a Frenchman by a Frenchman. That was the acid test. Though the first few recruits to the SOE were French, they were soon debarred from joining since they were recruited to the Free French led by de Gaulle. The SOE had to narrow down its recruitment drive to French-speaking Britons, which was not easy. Usually people who had one French parent or those who had lived a considerable time in France were recruited. Later, Canadians, Americans, South Africans and Mauritians were appointed.

It was crucial to get the right candidate because the wrong one might not only put his own life at risk but endanger the rest of the group as well. Even the weakest link in the chain had to be strong or lives were at risk. An agent unable to speak the French of a Frenchman could risk the exposure of his whole group.

Once the language issue had been cleared, the next test was that of character. There were many at the outset who felt that in order to counter the notorious Abwehr, the German security police, the SOE recruits would have to be drawn from among similar thugs who could beat them at their own game. But SOE officials did not favour this approach, finding that men with shady pasts often did unsatisfactory work. Instead they preferred a person with 'character and steadfastness of purpose'. 'Rugged honesty' was one of the things on the checklist for candidates. He or she could be a professional with no military background. Even physical fitness did not matter too much as the SOE officials were convinced that training could work wonders for anyone. 'We were vitally concerned with essential guts,' wrote Maurice Buckmaster.[9]

It was important to get the right person for the job, as the agent in the field would be working alone, often relying on himself with tenuous radio links with headquarters which could fail at any moment. The candidates were told that the job meant continuous strain, perhaps for years on end. There were no holidays, no home leave, no local leave, no Sundays or bank holidays. Instead the work involved endlessly pitting their wits against the German Abwehr and the French Milice (the pro-German French militia). Most serious of all, there was no protection, because the agents would not be in uniform, and they faced almost certain death if captured. Potential recruits were studied by psychologists at interviews and given full freedom to opt out if they felt they couldn't handle the task.

In April 1942, the War Cabinet passed a resolution to allow the SOE to use female agents in the field.[10] The argument was that women would find it easier to move around under cover of shopping or doing the daily chores and were less likely to be questioned than men.

And so it was that Noor was called upon to meet Selwyn Jepson, chief recruitment officer for the SOE. She had been under observation by Military Intelligence ever since her recruitment. She had already been trained in transmission and had increased her Morse speed during a specialist course. She had cleared the language test as her French was flawless. The rest would depend on the interview and her own willingness to join.

Selwyn Jepson was a writer of thrillers who sometimes also wrote under the name of E. Potter. The son of crime fiction writer Edgar Jepson, he had been educated at St Paul's school in London and at the Sorbonne in Paris. He was bilingual and had written several mystery books including *The Qualified Adventurer*, *That Fellow MacArthur* and *Love in Peril*. His book *Man Running* was later turned into a film by Alfred Hitchcock. Jepson was a skilled interviewer and appointed many of the women recruits in F-section. He generally used the bleak rooms at the Victoria hotel for his interviews. Jepson's greatest skill lay in the fact that he could judge a person's character fairly accurately in only a few meetings. He once said that he very seldom changed the impression a prospective agent made on him during the first quarter of a minute of their first interview.[11]

On 10 November 1942, Noor met Jepson in the Hotel Victoria. She thought she had been called by the War Office. Jepson found that with Noor he could come straight to the point. He had never felt this way with other potential recruits. He recalled later that 'in spite of a great gentleness of manner' she seemed to have 'an intuitive sense of what might be in my mind for her to do. Also, I realised it would be safe to be frank with her, that "her security" as we called it, would be good, that if she felt herself unable to take it on, she would not talk about the reason she had been called to the War Office.'[12]

This was in startling contrast to the other potential recruits who were told that if they repeated anything of what they had heard in the room they would be violating the Official Secrets Act and face dire consequences. Most agents had two or three interviews in which they were broken in and a third where they were asked to decide, but Noor was recruited after just one interview.

Jepson's main task at these interviews was to look at the person's motive and character. He needed to know why people would volunteer to risk their lives – was it patriotism, an unsatisfactory private life, a need for revenge or just recklessness? He also needed to ensure that the potential agent sitting opposite him was not impulsive. Prudence and caution were, according to him, an agent's most important qualities.[13] Jepson had a long talk with Noor about her family and background and then moved on to France and the war. He told her about the current state of affairs in France and the aim of the British war effort to interfere with German plans. He explained to Noor what her duties would entail: that she would be working as a clandestine wireless operator in the underground along with other British officers, helping the Resistance to sabotage the Germans. Throughout the interview they spoke in French. Jepson felt that Noor was almost perfect for the job of a wireless operator. He felt she was careful, tidy and painstaking by nature and 'would have all the patience in the world' – an essential characteristic for a wireless operator.

As Noor sat opposite him, Jepson told her that the assignment was one of extreme danger, that in the event of capture she could be interrogated by the Gestapo – a terrifying experience for anyone – and that since she would not be in uniform she would not have any protection under international laws of warfare. In short, that she could be shot and never return. She listened quietly as he spoke, absorbing the full implications of his words.

Jepson told Noor that there was no monetary reward for the mission. She would receive her ordinary service pay (tax-free for SOE), without increment or bonus and it would be held for her in England while she was in France. If she came back alive it would be paid to her, if not to her next of kin. Her only personal satisfaction would be the knowledge of the service she gave.

'I had scarcely finished when she said with the same simplicity of manner which had characterised her from the outset of our talk, that she would like to undertake it,' recalled Jepson.[14] He said that he would normally be uneasy and reluctant to recruit someone who accepted the situation immediately, because it meant that it was being accepted without proper thought, or for a motive other than the pure sense of patriotic duty. In Noor's case, however, he had no such misgivings, since he felt instinctively that she had thought about it deeply and would not change her mind.

As a writer himself, Jepson felt a natural affinity with Noor, as she had told him that she was a children's writer and broadcaster. He even told her that she might be of more value to society if she continued as a writer who would be able to communicate with children after the war was over and heal the young minds who had lived through the destruction. But Noor shook her head and refused the offer to get away. 'She was sure and confident. She would like to train and become an agent for us, if I thought she could make it,' said Jepson. 'I had not the slightest doubt that she could, and said so, and with rather more of the bleak distress which I never failed to feel at this point of these interviews, I agreed to take her on.'

Jepson saw Noor several times during her training and often had conversations with her about what she was going to do and the nature of the job, but he would never forget his first meeting with her and the impact it made on him:

> I see her very clearly as she was that first afternoon, sitting in front of me in that dingy little room, in a hard kitchen chair on the other side of a bare wooden table. Indeed of them all, and they were many, who did not return, I find myself constantly remembering her with a curious and very personal vividness which outshines the rest . . . the small, still features, the dark quiet eyes, the soft voice, and the fine spirit glowing in her.

Noor was now told that she would be discharged from the WAAF and enrolled in the First Aid and Nursing Yeomanry (FANY), also known as the Women's Transport Service. This department was the usual cover for women agents as it provided them with an excuse to train in the use of firearms (which, as WAAF, they were not allowed to do). It also gave them a uniform (which was useful during training) and gave them a reason to be away from home for long periods. It also served as a plausible cover story for family and friends and was used effectively by Noor. FANYs were employed in many positions, from drivers and telephone operators to wireless operators, canteen workers and prison guards. Since many female agents were both FANY and

WAAF there was always a slight confusion as to where they actually belonged. Noor's George Cross citation refers to her as a WAAF officer while a memorial to thirteen women SOE agents in Knightsbridge refers to her as FANY. Again the recommendation for the citation of her George Medal (which was later upgraded to the George Cross) was made out in the name of 'Ensign N. Inayat Khan, a volunteer FANY'.

When she joined the SOE on 8 February, Noor was in the WAAF. On 12 February she was enrolled in FANY. Noor was later given an honorary commission by the WAAF. This is why her WAAF records show her as being discharged from the WAAF on 15 June 1943 and being given an honorary commission on 16 June as Assistant Section Officer in the WAAF.[15]

Noor was made an officer because the SOE felt that the rank would provide her some degree of security, as a German officer might hesitate to shoot her if she was an officer. Promotion to officer's rank also meant an increase in allowance and Noor discovered that her mother would be eligible for a further allowance as a 'displaced person'. She was now told to return to Abingdon and await her orders.

The meeting with Jepson had transported Noor into a different world, but there was a calmness about her as she absorbed the implications. She had been determined to help in any way to fight Hitler's forces of occupation. She had also wanted to return to France, a country that she loved and felt most at home in. Despite the dangers of the job, Noor felt she was perfectly suited for it because of her language skills, understanding of French culture and her familiarity with Paris. She had no doubt in her mind that she wanted to take the challenge. Once she had made up her mind, the stubborn streak in her kept her going through the days ahead.

There was only one thing that troubled her. Noor was apprehensive about how her mother, still extremely frail and dependent on her, would take the news of her going away on service work. On 11 November Noor wrote to Jepson from Abingdon, having given some thought to the interview. Her formal letter of acceptance showed the courage and forthrightness that Jepson had noticed in her. She told Jepson that winning the war was more important than family ties.[16]

Signals
RAF
Abingdon
Berks
11/10
Capt Jepson

Dear Sir,
After the interview I had at your office (Tues 10th) I have spoken with my mother and my worries in this connection are more or less wiped out. Firstly, I realise that in time my mother will get used to the idea of my going overseas. Secondly, I may be able to provide her with more efficient financial help which would relieve me tremendously, as my war time writing income is quite inadequate.

Besides, I realise how petty our family ties are when something in the way of winning this war is at stake.

I shall therefore accept gratefully the privilege of carrying out the work you suggested. I feel I may be of some use as long as the work is purely operational.

Thanking you sir, for asking me
Yours faithfully
N. Inayat Khan

P.S: If there was a question of choice, I should prefer to remain RAF if possible. I have grown more or less attached to the service.

Jepson replied on 13 November that he appreciated her anxiety about the 'kind of work about which we spoke' and promised to do all he could to arrange everything.

Noor's personal files have the following note dated 18 November 1942. 'To be engaged as an agent after training – date not yet arranged.'

Noor wrote to Vilayat that she had been accepted as an Air Force officer and would be working in the combined Navy, Army and Air Force Intelligence Service. She told Vilayat delightedly about her officer's allowance and said that they would probably be able to manage a flat in London sometime in the future. Back at Abingdon, she waited eagerly for her orders.

By the time Noor was recruited to the SOE, it had been in existence for two years. In May 1941 the first SOE agent, George Bégué, had parachuted into France and gone into a large house owned by a man sympathetic to the Resistance. The man was a friend of F-section officer, Maurice Buckmaster.

In November 1941 Maurice Buckmaster took over as head of F-section. Buckmaster had studied at Eton and worked as a reporter for *Le Matin* and *Paris Soir* in France. He had dabbled in banking and then joined the Ford Motor Company as manager of the Paris branch. He spoke fluent French and knew the towns and countryside of France well. When the war broke out he joined the British Expeditionary Force in France and returned to Britain, where he was recruited to the SOE. He was committed to his agents, often trusting his own instincts about them rather than their training reports. The ultimate decision to send someone into the field lay with him.

Buckmaster's assistant was Vera Atkins, a formidable woman of thirty-three who had been to school in France and graduated from the Sorbonne. She, too, spoke fluent French and was well acquainted with French manners and customs. It was she who accompanied each agent to the airfield before they left and kept in touch with their families afterwards. After the war, Atkins set out to investigate the fate of some of the agents who had not returned and painstakingly uncovered their stories.

From 1943 the SOE was led by Brigadier Colin Gubbins, a professional soldier, who became its Executive Director. Gubbins had joined the SOE in November 1940 as Director of Operations and Training and had made an immediate impact. He was a proud Scotsman whose mother's family had come from the Highlands. He was an energetic man who would work till midnight and make merry till the early hours of the morning. He was once seen at five in the morning doing handstands surrounded by cheering colleagues.[17] Gubbins brought a new drive to the SOE. He was a great believer in guerrilla movements and wanted to ensure that agents were well trained in arms and explosives and had a complete idea of the ethnology, politics and religion of the place they would be working in. He secured remote country houses in the Highlands of Scotland to train his agents in arms.

Gubbins' hard work in the formative years of the SOE started paying results by the time he took over as chief of the organisation. An internal report of 24 March 1941 said that the SOE had despatched explosive material and devices into most countries in Europe in large quantities, provided money to subsidise opposition parties and wireless sets and established courier services to facilitate communication.[18]

SOE agents in France had brought back details of factories where the British would find sympathisers and lists of French Resistance supporters who would help against the Germans. They had drawn up names of petrol stations and oil dumps all along the French coast from Marseilles and up to Bordeaux, Le Havre and Dunkirk. They had done their homework on living in an occupied country, securing ration books, permits, controls and details of train services: everything to help the agent in the field. They had also got the crucial feedback that many Frenchmen were willing to help the SOE in sabotaging the Germans in the occupied areas. They learnt that after the initial shock of occupation, resistance to the enemy was growing. Much of SOE's work was dependent on chains of communication with locals who were crucial in providing safe houses for agents, letter boxes for couriers and the numerous farmers and villagers who agreed to have arms and armaments dropped in their fields and hide them in their barns till they were collected by the agents. Among the biggest supporters of the SOE were French railway workers, postal workers and factory workers who took great risks for the cause.

The SOE had a large number of establishments and workshops operating round the clock to provide equipment for its agents. The most innovative gadgets were used: dead rats fitted with explosives, secret wireless transmitters concealed in bundles of logs and sticks or petrol cans, exploding animal droppings (horse droppings were collected from Hyde Park), TNT painted to look like coal lumps, exploding nuts and bolts, exploding fountain pens and milk bottles and improved plastic explosives. There were even some exploding Buddhas which SOE agents, disguised as hawkers, could sell to Japanese troops. All these were manufactured in laboratories at the Victoria and Albert Museum, the Natural History Museum and the

Thatched Barn Roadhouse at Barnet. The tiniest of spy devices too were produced: microfilm dots on spectacles, button compasses, miniature escape saws, silk-scarf maps, forged papers, clandestine radios, invisible ink and much more.

To say it was the stuff of spy fiction was not far from the truth. Ian Fleming's creation of Q, the gadget man for the James Bond novels, was inspired by the 'toy shop' at the Natural History Museum and the inventors who produced these devices. In April 2004, a plaque was unveiled at the site at the Natural History Museum where the SOE had its secret 'toy shop'.

By October 1941, French section had 33 men in France. By the time Noor joined the ranks in 1942 this had reached 50. By June 1943 there were 120 recruits and more ambitious operations were planned. In all 480 active agents were employed by the French section. Of the 39 women sent to France by F-section, 13 never returned. It was in 1943 that the French section of the SOE really took off operationally, yielding results.

Noor was yet to learn about the establishment she had unhesitatingly agreed to join. She was impatient to get started, but had been asked to go back to Abingdon and await orders. The few months spent waiting were torture for her. By now her mother had secured a job at the Red Cross and was living at 4 Taviton Street, London, a few houses along from her friend Jean Overton Fuller. Noor came frequently to London to visit her mother and sometimes went to the British Museum or the Library. Sometimes she would stay with Jean. Her friend had a spare room in her flat in Gordon Square and Noor loved spending the night in the cosy room. Jean had a collection of oriental and Middle Eastern artefacts that Noor loved, and she also liked to browse through her friend's book collection. The women would stay up till late at night discussing art and philosophy.

'She sought solace in my house,' recalled Jean. 'My room was a refuge for her from the war. Here she could talk about books, spirituality, art, culture and matters of the soul.'[19] Noor often talked about life after the war. She told Jean about her plans for the future: to learn Sanskrit, to continue writing, to play the harp, get married and have children.

Though they were both only in their twenties, Noor and Jean were more serious and philosophically inclined than most women of their age. 'We were certainly not carefree,' said Jean.[20] Their common interest in oriental philosophy and spirituality also drew them close. Noor loved a Tibetan prayer wheel that Jean had in her flat and said holding it gave her a sense of peace. She had a premonition that she would not live long as she had a short lifeline and often spoke to Jean about it. At the same time, she talked about her life after the war. Jean got the feeling that she always wanted to go back to France and had felt that way ever since they had left the country in 1940.[21]

Noor thought of herself as an international person who did not belong to any one place. She was born in Moscow to American and Indian parents and brought up in a Sufi tradition in London and Paris. She had visited India, which she loved. But she felt her natural home was France. After the war she wanted to write and play music, both of which she missed greatly. The struggle for Indian independence was also on her mind and the imprisonment of freedom fighters like Gandhi and Nehru affected her.

Noor hoped that her international background could be used by the Allies after the war. She visualised the Allied forces of Britain, USA, France and the Soviet Union converging in Berlin at the end of the war and felt she could be useful as a liaison agent between the western world and the Soviet Union, because she had been born there and had an understanding of oriental culture.

The conflict between Noor's own Sufi faith of non-violence and the path she had chosen in the war would sometimes arise, but she had thought about it deeply. She would say it was possible for a spiritual person to take up the sword if they were not motivated by hate. Though a Muslim, she took solace in the Hindu spiritual text, the Bhagavad Gita (as her father had done before her) and its teaching that action was superior to inaction. She was influenced by the lines from the Bhagavad Gita where Lord Krishna tells the warrior prince Arjuna – who is hesitant to go to war against his own cousins – that he must do his duty without thinking about the results. She felt it was her duty to resist Hitler's occupying forces and all other considerations of family and faith were secondary.

Noor herself had chosen the violent option in the war. Not satisfied with working with trainee pilots in Abingdon, she had wanted to be in active service on the front line, knowing it could entail the use of weapons and firearms. Yet she never hated the German soldiers. It was the Gestapo and the secret police at whom she aimed her wrath.[22]

Meanwhile, Noor carried on with her work. Over the next few months she formed a friendship with a young WAAF meteorologist, Joan Marais. Joan was born in India and brought up in Bombay where her father was a civil engineer and lectured at the Victoria Jubilee Technical Institute. Joan's family left India when she was eleven. She retained a deep attachment to the land of her birth. Noor and Joan were drawn together by their common background and bonded immediately. They shared quarters in a house in Abingdon called Defiant, and Joan recalled Noor as being 'beautiful . . . with a luminous smile' and having 'a lively intelligence and sense of fun'. In temperament they were poles apart – Joan was a socialist and atheist and Noor was deeply spiritual – but they shared a common sensitivity and humanity. Over cups of tea in Defiant, they discussed religion and spirituality, Gandhi, Nehru, and the philosophy of loving one's fellow men. Joan recalled later: 'Two WAAFs, in blue-penguin greatcoats, pedalling through the silver straws of rain . . . on black-enamelled service issue bikes. Noor di-di-dahed with the wireless operators, while I floated hydrogen weather balloons to 20,000 feet . . .'[23]

Unknown to Joan, Noor was already entering a secret world. On 25 January 1943 the personnel form at the SOE entered Noor as Norah Inayat Khan, WAAF no: 424598. Age 29. It requested a month's attachment and called her once again to Hotel Victoria, on 8 February at 1000 hours. The short memo said, 'If satisfactory after training will be used in important operational role for which she has special linguistic and geographical qualifications.' The note also said that 'she should have her kit . . . with her in London but should not bring it with her when she reports'.

On 10 February, Noor was attached to the Air Ministry Unit for service under Air Intelligence (A.I 10) for a period of one month. Air Intelligence was another cover used by the SOE, useful since Noor had been recruited from the WAAF. Her field salary was fixed at £350 a year paid quarterly into her Lloyd's Bank account.[24] On 15 February, Noor signed the Official Secrets Act. Her formal initiation into the SOE was complete.

In Abingdon, one day in February 1943, Joan discovered that Noor had simply 'disappeared. Just like that. No word, no sign, no letter to explain a sudden posting. Just her blankets stacked neatly on the bedspring, and a few hurt feelings among her friends.'

FIVE

Codes and Cover Stories

As the train pulled out of Waterloo, Noor felt nervous at the thought of her first assignment with the SOE. She had exchanged her blue Air Force uniform for the khaki FANY dress which flattered her slight figure and oriental features. Life had changed dramatically for Noor in the last two years. The house in Suresnes seemed to belong to a distant past. She longed to play her harp and go to a concert or write a story, but her head reeled instead with Morse and the sound of aircraft engines.

From the window she could see the backs of the houses that lined the railway track. Cramped balconies with washing lines gave way to unkempt gardens, as Londoners found little time to tend their herbaceous borders in the war. Soon the scenery changed and she felt better as the rolling greens of the Surrey countryside unfolded before her.

Noor had been asked to report to the commandant at Wanborough Manor. It was a fine Tudor house on the Hog's Back near Guildford in Surrey with large rooms and a private park. This was the first of the Special Training Schools (STS) for F-section agents and one of SOE's forty-one training schools spread across Scotland and England. The SOE's collection of fine country houses had earned it the nickname 'Stately 'Omes of England'. Training Noor at Wanborough was ex-Coldstream Guards officer, Major Roger de Wesselow, and her escorting officer was Joan Sanderson.

At Wanborough, Noor met Yolande Beekman and Cecily Lefort. In the pleasant surroundings of the manor, the three girls did not know that their fates in France would be tragically linked. Cecily and Noor would leave for France on the same day. Cecily would die in Ravensbruck concentration camp. Yolande and Noor would meet again on the fateful journey to Dachau.

Every morning the recruits were made to do a ten-minute run before breakfast with Major Wesselow himself leading them. Then they were taught to shoot, throw a hand grenade, and handle explosives. The course at Wanborough consisted of a preliminary round of military and physical training and the basics of wartime operation: the Morse code, map reading and the handling of pistols and sub-machine guns. Wanborough trainers watched them closely to assess their personality and the sort of work they would be suitable for. Yolande and Noor were chosen to be radio operators while Cecily was trained to be a courier. The bar at Wanborough was well stocked and agents were encouraged to drink in their free time. They were then watched to see if they got drunk and, if so, what they revealed. It could mean an early elimination for some if they were found to be easily inebriated. Agents who talked in their sleep were also watched over. What did they talk about and, crucially, in which language? If they were going to France they had to speak French at all times. Because the agents often carried large sums of money, the vetting process had to ensure that they were reliable and not prone to gambling.

Noor threw herself into her training, determined to do well. She enjoyed the atmosphere at Wanborough and seemed to find a renewed purpose in her life after the stagnation of Abingdon. 'I am a busy little girl now,' she wrote to Vilayat,[1] giving him the news that Claire was well and had joined the Army Territorial Service (ATS). They had also heard recently that their brother Hidayat was safe, which was a huge relief for her. Vilayat meanwhile was at sea on HMS *Quantock* and none too happy with life on the deck. He wrote complainingly to Noor that all he did for three days was carry potatoes, that the lower deck made him ill, and that he would leave and join the Resistance if this carried on any longer. His letter alarmed Noor, who was well aware of her brother's hot temper and impulsiveness. She was worried that if he carried out his threat and left, he would be regarded as a deserter. Her training officer, Joan Sanderson, knew Noor was fretting about her family and was struck by how close she was to them.

A report in Noor's Personal File[2] from Wanborough Manor (STS 5) by Lieutenant Tongue dated 23 February said: 'Has been doing arthritis (SOE for radio work) for two years, is in good physical condition.'

With all the intense training she was undergoing, Noor began to improve her fitness levels. On 10 March, her instructor from Wanborough noted that Noor could run very well, something that would prove very useful to her later in the field. Her instructors also decided that Noor was 'unsuitable for jumping'. This meant that for some medical reason, she could not train for parachute jumps. The reason why she was not considered suitable for parachute training is not mentioned, but it could be any factor from ankle injury or foot problems to an earlier operation for an inflamed appendix that she had undergone in Paris.

Although she had spent over a year in the RAF, Noor had never quite got to grips with the regimental side of being in the services. She also disliked the physical aspects of the training, having no aptitude or enthusiasm for PT. Training in explosives and demolitions was another problem. Though Noor had a full understanding of the theory and she put in her best effort, her natural clumsiness was a drawback when it came to the practical side. But she was determined not to fail. She tried very hard and to her instructors seemed 'very keen and interested'. Handling weapons was never going to be easy for this dreamy, sensitive writer of children's stories. It was not surprising that her instructors noted she was 'pretty scared of weapons'. They were, however, impressed by the fact that she tried hard and had improved greatly in a few days and concluded that 'with a little more training [she] should be quite good'.

Noor's results on the whole were fairly balanced at this stage. It was clear to her instructors that she was finding the training very different from what she had done previously, but was slowly settling in.

Having improved her Morse in Abingdon, Noor had to now cope with all the other skills an agent needed to function in the field. She enjoyed map reading and soon became quite good at it, though she was said to be 'useless at field sketches'. Though she had got off to a slow start, Noor gradually built up her confidence in Wanborough. Her instructor now described her as: 'Active, [with] plenty of spirit and could be relied on to come up to scratch when the occasion arose.'

Noor's earnestness and warmth had made an impression on everyone at Wanborough. On 11 March 1943, she received a glowing report from her training officer Lance Corporal Gordon:

> She is a person for whom I have the greatest admiration. Completely self-effacing and un-selfish. The last person whose

absence was noticed, extremely modest, even humble and shy, always thought everyone better than herself, very polite. Has written books for children. Takes everything literally, is not quick, studious rather than clever. Extremely conscientious.

The most important report came from her Commandant, Major de Wesselow. He was positive about Noor's progress: 'Hadn't the foggiest idea what the training was going to be about. From a shaky start has developed a certain amount of confidence. Energetic. Experienced W/T operator though she dislikes the work: extremely earnest in her intentions, and despite a timid manner would probably rise to an emergency.'

The report by Major de Wesselow was sent to Baker Street, where officials monitored Noor's progress. Both Maurice Buckmaster and Selwyn Jepson had complete faith in Noor, confident that she would pull through in the end because of her strength of character and positive attitude.

Noor had cleared the first stage of her training. To Buckmaster, Noor's determination to overcome her weaknesses and her courage were her most important qualities. All else would fall into place since the training course for agents was rigorous. In the very first month Noor was trained in the use of codes, unarmed combat, fieldcraft, shooting, sabotage (including the use of explosive and the knowledge of where to use it to inflict the maximum damage on specified targets), methods of contact and psychological tests. It was now time to move to the next stage.

On 13 March 1943, there was a note about Noor. 'We should like to have a vacancy for this student at STS 52.' Noor was ready for her next move. Five days later she had her security clearance. She was now to proceed to Group B.

But first Noor had to visit her chiefs at Baker Street again. One day, probably around mid-March, Jean was sitting on a bench and reading a book in Gordon Square when she saw Noor walking up to her. Instead of her regular Air Force blue she was wearing khaki. When Jean asked her why, she said she had joined the FANY.

'I knew Noor had done some nursing training but was puzzled about why she had moved. She then told me that "it covers a lot of things".'[3] Jean gathered that she was doing some sort of intelligence work and did not probe any further. Noor's mother, who thought service life was too harsh for Noor, was relieved, thinking that the FANY would not involve military training but be composed of nursing and first aid.

While in London, Noor enjoyed the cosiness of domesticity. She spent her time with Jean and her mother and caught up with all the news about Claire and Vilayat. Feeling confident and happy, she wrote to Vilayat that life was full of 'activity and interest'. She missed him and longed to see him soon. The family was getting on well: Claire had settled into an army secretarial course and Amina was expecting a promotion to the post of Red Cross Deputy Superintendent. Vilayat was proceeding to Lancing College and was on training for a commission. Noor felt that things were looking up again for the family. She spent her time reading at the British Library, discussing oriental philosophy with Jean and was keen to read modern popular German fiction (possibly to familiarise herself with German culture and the German psyche). All too soon it was time to leave for duty again.

On 29 March 1943, Noor reported to Thame Park in Oxfordshire (STS 52) for specialist signals training. She was the first of the women agents to be selected for this intensive course. She was now to spend long hours in the laboratories learning about the composition of her set, fault diagnosis and how to repair it. She also had to increase her Morse speed. Wireless operators developed a 'fist' or style by which those receiving their transmissions could tell who was transmitting – a kind of fingerprinting in Morse. It was, however, far less accurate than fingerprinting by police, and Abwehr agents in Holland reckoned that after listening to an SOE agent's key-work three or four times, they could imitate it perfectly.[4] The signals course was extremely technical and specialised. Agents learned about wavelengths, atmospherics and jamming, as well as basics such as how to hide radio sets and put up aerials. They were taught to incorporate certain security checks in their messages so that the receivers in England could tell whether they were genuine or sent by the Germans.[5] The SOE was always chronically short of radio operators, as the post was recognised as one of the most dangerous and vulnerable in the field. Training agents in clandestine radio operations (as opposed to ordinary wireless transmission) was a difficult task, and was not helped by the fact that very few sets were available at the time. Radio operators suffered the highest casualties among agents and there was a constant demand for replacement operators. Noor was clearly ahead of the others, thanks to her previous RAF training, and she now became the focus as the first woman radio operator likely to be sent to France.

In the early years of the SOE, wireless operators were taught the Playfair code, which used a 5-by-5-letter square and a single word as the Playfair key. It was taught as a mental exercise but rarely used in the field. The key was later changed from a single word to a single line of verse which was carried by the agent as a personal code and had to be memorised. The transpositions were done on the word square on the basis of this poem code. The phrase was chosen by the agent so that it could be easily remembered. (Noor based hers on a poem that she had composed.)[6] This was harder to break compared to previous ciphers. However, even these codes were eventually cracked by the Germans because if they discovered the poem or phrase it was all they needed to know to decipher the whole code. By 1942 another ciphering system called double transposition was introduced. For this the agent had to memorise two sets of random numbers. The plain text was written out under the first random numbers and then transcribed on to the second set. In 1943 a further modified version of the Playfair code, using numbers as well as letters, was used. By mid-1944 a much safer and practically impenetrable cipher had been introduced. The agent was given a number of small silk cloths, each printed with several columns of random letters or figures from which any message could be enciphered or deciphered. After the agent had used a letter he was supposed to cut it out and burn it. This ensured that he could never give the codes to the Germans since he had destroyed it and would be unlikely to remember it. The duplicate of the silk cloth was kept by the home station. This was called the one-time pad. Noor learnt to operate using the Playfair code and double transposition.

Agents also had to learn how to incorporate security checks in their transmissions. This was crucial for the operator to warn home station that he or she had fallen into enemy hands. These checks were individual to the particular operator and consisted of a deliberate spelling mistake or a series of mistakes – like getting the seventh letter of each text wrong, or replacing the twelfth letter by the letter preceding it in the alphabet. The Germans soon caught on that there was a security check and pressured captured agents to reveal them. Agents then began to carry a double security check: a bluff check which they could reveal to the enemy under pressure and a true check to keep to themselves. The deciphering staff knew which checks each operator was supposed to use. So if their notes said, 'Bluff check present, true check omitted' it meant that the operator had been captured and was under duress. These checks were vital for head office in London but they were often not heeded by the receiving staff, with disastrous effects on Noor and her colleagues in the field.[7]

Head office also checked the genuineness of an operator by sending bogus messages. An agent could be sent a message asking: 'Have you contacted Nicole as ordered?' where Nicole was a fictitious person and no order had been given. If the surprised agent replied, 'Who the hell is Nicole and what order?' head office would know he was genuine. If instead they received a reply such as 'Where shall I meet her?' or 'Am arranging it, send further details', or simply 'will do' they would know they were talking to the enemy.

Messages from the field would go to a specialised group of listeners – mainly the FANY – who listened out permanently for these transmissions and replied to them. Colin Gubbins called the work of the SOE wireless operator 'the most valuable link in the whole of our chain of operations. Without these links, we would have been groping in the dark.'[8]

Noor progressed steadily at Thame Park. As she had already trained in Morse she had a head start over all the other trainees, who had to begin from scratch. Noor used the opportunity to improve her performance. Every week her speed was noted down, along with general remarks.

After 40 hours of training at Thame Park, she reached a Morse speed of sending at 16 words per minute and receiving at 19 words per minute. Her instructor noted that she was 'in need of practice and tires quickly but is working well and should make progress'. A week later she had increased her speed to 18 wpm (sending) and 20 wpm (receiving). By 16 April, Noor's Morse speed was 18 wpm (sending) and 22 wpm (receiving). This was noted with satisfaction by her instructors as it was the fastest for any trainee operator. She had also at this stage moved on to practical work on the A Mark II (radio used in the field). Her report said she was finding it a 'little strange but making good progress on the whole'.

Clearly, Noor had settled in well. Her aptitude for radio transmission marked her out from the rest of the recruits. The only aspect of the training she did not enjoy was the physical work, including intensive weapons training. She was, however, determined to work at it, as her instructors noticed.

On 19 April 1943, another report from her instructor, Lieutenant Holland, praised her progress and attitude.

> This student, like her two FANY companions of the 27X party, has thrown herself heart and soul into the life of the school. She has any amount of energy, and spends a lot of it on voluntary P.T. with the object of overcoming as far as possible feminine disabilities, very eager to please, very ready to adapt herself to the mood of the company, or the tone of the conversation, interested in personalities, capable of strong attachments, kind-hearted, emotional and imaginative. She is very fond of her family (mother, brother in the Fleet Air Arm and sister) and was engaged for about five years, but broke it off. The motive for her accepting the present task is, apparently, idealism. She felt that she had come to a dead end as a WAAF and was longing to do something more active in the prosecution of the war, something which would make more call on her capabilities and perhaps demand more sacrifice. This appears to be the only motive, the broken off engagement is old history, nor does she appear to have any romantic ideas of the Mata-Hari variety. In fact she confesses that she would not like to do anything 'two-faced', by which she means deliberately cultivating friendly relations with malice aforethought. The fact that she has already given some thought to preparing her mother for the inevitable separation and cessation of correspondence shows that she has faced some, at any rate, of the implication of the job. It is the emotional side of her character, coupled with a vivid imagination, which will most test her steadfastness of purpose in the later stages of her training.[9]

This detailed report shows how interested the SOE was in the background and psychological make-up of their trainees. Noor had clearly discussed her personal and family life, her anxieties and apprehensions, at some depth with her instructors. Though it was clear to them that she was emotional, they saw reserves of strength and courage in her. Her maturity and forthrightness had impressed her instructors but there was a lot more to be done. Apart from her radio and technical training, Noor had to learn the crucial art of becoming a secret agent and surviving as one. After the initial training at Wanborough and the specialist training schools, most F-section agents were sent to the Group A Special Training School Number 26 at Arisaig in Scotland. Here F-section had found an ideal training ground – a number of large houses in one of the most inaccessible parts of the Scottish Highlands. In these remote mountains, often battling severe weather, the trainees were taught how to blow up bridges using dummy explosives and to carry out other acts of sabotage. The training was intensely physical and the recruits had to learn how to handle arms, load slippery weapons in the dark, make their way across rough country and creep silently through the undergrowth. They learned how to wade through rock-strewn streams, how to avoid the skyline, how to live off the land and kill silently. They were made to cycle for miles in the mountains building their physical fitness to peak levels which would stand them in good stead in the field. There is no evidence from Noor's training files that she went to Arisaig. As a radio operator, it was probably thought better to concentrate her training in her specialised field.

After the training at Arisaig (A-school), agents were sent to further special schools to specialise in their field of work. Some did courses in industrial sabotage, some learned the skills of choosing and describing outdoor zones and creating special reception committees for parachuted supplies, others learned the art of safe-breaking and lock-picking and the use of armaments. One of the final courses was for parachute training at Ringway Airfield near Manchester. From here, they were air-dropped into Tatton Park. The trainees usually did four or five practice jumps, one at night and one with equipment strapped to the leg. However, Noor did not go to Ringway as her instructors had already excluded her from parachute training.

One of the last stages of training for all agents was the Finishing School. For Noor, this was Beaulieu (B-school) STS 36 in Hampshire. She was given instructions to travel with four other colleagues from Waterloo to Southampton on Sunday 9 May. From there they would go on to Beaulieu, the jewel in the crown of the SOE training schools.

Here, deep in the New Forest, in the spacious grounds of the Montagu family estate and the ruins of one of Britain's oldest abbeys, built in 1204, agents learnt the art of surviving behind enemy lines. After the rigours of training in Arisaig, this country house with its log fires, views overlooking a lake and relative luxury offered the agents a chance to unwind. A plaque on the abbey ruins today commemorates the agents who trained for their dangerous wartime missions here.

The SOE had eleven houses scattered through the estate which served both as specialist training schools and as cottages to live in. Beaulieu Manor (now the National Motor Museum) was the headquarters of the Group B school. The Montagu family themselves lived at Palace House in the grounds. Palace House was also used as the local Air Raid Precautions (ARP) and Red Cross headquarters and was later earmarked as a stand-by headquarters for General Dwight D. Eisenhower, the Allied Supreme Commander. The main classes took place in The Rings, a rambling 13-bedroom mansion (now demolished). All the houses had different names. Boarmans was favoured by F-section, and it was here that women agents like Noor were trained. Warren House, further down the river, near Needs Oar Point and the House on the Shore at Sowley overlooking the Solent, were used for training agents to fire a variety of weapons. Inchmery House on the east bank was used as a commando training school for Polish and French troops of the Free French Combat Parachute Company. Clobb Gorse was also taken by F-section.

The picturesque village of Beaulieu provided the base for some of the most clandestine work that would be done during the war. The tranquil surrounds of the New Forest with its wild ponies and ducks nestling along the riverbank was the setting for highly secret and dangerous missions. Preparations for D-Day saw components for the floating Mulberry Harbour being constructed in the oyster beds on the west bank of the Beaulieu river while over 500 landing craft and barges used the river during Operation Overlord. Units of frogmen and a secret underwater survey team were concealed in the grounds of the houses, along with SOE agents and commandos, while naval scientists experimented with new weapons. The whole area of Beaulieu and neighbouring Bucklers Hard were restricted areas during the war. On the east bank of the river was Exbury House, home of the Rothschilds, which was requisitioned by the Navy and came to be known as HMS *Mastodon*. Among its residents was the famous writer and engineer Nevil Shute, who experimented with a rocket-propelled pilotless aircraft called the Swallow, the precursor to the modern cruise missile.

Beaulieu had included among its list of instructors the flamboyant Kim Philby, later discovered to be a Soviet double agent. He taught propaganda at Beaulieu. Ironically, Philby had himself learnt his skills from the Soviets since he had been working for them since 1933. By Noor's time he had left for his career in MI6 but he was remembered in Beaulieu as a brilliant instructor who taught agents to live under a regime they detested without showing that they hated it.

The training at Beaulieu was considered most crucial by the SOE. It was at Beaulieu that agents learnt to recognise their enemy and survive in the field. They were taught how to tell whether they were being followed and how to give the enemy the slip, how to contact a source, how to establish safe letter boxes, how to pass messages, and how to set up radio aerials. Agents were sent on field trips and often arrested to see if they could stick to their cover stories. Everything was a preparation for the final mission.

Maurice Buckmaster would often come down from headquarters to cross-question recruits and subject them to Gestapo-style interrogation in order to break their cover stories. Agents would be dragged out of their beds in the middle of the night by someone dressed as a Gestapo officer. They would then be taken to an interrogation room, have a strong light shone on their face, and made to face a panel of what looked like Gestapo officers. This was done so the trainees would get some idea about the ruthless nature of these interrogations. They would have to repeat their cover story so many times that by the end of the interrogation it would be ingrained in their minds. If they survived without cracking, their confidence would be greatly increased and they would be able to face the thought of a genuine German interrogation. The rehearsals were grim affairs and the recruits were not spared. They were stripped and made to stand for hours in the light of bright lamps and though physical violence was never used on them, they knew that the real interrogation would probably include torture as well.

If the recruits cracked badly under the strain, they were unlikely to be sent into the field. Buckmaster recalled later that the cruel jibes, the repeated and shouted questions and implacable persistence broke a man's spirit, but he could console himself with the fact that this cracking at a rehearsal might well have saved his life – and others' – by preventing the possibility of his doing the same thing with the enemy. It was no game.[10]

Noor is said to have been terrified during her mock Gestapo interrogation at Beaulieu and become practically inaudible as the officers shouted at her. Dragged out of bed at night and rounded up by men in Gestapo uniform terrified her. Joan Sanderson said later that she found Noor's mock session

> almost unbearable. She seemed absolutely terrified. One saw that the lights hurt her, and the officer's voice when he shouted very loudly. Once he said, 'Stand on that chair!' It was just something to confuse her. She was so overwhelmed, she nearly lost her voice. As it went on she became practically inaudible. Sometimes there was only a whisper. When she came out afterwards, she was trembling and quite blanched.[11]

At Beaulieu the agents were also taught to acquire French mannerisms, as this was crucial to their survival in France. Everything the agent did had to be done in a French style, whether it was combing their hair or leaving their knives and forks on their plates, answering the telephone or calling for a waiter. Often a man could give himself away by using an incorrect idiom in French, even though his accent and the individual words of a phrase might be perfectly correct.

Trainees were told about the experiences of returning agents so they could learn from them. They were told how an agent once went into a café in France and asked for café noir (black coffee). This surprised the waitress as there was no other coffee available at that time in France. Such small slips, however insignificant, could arouse suspicion.

Noor was told off in France for pouring her milk in her tea first in the English manner. The smallest indiscretion could give you away as there were informers everywhere.

Maurice Buckmaster noted that another small example was telephone manners. The French never say *Tenez la ligne* (hold the line) as the English do. Instead they say *Ne quittez pas l'écoute* (literally – don't stop listening) or more simply *Ne quittez pas*. The use of any other phrase would automatically make a Frenchman suspicious and could lead to the death of an agent if the Frenchman was a Vichy supporter.[12]

The agents were taught how to coordinate with Baker Street from their stations in France through a series of postboxes which took messages from Paris all the way down to the Spanish border, over the mountains and to various agents in neutral capitals.

Though Noor had lived in pre-war France, it was a very different place now it was under the Germans. Her rigorous training prepared her for survival in a city that was occupied by the enemy. She learnt about the conditions of life in France, what identity card she would need and hundreds of other relevant details. She was taught to recognise the uniforms of the different police forces and learn how closely the local police worked with the Germans. At classes in The Rings and Boarmans she was shown photographs and taught to recognise the faces of the enemy: the German soldiers and the French Milice (pro-German French police). She was taught to look out for the Abwehr, the military arm of the Germans, based at the Hotel Lutetia on the Boulevard Raspail in Paris, and the SD or the Sicherheitsdienst, the intelligence wing of the SS based at 82–86 Avenue Foch. She attended lectures on the Nazi party, the German army and the Gestapo and heard returning agents describe how to deal with interrogations.

There were also lessons on codes, map reading, micro-photography and how to recognise and make forgeries. Agents were taught how to use and arrange messages on the BBC which would alert them in the field. The French service of the BBC was used regularly by the SOE to send coded messages to the agents. Before each drop, reception committees in France would listen for news of an expected delivery of agents or arms and supplies. After the evening news bulletin read in French, the announcer would give a series of personal messages called *avis*. These would be broadcast every night at 7.30 p.m. and then again at 9.15 p.m. from the BBC World Service headquarters on the Strand in London. Among the items of trivia and poetry in the programme were scattered lines in prearranged codes which would tell the agents on the field about arrangements for a drop. So the announcer in slow clear tones would say '*Moïse dormira sur les bords du Nil*' (Moses will sleep on the banks of the Nile), which could mean that an agent was arriving by Hudson aircraft.

The early evening broadcast would alert the agent. If it was repeated on the later broadcast, it was a confirmation. They would then get ready to receive the agent or the parachute drop in the fields. Very often meaningless sentences were added just to make the *messages personnels* sound genuine.

The methods at Beaulieu were classic spy school. Noor was taught how to be constantly vigilant, how to organise safe houses, how to pass a message to someone in a crowd without attracting attention and how to keep her identity a secret. Every single aspect of the training was aimed at helping the agents to save themselves and function effectively.

Noor immersed herself completely in her training. For the first time she felt she was working towards a positive goal and was doing something worthwhile. On one of her visits to London from Beaulieu, Noor told Jean that she had been promoted to something special and she was working with girls who were of a 'superior type'.[13] She also mentioned that she was staying in a beautiful old house with stained-glass windows. Jean remembered her being very keyed up and excited and looking better than ever.

Meanwhile, the shortage of radio operators in the field was reaching crisis proportions. An SOS from Paris led the SOE to ask Noor if she was prepared to go straight away, without completing her training. Typically, she agreed immediately. Vera Atkins gave her a cover story and prepared her for the final stages before departure. Noor was to be flown in by Lysander aircraft and landed on the ground. There are no details of the flight except the flight records kept by the Air Ministry. They show that on the night of 21/22 May, Noor and another agent, Jacques Courtaud, were flown into France but the flight had to come back from Compiègne because there was no reception committee.[14] The field agent in Paris had not heard the radio instruction because of jamming. Noor suffered the anxiety of this flight in vain.

There is slight confusion in Noor's personal files at this stage. They make no mention of her flight to Paris in May, but show that from Beaulieu she was sent on a training operation to Bristol.

It is unclear whether Noor made her first trip to Paris during her trip to Bristol or immediately afterwards. Her file says she was in Bristol between 19 and 23 May 1943 as part of a 96-hour scheme.

These clash with her dates for the Paris flight. It is unlikely that Noor would have been sent to Paris without completing her 96-hour course in Bristol. This final training-push gave recruits the most realistic idea of what it was like to work in the field and was considered essential.[15] It is likely therefore that Noor left for Paris after returning from Bristol, which means her Bristol test run would have been around 17 May.

Noor's assignment was to visit Bristol with a workable cover story, recruit contacts, fix up live and dead letter boxes (people and places from where agents could retrieve messages) and find a flat from which it would be safe to transmit. She would have to take all the precautions of security, watch out for being followed and handle the police if she was caught and questioned. She would be watched by SOE staff to see if she made any mistakes. Her detailed notes of the exercise are in her file.[16]

Noor decided to go to Bristol in the guise of gathering children's impressions of air raids for a book and providing articles for the BBC on this subject. This was considered a good cover story as she was a writer of children's stories and had been broadcast on the BBC. To make it look even more genuine, she actually interviewed children at Bedminster and at the Mangotsfield War nursery. She chose the cover name of Nora Kirkwood. The SOE thought this was very workable. Noor also chose a permanent cover story while at Bristol. She chose to say that she was a secretary at BOAC and that she was an Air Raid Patrol (ARP) warden with night duty three times a week. This would give her the excuse to go out at night without coming under suspicion.

The first thing Noor had to do was find herself a safe place to stay where she could work comfortably. She rented a room in a boarding house belonging to a Mrs Harvey at 30 Richmond Park Road, Clifton. But Noor found Mrs Harvey to be a very inquisitive person and she would have left the place if accommodation had not been so difficult to find. Mrs Harvey, she said, was 'frightfully conventional and police-minded'. She also wrote that 'general accommodation was very scarce and landladies as a whole (were) uncongenial'.

All the while Noor was observed by the SOE. They noted that she took the usual security procedures against search and surveillance. She did not carry any incriminating papers with her as she memorised her orders before leaving base.

Noor's first point of contact was a Mrs Laurie, head of the Irish Traveller's Censor Office, who had been instructed by the SOE. The first interview was arranged by letter. Noor set up a meeting on the pretext that she was looking for a job in the Censor's Office. During the meeting she introduced the password naturally in the conversation as she had been taught to do in Beaulieu.

She arranged a second meeting with Mrs Laurie on the cover that she would come to hand in her completed application form. Noor now put forward her real proposal to her contact. She did so with ease, asking Mrs Laurie to cooperate in a line of communication in the event of an invasion. Mrs Laurie agreed to all her suggestions.

Both Noor and Mrs Laurie had to make reports to the SOE about the meeting. Noor reported that Mrs Laurie was a 'very suitable contact'. She described her as 'responsible, understanding and tactful, security minded from experience and duty conscious as far as own country interests were concerned'. Mrs Laurie reported that Noor had 'put up a good show' but added that there was something very suspicious about Noor's manner. SOE dismissed this as nerves.

Next Noor had to locate a place to set up a live letter drop. This would be a person who would be used by her and other agents as a letter box to pass messages. She did this successfully with a porter at Bristol University and a secretary at the Empire Rendezvous in Whiteladies Road, explaining that she was moving to Bristol but as yet had no address.

She then selected two dead letter boxes. Dead letter boxes were unused hidden places where agents could exchange messages. Noor chose an oblique angle in the stone steps of the ruins of Bethesda Chapel in Great George Street and behind a fuse case in the call box at the end of Queen's Road, Clifton. The SOE found both of these 'very suitable'.

In the short time that she had, Noor had to now establish six rendezvous where she could set up meetings with contacts. The SOE had given her detailed instructions on the nature of the arrangements. Three of these were to be for a person of the same social standing as the agent. For these, Noor chose the University Library between 1 and 6 p.m., the Clifton Lawn Tennis Club on Beaufort Road before 12 noon on a Sunday, and the entrance to the Victoria Rooms after 11 p.m. She noted that the dances and parties at the Victoria Rooms finished at 11 so it would be relatively safe to meet there.

The other three rendezvous were to be with an elderly working-class woman. For these Noor chose the waiting room at the bus station at the Knowles Centre between 1 p.m. and 6 p.m., St George's Church on a Sunday at 12 p.m. and the waiting room on platform 9 at Temple Meads station after 11 p.m. Again the SOE thought the choices were good.

Noor used her Beaulieu training and observation skills to complete the rest of her project. She had to identify three operational sites where a wireless could be set up and used. This meant posing as a tenant and searching for flats available for rent. She did this with considerable speed. The first flat she chose was 9/34 Cornwallis Crescent, where the rent was £80 and the electric supply of 210 volts. Noor noticed that there were two parts of the flat to be let, the top maisonette and the basement flat. She reported that the two intermediate floors were occupied by a Mrs Sutton (the proprietor), who lived alone. She was aged between seventy-five and eighty and was very deaf. Noor found her to be a kindly old lady, most helpful and rather 'half-witted'. She noted that this was very suitable for the job as she would not know what the flat was being used for. The next step was finding a place for the aerial. Noor moved quickly around the apartment without arousing any suspicion and found that the top maisonette was a complicated structure offering several places of concealment. There was one exit by the door. The back window gave way to a long balcony which would provide roof escape.

The basement flat was separate from the rest of the house. It had two exits – one on to the crescent and one on to a wooded garden at the back facing the avenue. Noor noted that there were two main rooms and a place of concealment. There was an area in the middle between the conservatory and the garden where a wireless set could be buried under the fence. The SOE appreciated Noor's detailed report.

The second flat selected by Noor was at 99 Pembroke Road with a rather higher rent of £120 per year. She noted that it had a spacious loft in which to conceal a wireless set and offered an easy place to fix the aerial. There was no danger of being overheard and good means of police warning and escape.

A third address was at 10 Whiteladies Road, where the rent was £75, and the electric supply of 210 volts. It was a first-floor flat with one exit. This the SOE found very suitable.

Noor had to now find some reliable colleagues to act as cut-outs. These were people who would convey messages and help the agent. Noor identified Mr T.A. Leach, secretary of the Bristol University Union at Victoria Rooms. She chose him because he was very popular among Bristol students and was a great sport with close connections with the boat club. She also described him as a clever organiser.

Her second contact was Dr Hope Scott, a surgeon based at Clifton Down Road, Bristol. He was in practice with a Dr Carter, who lived at 55 Old Market Street, Bristol.

Noor found Dr Carter to be a sporty man with a 'high sense of responsibility'. She also found that he was popular among both wealthy and poor people. Noor described him as 'extremely active, genuinely English. Most precious as potential cut-out'.[17]

Noor noted that the 'Bristol area as a whole was suitable for operations. Security precautions and well founded cover most essential as police service is extremely efficient being a coastal area.'[18]

As part of the operation, Noor had to send a letter to the Bullring (this was probably a secret address in Birmingham where the SOE received letters). She successfully deposited a letter with a commando, who would have been the most reliable way of getting it delivered without the letter being traced back to her. This letter was handed over on the London train. But the SOE remarked that this gentleman, unfortunately, returned to the Bristol area before posting the letter. It was actually sent from Weston-super-Mare two days after the exercise had finished.

The most difficult part of the Bristol scheme was the interrogation. In a set-up by the SOE, Noor was arrested and taken to the police station to test her ability to improvise and stick to her cover story. Here, however, she did not perform well. The SOE noted that Noor made 'stupid' mistakes that she could easily have avoided with a little forethought. They also reported that Noor 'always volunteered far more information when being questioned'.[19]

The SOE officer concluded that Noor had worked very hard and 'shown interest in the exercise, but however, she must learn to be more discreet. Apart from the police interrogation, I consider this quite a good scheme.' This would go against Noor in her reports, leading to divisions among her instructors as to whether she was capable of becoming an agent.

Once Noor finished at Beaulieu, she had to wait for the next full moon to be flown to France. Agents were flown in on full-moon nights so that the pilot could have greater visibility of the area. While most agents went after Beaulieu for further specialist training – parachuting, lock-picking and safe-breaking or clandestine wireless techniques in Thame Park – Noor was urgently needed in the field and had to make her final preparations. Meanwhile, opinions about her capability were divided. Her nervousness had clearly gone against her. Some of her instructors were concerned that she did not have a sense of security and was too emotional. They blamed her emotional state on her father, as word had got around that he had been a Sufi preacher. Noor became one of the most controversial agents in Beaulieu as instructors clashed over their assessment of her. She was considered by some to be too beautiful and exotic, a person who would attract attention to herself rather than blend in the background. Some thought she would be a security risk while others considered her a very capable potential agent and an excellent radio operator.

Even Noor's colleague in Beaulieu, Yvonne Cormeau, a successful agent herself who survived the war, described Noor as a 'splendid, vague dreamy creature, far too conspicuous – twice seen, never forgotten' who had 'no sense of security' and should never have been sent to France.[20]

The training schools, however, often had reports which did not match the agents' actual performance on the field. A report from Beaulieu on Francis Cammaerts, one of the SOE's most successful agents, described him as 'rather lacking in dash' and 'not suitable as a leader'.[21] By 1944 Cammaerts had trained and armed nearly 10,000 men who were all in place by D-Day ready to delay German reinforcements. Violette Szabo, who later got the George Cross for her bravery, and was a crack shot, had reports which said: 'I seriously wonder whether this student is suitable for our purpose. She seems lacking in a sense of responsibility and . . . does not appear to have any initiative or ideals.' Szabo was also described as being 'uncertain of her own mind and to have no definite purpose'. Even her final report described her as 'temperamentally unsuitable for this work'.[22] Yet in these and other cases, Maurice Buckmaster and Selwyn Jepson took the final decisions on the agent, trusting their own instinct rather than the reports from the training schools.

Noor now remained on standby. From Beaulieu, she was to be sent to Chorleywood in Hertfordshire where agents were taken just before they went into the field. The actual house was at Chalfont St Giles in Buckinghamshire, but Chorleywood was the name of the nearest railway station. It was a large country housc full of agents leaving on different missions and all, understandably, a little nervous. Here the training continued, with codes, map reading and cover story familiarisation. Noor was by now expected to finish her training by the end of June. Yet she knew she would have to leave before that, possibly by mid-June.

Before she left for Chorleywood, Noor had to say goodbye to her mother and sister. She did not know when she would meet them again. She went to London and tried desperately to organise the paperwork on the financial front so that Claire could look after her mother when she had gone. She told them she was going away for a long time and would not be able to write letters. Her mother thought she was going to Africa. Claire thought she was going to some island and had no idea that she was heading for France.

But almost on the last day, Noor sprang another surprise on her family. She told them she was engaged.[23] Her fiancé was someone she had met at the War Office and they would be married when she returned. The family had little time to react. They had noticed that a gentleman often used to telephone Noor when she was in London, but had not thought much of it.

Noor told them briefly that he was a British officer. His father was English. Noor said they had hoped to get married before she left but it had not been possible. Nevertheless, she told them that she considered the engagement formal. Noor would not reveal the young man's name or address to her family, but later Claire thought she had said his mother was Norwegian or that he had lived in Norway for a while.

Noor also told Claire that if she was ever called upon to do something called 'liaison work' she was to refuse. When Claire asked why, Noor explained to her that if her knowledge of French and upbringing in France led to her getting a call from the War Office, she was not to accept the job. The request made no sense to Claire, but she promised Noor because her sister seemed so serious about it. It did not occur to Claire that Noor herself may have been off on just such an assignment.

Noor did not manage to say goodbye to Vilayat, who was now at Lancing College. He had always been her closest friend and soulmate and she was still worried about him and his threats to leave the Navy. She gave a sealed envelope to Claire with instructions that if he failed his commission and was about to do something reckless, she should give him the letter and tell him to try and do what she had suggested in it. Later Vilayat discovered that Noor had written the name and address of an officer of the French section in it.

It was time for the final farewells. After kissing her mother and sister, Noor walked away. But something made Claire cling to her for a few more minutes. She took Noor's hand and started walking with her. Noor didn't ask her to go back. Both girls took the tube from Euston Square to Baker Street. At Baker Street station she hugged Claire again and simply said: 'This is where we say goodbye.'

Her last words to Claire were 'Be good'. Claire watched till the last, as Noor's slight figure melted into the crowd in Baker Street.

SIX

Leaving England

Before going to Chorleywood Noor had to meet her section chiefs in Baker Street, who were facing a crisis. The wireless operator of their team in Paris had asked for emergency help because his workload was too heavy to handle alone. He needed immediate relief. Though she had still not finished her training, Noor was the only one available, and she knew she would be taking the next flight out. It was scheduled for the next full moon, 16 June.

Feeling a little low after having said goodbye to her family, she reached Chorleywood and met her escorting officer and colleagues. Here in the large country house, Noor's training continued. Along with other agents she pored over maps, practised her cover story and had further instructions on codes and wireless training. Noor was given revision in Innocent Letter Conventions (long reports written in code which were carried on aircraft rather than transmitted by radio), training in writing practice letters, wording messages, revision of double transposition and envelope opening. But even as she made her preparations to go, there were some last-minute hitches. Her final reports were negative, questioning her suitability for the field. In a report on 21 May, Colonel Frank Spooner wrote: 'Not overburdened with brains but has worked hard and shown keenness, apart from some dislike of the security side of the course. She has an unstable and temperamental personality and it is very doubtful whether she is really suited to work in the field.'[1]

This controversial note is heavily underlined and the words 'not overburdened with brains' have a comment by Buckmaster in the margin saying 'We don't want them overburdened with brains'. The bit about the 'temperamental personality' is also underlined, with 'Nonsense' written next to it in the margin. There are further scribblings from Buckmaster, 'Makes me cross', and finally, 'she ought to work as S2'. While Buckmaster's comments about not wanting his agents 'overburdened with brains' may smack of arrogance, implying that brains were needed only for the senior people, it was also a reflection of the SOE's desperate situation. Buckmaster may have made the throwaway remark because he was anxious to send Noor into the field as soon as possible. F-section was under tremendous pressure. To get a trained wireless operator was difficult enough – to get one who was fluent in French as well was almost impossible at short notice. Noor was almost tailor-made for them and her chiefs were confident she should go.

Colonel Frank Spooner later told Noor's friend Jean Overton Fuller that he had prepared the harsh report just to protect Noor and prevent her going into the field. He was opposed on principle to women doing this work and felt particularly strongly that Noor would not be able to cope. The word had spread in Beaulieu that Noor came from a mystical Sufi background and there were many doubts about whether she had the inner toughness to be a secret agent.

These concerns were expressed in another memo of 24 May 1943: 'From reports on the girl I suggest that care be taken that she be not given any task which might set up a mental conflict with her idealism. This might render her unstable from our point of view.'

Noor had performed terribly at the mock Gestapo interrogation which took place at the end of her training period. The contradictory reports made the SOE keep a close watch on her. There was one thing all the instructors agreed on: her radio skills were excellent. Besides, she was the only one who could go, since the others in her batch were well behind her in speed and wireless training. Noor by now had completed her course on the A Mark II transmitter and could handle the controls quite efficiently. She had a few problems with systematic fault-finding and technical intricacies but understood her code theory very well. Her trainers noted that she needed more practical experience to become fully proficient.

It wasn't just the report from Spooner that cast doubts in the minds of the SOE. Two women agents who were staying with Noor in Chorleywood wrote to Vera Atkins expressing their doubts about Noor's suitability for the field. Troubled by the reports, Vera took Noor out to lunch at Manetta's in Clarges Street. Taking a corner table where they could not be overheard, Vera told her about the letter she had received and asked Noor how she felt about the women's views. Noor was shocked and hurt.[2]

Vera put it to her that she could still opt out without any trace being left on her file if she had doubts. She explained to her that there was nothing wrong in admitting it. It was worse to go into the field and let your comrades down. But Noor was firm. She said she knew she was the proper person for the mission and had never had any doubts. She told Vera that saying goodbye to her mother and sister in London had been the most painful experience of her life. She also confessed that she was worried about Vilayat's examination results.

Vera told Noor that she would inform her in Paris how Vilayat had done in his exams. By the end of the meal, Vera was convinced that it was only the pain of parting from her family that had dampened Noor's spirits. She, along with Maurice Buckmaster, had complete faith in Noor.

Noor asked Vera to send periodical bulletins to her mother informing her that she was well. If she was missing they were not to tell her. She wanted Vera to keep up the bulletins till they had definite information about her (even if it was after the war was over). Vera asked her if this would make her happier and she said it would.

On 4 June, Selwyn Jepson sent a memo from F-section asking if Noor could be discharged from the WAAF and given an honorary commission in that service. 'She will be leaving for the Field very shortly and I should be glad if the necessary action could be put in motion,' he wrote.

Noor was still at Chorleywood preparing her cover story and doing some crucial map reading and further wireless training. On 5 June 1943 her progress report stated: 'Has now completed a shortened course at the request of Country section. Her scheme [training exercise] was curtailed through a technical fault, but she gained some useful experience and is now more confident of her operating.' Her final report from Thame Park confirmed that her training had been cut short and she was being sent to the field.

> This student was withdrawn during the month at the request of her Country section. While she cannot be considered a fully trained operator because of her shortened course, she is quite capable of handling her set, and of passing messages. She should, however, gain more confidence in time. While at this school she showed signs of being easily flustered when difficulties cropped

up, especially if they were of a technical nature, and it is doubtful if she will ever be able to fully overcome this.[3]

Noor knew she would not be completing her training and went to say goodbye to Joan Sanderson, giving her a pair of cufflinks she had been wearing as a memento.

On 7 June Noor had a final appointment to run through her codes before she left. She had to go to London to meet Leo Marks, master code-maker and head of communications at SOE. He was the son of Benjamin Marks, owner of the legendary London bookshop at 84 Charing Cross Road, and had joined the SOE aged twenty-two in 1942. A cryptographer of genius, he had made the codes to be used by agents in the field.

Many years later Marks gave an amusing account of the meeting with Noor and an impromptu meeting with Buckmaster that preceded it.[4] Late one night Maurice Buckmaster knocked on his door, hungry and exhausted, complaining that the canteen was shut.

Once Marks had supplied him with his mother's home-made sandwiches and cakes, Buckmaster blurted out a name: 'Noor Inayat Khan.'

He told the bewildered Leo Marks that she was a wireless operator who had finished her course in Beaulieu and was due to be dropped into France in around ten days' time. Buckmaster told Marks that the problem was that 'the bastard Spooner' had 'taken against her' and had written a report saying that she was 'temperamentally unsuitable' to be an agent, and would be a major security risk if she were sent to the field. 'Which is absolute balls,' said Buckmaster. He admitted, however, that Noor's other instructors agreed with Spooner.

'What else could one expect from that mob of second-raters?' he burst out. He also said that 'that damn busybody' had sent a copy of his report to Baker Street and the question of whether Noor should be allowed to go to France was now in the balance.

In fact Spooner had sent a copy of the report to Robin Brook, controller of the French, Belgian and Dutch directorates and to Eric Mockler-Ferryman, director in charge of operations into all Western Europe, hoping the latter would refer the matter to the SOE chief Colin Gubbins. Marks knew that one attempt had already been made to fly Noor into Paris. So desperate was the SOE that on that occasion she had left without even the required final code briefing from him. He had only heard about it later. Maurice Buckmaster admitted in his book *Specially Employed* that sometimes the training school's commandant's report on an agent was at variance with their own, but that 'it was necessary, for overriding reasons of shortage of specialists – particularly wireless operators – to stretch a point in favour of a candidate'.[5] Noor was clearly one such case.

Buckmaster told Marks that Noor's character needed more understanding than Spooner and co. were capable of. He described Noor as a 'sensitive dreamy girl' whose father, an Indian prince, had given her a mystical upbringing. She had spent her childhood in France and thought her knowledge of French could be more useful to the Resistance than to the RAF. He also told Marks with paternalistic pride that Noor had a book published.

Buckmaster asked Marks for a favour: to give Noor an 'extended briefing' to help her memorise her code conventions so thoroughly that she would not forget them when she reached France. He asked him not to give her one of the new silk codes since it would thoroughly confuse her and she would just leave it lying around. 'I must admit that Noor has a tendency to be absent-minded,' remarked Buckmaster.

He asked Marks to send him a written report after the briefing. Marks made it a point to change the time scheduled in his diary for Noor from the customary one hour to three. 'Any longer than that and I might emerge as an Indian mystic,' he wrote. He also ordered a copy of Noor's *Twenty Jataka Tales*.

Reading Noor's files, Marks discovered that her instructor at Beaulieu had said her coding was 'completely unpredictable'. He rang the instructor up for a chat. The instructor confided in Marks that the 'potty princess' had caused more dissension than any pupil in the history of Beaulieu. Yet no one could deny that she was an excellent radio operator.

Pressed further by Marks, the instructor described her father as a 'crackpot' and head of a mystical sect who had founded the House of Blessing in Paris where Noor spent her childhood. They all agreed at Beaulieu that the 'crackpot father' was responsible for her eccentric behaviour.

'Do you know what the bastard taught her? That the worst sin she could commit was to lie about anything,' the instructor told

Marks helpfully. He also told Marks about an incident that underlined just how unpredictable and ingenuous Noor could be. Once when Beaulieu had sent her on a radio exercise, and she was cycling towards her safe house to practise transmitting, a policeman stopped her and asked what she was doing. 'I'm training to be an agent,' she said. 'Here's my radio – want me to show it to you?' She then removed it from its hiding place and invited him to try it.

The instructor also related how after Noor's mock interrogation by Bristol police, the superintendent in charge told Spooner not to waste his time with her 'because if this girl's an agent, I'm Winston Churchill'.

Marks prepared himself for a daunting meeting with the Indian princess. In the meantime he read each of the twenty stories from the *Jataka Tales* twice and knew one of them by heart. It was a story about a monkey chief who led 80,000 monkeys to their freedom by sacrificing himself and offering his body as a bridge. The monkeys were trying to flee the wicked king Brahmadatta. But one of the monkeys jumped so hard that he broke the monkey chief's back. The story was about sacrifice and how the monkey was happy to sacrifice himself to save the others. Even the wicked king learnt that ultimately it is love that conquers.

'Oh, Noor. What the hell are you doing in SOE?' thought Marks.

Marks had anticipated he would conduct the briefing with an air of detachment, but when Noor entered the room, he was thrown. 'As soon as I glimpsed the slender figure seated at a desk in the Orchard Court briefing room I knew that the only thing likely to be detached was one (if not both) of my eyeballs. No one had mentioned Noor's extraordinary beauty,' wrote Marks.

Marks asked her to compose a message of at least 250 letters and encode it for transmission. Noor got to work immediately writing the message in French but then spent five minutes changing it. She gave a satisfied smile at the end and completely forgot to encode it. Marks gently reminded her that London was waiting for the transmission. She apologised profusely and produced a poem code from her handbag. She told him it was her own poem and began to work on the encoding. After a shaky start she suddenly changed gear and finished her first transposition faster than any agent Marks had briefed. She handed it over with a pleased smile but forgot that she hadn't finished encoding the rest of the message. Again she apologised, but completed the rest in under ten minutes (again faster than anyone Marks had seen).

He then asked her to decode it herself. She took twenty minutes to do that. When Marks examined the worksheets he found she had made a number of mistakes. Noor looked as if she was close to tears. 'You've made fewer mistakes than most,' he told her, 'but those you have made are very inventive.' That made her feel a bit better.

Marks then decided to tackle 'the princess' in her own style. Basing his words on her stories, he told her: 'Coded messages have one thing in common with monkeys: If you jump too hard on them you'll break their backs – and that's what you have done to this one. I doubt if Brahmadatta himself could decipher it, I know my monkeys in the code room couldn't,' Marks told Noor.

Noor looked up in surprise. 'You've read my book,' she said.

Marks recalled that the 'intensity of her look reduced him to chutney'. He told her he had enjoyed it and it had taught him a lot. And then he told Noor that she had told him a lie, and made the code tell a lie.

Noor sprang to her feet and exclaimed, 'I've *what*?' The word 'lie' had had the desired effect. The Beaulieu instructor had been right after all. Marks tackled her. 'You have given the wrong indicator-group. What else is that but a lie?'

'I hadn't thought of it like that,' replied Noor.

Marks went through her work and said there were six lies and one half-truth. He said it would take 10,000 attempts before Colonel Buckmaster could read the message, to which Noor whispered, 'Oh no.'

Marks then told the despairing agent: 'I believe your Jataka Tales could help you to become a very good coder.'

Noor looked up in astonishment. 'How?'

He replied:

> Every time you encode a message think of the letters in it as monkeys trying to cross the bridge between Paris and London. If they fall off, they'll be caught and shot . . . but they can't cross by themselves, and if you don't help them by guiding them slowly and methodically, one step at a time, giving them all your thoughts and all your protection, they'll never reach the other side. When there's a truth to pass on, don't let your code tell lies.

Noor asked if she could try again. She now encoded at half her previous speed (which was still faster than most) and copied out the code-groups carefully. She ran her fingers across the messages as if searching for injuries before giving them to Marks. Both were perfect.

'Thank you, thank you – but will it be all right if I think about pigs sometimes?' she asked Marks. (One of her stories was about two piglets named Mahatundila and Cullatindila.) Marks told her that she must do whatever helped to cross that bridge and then asked her if she was sure she could keep it up.

'Mr Marks, I promise you I will,' she said.

Noor asked Marks what he wanted do after the war. He told her he planned to write a play, and she expressed such interest in this that he found himself discussing it with her, even though it had nothing to do with the purpose of their meeting. The play was about a girl who couldn't laugh. She had stopped laughing at the age of five and was now eighteen. Many attempts had been made to get her to laugh, but nothing worked. Then one day she saw a dirty old tramp and burst out laughing. He was brought into the house and she found him even funnier. But the tramp refused to stay because he didn't like being laughed at.

The tramp decided to find out what had stopped her from laughing. He discovered that someone had inflicted enormous pain on her. But the moment the tramp discovered this, the girl was cured. Ironically, the moment she was cured, she saw the tramp for what he was – a dirty old vagrant – and he had to go.

Noor thought the story was sad and funny and hoped that the tramp would go away without letting the girl know how much she owed to him. She asked Marks if the play had a title. Looking at Noor, Marks immediately thought of the title: 'The Girl Who Couldn't Quite!'

Noor told Marks that she was sure lots of people would come to see the play and promised that she would come if she could. It left Marks hoping that she would fail her test so she would not have to be sent to the field.

Then it was time for Noor to learn her security checks, the all-important means by which the SOE would know whether her radio messages were genuine or not. Marks realised he might have another uphill battle about 'not having to lie'. Noor had used her security checks correctly, but she may not have realised that she would have to lie about them if caught.

'Why should I do that?' Noor asked. Marks explained that if she told the Germans the real check then they would pretend they were her and send messages to England in her name, thereby lying to England.

'But there's a better way. Suppose that I refused to tell them anything at all – no matter how often they ask?' said Noor. Marks realised that she would rather die than tell a lie. To get around this problem, he gave Noor a security check that was completely new and said she would not have to lie about it because no one but Noor and he would know about it. 'All you have to do is remember one thing. Never use a key phrase with eighteen letters in it – any other number but not eighteen. If you use eighteen, I'll know you've been caught.'

'Eighteen's my lucky number,' said Noor. 'Yes, I could do that. And I promise you not to forget it. I promise you, Mr Marks.'

Marks wasn't taking any chances with Noor, however. He told her to encode three messages at least 200 letters long and have them ready for him by midday next day. She had to include her true and bluff checks. When he left the room, Noor was saying to herself: 'I mustn't use a key phrase eighteen letters long', and reaching for her pencil.

Marks was still hoping that she would fail the test so he could give her a bad report. Noor's beauty and sensitivity had captivated him. He did not want to expose this delicate person to the Gestapo, possible torture and death. But Noor encoded six new messages and every one of her monkeys crossed the bridge securely, including her security checks. She numbered a key phrase eighteen letters long and handed it to Marks proudly.

On 10 June Leo Marks reluctantly gave the full go-ahead to Noor and sent the report to Maurice Buckmaster. He remembered his meeting with Noor all his life. *The Girl Who Couldn't Quite!* was performed at the St Martin's Theatre in 1948.

The next few days were a rush for Noor. Paris needed her urgently and it was just a few days till the next full moon.

The week before she left, Noor was brought to the flat at Orchard Court, manned by the famous butler Parks, where agents stayed before they left on their missions. The flat had a black-tiled bathroom that became quite a legend in the service. Often agent

Peter Churchill would be seen here, fully dressed in a suit, sitting in the empty bath with his feet resting over the taps doing *The Times* crossword. At other times an agent might be found perched on the side of the bath going over the last details of his or her cover story.

The time the agents spent at Orchard Court was a brief period of luxury before their gruelling, dangerous stints in the field. Here the last checks were made, cover story rechecked, details pored over. The agents were given the latest news from France and their own specialist operations. If a certain operator was suspected of working for the Germans they were told to take appropriate action against him.

Parks presided over Orchard Court with skill. He was a former messenger at the Paris branch of the Westminster Bank and he had an excellent memory. He knew every agent by their training pseudonym and made each one feel welcome when they came to the flat for their last briefing. Parks knew exactly how to ensure that the agents did not bump into one another during their time in the flat. It was SOE policy to discourage the agents from meeting in the field, and the best way to do this was to make sure they did not meet too much in England. It was particularly important for agents never to tell anyone where in occupied France they were going. As it was highly likely that two agents who were due to go into the field would discuss this if they met in the flat, Parks had to make sure they never had the opportunity to do so.

Parks somehow managed to spirit people from room to room with complete delicacy. Sometimes he even spirited them into the bathroom. This might have become somewhat inconvenient for the visitors at the flat but the agents knew why Parks had to do it, and the genial butler was very popular with F-section.

At Orchard Court, where the walls were covered with maps of France and Paris, the agent was given suitable clothes to match his or her cover story. Maurice Buckmaster did not favour his agents carrying any spy devices: no hollow pens, false-bottomed briefcases or detachable heels. He thought these were on the whole more risky, as discovery by the German Abwehr would certainly lead to imprisonment or death. It was easier for an agent to bluff his way if he were found without any incriminating evidence and gadgets. It was better to carry a message in a folded newspaper. In a tight spot it could be discarded. It was, of course, best if the agent simply memorised messages and instructions.

Appearance was most important and a thorough check on French mannerisms and style was crucial. If the hairstyle was not suitably French, it had to be changed. If the agent had an English-style dental filling, then that would have to be replaced by an expensive-looking gold plug as was usual on the Continent.

All the agents' clothes were specially tailored by Claudi Pulver, a refugee from Vienna, who put her design skills to use and tailored clothes for the agents in the European style. Shirts, skirts, even underwear was stitched in the most meticulous Continental style after careful research into clothes brought in by refugees. Sometimes spare French clothes brought by refugees and agents were reissued. Noor had to go to the showroom in Margaret Street to be fitted for her clothes.

The collars, the cuffs, and most importantly the labels were carefully checked. All laundry instructions had to be removed. An English label could give the game away, as could a wrongly sewn button, or the style of the collar. Name-tabs of tailors in the arrondissement of the Etoile were sewn in. A Jewish German tailor who had escaped the Nazis was also recruited. He could look at a suit and say whether it came from Czechoslovakia, Italy, Spain or Germany. For agents going to Germany, he made German-style suits and then aged them, since few people in Germany were wearing new suits. The clothes also had to be suitable for the person's cover story. Noor, playing a nurse, needed a few simple dresses.

Every caution had to be taken to see that the cover story was watertight. If the agent had a slight trace of a foreign accent, the cover story would be made up to suit it. So if a person had a slight Canadian accent then a Canadian background would be worked into the cover story. Sometimes a Belgian accent would merit a story about Belgian education or childhood in Brussels.

Cover stories were meticulously checked and rechecked. The identities were created from places where the town halls had been bombed or destroyed and the records scattered. Sometimes an obscure town overseas which was in French possession was given as the birthplace, so it would be nearly impossible to check the details. Considerable research was done on the background. Aunts, uncles, whole families were all woven into the cover story and were located in districts where search was difficult or impossible. Real streets and real house numbers were always used.

These were found with the help of French post office guides and telephone books.

A full-time forgery department based at Roydon in Essex worked on the passports and papers. The latest ration cards were immediately rushed back through agents on the field and copied. Ration cards, identity cards, birth certificates – nothing escaped the skilful forgers, who worked overtime to provide the agents with their papers.

Noor had already been given her cover story by Vera Atkins. She was to be Jeanne-Marie Renier, a children's nurse. All the details had been carefully worked out.[6] Jeanne-Marie was born in Blois on 25 April 1918. Her father Auguste had been a professor of philosophy in Princeton and her mother, Ray Baker, was American by birth and French by marriage. Her father was killed in the 1918 retreat on the Marne in the First World War. Her mother returned to Paris after the Armistice, and went back to America just before the collapse of France in 1940.

Jeanne-Marie had been to school in St Cloud, and passed her Bacchot at the Lycée de St Cloud, then went to the Sorbonne in 1935. She studied there till 1938, specialising in child psychology. She looked after children in various families, and when the war broke out she worked as a nurse in Paris. Some of these facts for the cover story were drawn from Noor's real life. Noor went to school in St Cloud and had a degree in child psychology from the Sorbonne.

When the Germans broke through, Jeanne-Marie went south and stayed for a while in the Bordeaux area. She was employed as a governess by a family named Jourden in Royan. She spent Christmas 1941 in Paris and obtained there her new ration card on 30 December 1941. She also obtained a new identity card early in 1943 when she was in Bordeaux looking for a family who would need her services as a governess. Her textile card was obtained in Paris. The SOE's skilful forgery department issued 'Jeanne-Marie' with a fake identity card, a ration card and a textile card.

On all social occasions Noor would be referred to as Mademoiselle Renier. Apart from the cover name, all agents also had a code name by which their colleagues in SOE would refer to them. Noor's code name was Madeleine, based on one of the characters from her stories. She would use the name Madeleine only with members of the French section and it would be closely guarded. Her radio post would be called Poste Madeleine.

Noor had asked Maurice Buckmaster if she could work in the Paris area, as she was familiar with it. Though this posed the danger that she might be recognised, Noor was confident that she would be most effective in that region. Occupied Paris was also the most dangerous place to operate as the city was crawling with the Gestapo.

As a telegraphist, or 'pianist' as the job was called by SOE, Noor would need a transmitter. Since she was a petite 5ft 3in and weighed under 8 stone, she needed lightweight equipment. Transmitters were always in short supply and were imported from US manufacturers and then adapted for installation in a suitcase.

Finally, the agents were given a set of four pills. One was a type that would induce sleep for six hours and was to be administered in the enemy's tea or coffee if the need arose. The second pill was a stimulant, Benzedrine, which would keep the agent awake in an emergency if she was dog-tired but had to go on. The third could produce stomach disorders. This was for the agent if she wanted to sham an indisposition. The fourth was the L pill, a suicide pill containing cyanide in a little rubber coating, which the agent had the option of taking if they were captured and did not want to face Gestapo interrogation. The L pill would work only if it was bitten and would be ineffective if it was swallowed whole. The set of four pills was handed over to Noor by Vera Atkins.

Once the agent was absolutely clear on the background of their mission, they were passed on to an escorting officer who stayed with him until the very moment when they boarded the plane. The officer was responsible for going through the agent's pockets to make sure that no English cigarettes or money was slipped in at the last moment. A small lapse like this could cost a life and wreck weeks of careful planning. Noor's escorting officer was Patricia Stewart-Bam, who clearly remembered the young woman's courage years later.[7]

Maurice Buckmaster made a point of meeting every agent personally before they left for the field and gave each one a small gift. The men got a pair of gold cufflinks or a cigarette lighter, and the women a gold compact. When the agents were alone in France the gift would remind them that their colleagues back home were thinking of them. If an agent was in dire straits, they could even sell the item to raise cash. Buckmaster tried to go to the airfield with as many agents as he could as it was always in the last few moments before they left the country that they would feel the most nervous and vulnerable.[8]

A few days before she left, Noor paid an unexpected visit to her friend Jean. This was probably after 10 June when she had been given the all-clear for France and was living in Orchard Court. She arrived late at night at Jean's flat and the two of them talked long into the night. Fuller remembered that Noor was looking very beautiful, that her skin was glowing and there was a shine in her eyes. Noor told her she was very happy. Jean thought she was in love. 'Everything I have ever wanted has come at once,' she told Jean.[9] She was wearing her khaki FANY uniform and was very keyed up. 'There was an extraordinary degree of excitement in her,' said Jean.[10] 'She had stars in her eyes. She wanted to go.'

Noor was, in fact, very much in love and engaged to a man at the War Office, as she had told her family. Strangely, she did not tell Jean about her romance. Perhaps this was because her relationships had so often gone wrong, and there was so much uncertainty in her life at the moment that she did not want to tempt fate by telling too many people. She had given only sketchy details of her fiancé to her own family and not given them any contact details either. He remained a mystery to them and they never discovered who he was.

That night Noor asked Jean to read her palm and tell her what the future held for her. At one point in the evening she remarked that she had always been afraid of being tortured. As a child she had read about martyrs and lain awake at nights worrying about them; she had nightmares that she was being tortured so she would reveal a secret. She wondered how she would cope in a Nazi concentration camp if she were tortured. 'I don't see how one can know . . .' she said, and then added: 'I don't think I would ever speak.'

As they talked Jean was struck by the change in Noor's personality. Though Noor had always been a highly strung person, Jean had never seen her like this before. After breakfast, Noor got up and said 'I am going to go now', and hugged and kissed Jean. It was the last time Jean saw her friend. For a long time she assumed that when Noor said she had to go 'overseas', it meant across the oceans to another continent. She did not think that Noor was just going across the Channel to France.

On 15 June 1943, Noor was released from the WAAF and on the following day she was awarded an honorary commission in the

WAAF as Assistant Section Officer. It was nearly a year since she had attended the interview for her commission in the same service, where she had spoken emotionally about Indian independence and almost ruined her chances. But life had taken a different course for her. Now she had been given an honorary commission and was to be sent on a dangerous mission for King and country.

On the afternoon of 16 June, Vera Atkins called for Noor at Orchard Court in an open car. (This estate car had been nicknamed 'the hearse' by the SOE.) They drove through the Sussex countryside in full summer bloom with honeysuckle and marguerites. Noor hardly said a word. Vera Atkins noticed she had a serene expression on her face and a half smile playing on her lips. She always felt that Noor was very self-contained and had an unworldly idealism.

It was nearly evening by the time they reached Tangmere in Sussex and stopped outside the little ivy-covered cottage just opposite the main gates of the RAF station. It was partly hidden by tall hedges and could hardly be seen from the road. Though it was a summer evening all the doors and windows were shut and the silence was almost eerie. But as the two women stepped inside, they found the hall was full of smoke and they could hear men's voices.

Tangmere Cottage was a seventeenth-century house with low ceilings and thick walls. On the ground floor were two living rooms and a kitchen. One of the living rooms was used as an operations room for the crew and there was a large map of France on the wall, a table and a map chest. There was also an ordinary telephone line and a 'scrambler' phone line for confidential conversations. The second living room was used as the dining room and had two long trestle tables where agents and pilots often had their supper before they left. Upstairs there were five bedrooms functioning as dormitories for the pilots.

After a hearty farewell supper, Vera Atkins led Noor upstairs to a room. On one of the chairs lay a novel called *Remarkable Women*. Noor remarked that the men probably enjoyed reading about remarkable women. Vera Atkins replied that perhaps one day someone would write a book about the 'most remarkable women of all'. She commented to herself: 'That book will have to be rewritten after these girls have done their stuff.'[11] Noor started to get ready, putting on her green oilskin coat. In her handbag was a French identity card, ration card and her Webley pistol. The rest of her belongings – radio, clothes and personal effects – would be parachuted separately, so she did not have to carry them with her. She needed to carry the pistol on her in case they were ambushed as soon as they landed.

Vera Atkins did the usual last-minute pocket-check for English cigarettes, English bus tickets or English money – anything that could risk the agent's life if discovered. As she was getting ready, Noor noticed a silver bird on Vera Atkins' suit and remarked how lovely it was and how Vera always managed to look so smart. She herself, she felt, inevitably looked plain. The older woman took off the bird and pinned it on Noor's lapel. When Noor protested she said: 'It's a little bird, it will bring you luck.'[12]

Soon there was a knock on the door signalling that it was time to go. The full moon shone high in the sky. A large Ford estate car was waiting to take them to the airstrip. There, silhouetted against the night sky, she could see the two Lysanders waiting for their passengers. Noor stepped out into the night and walked on English soil for the last time. She felt she was keeping her promise to the people of France. She was going back.

In France that evening, waiting agents received a message in the middle of an entertainment programme on the BBC French service. It said: 'Jasmine is playing her flute.'[13] It was the code telling them to prepare for the arriving agents.

SEVEN

Joining the Circuit

On the night of 16/17 June two Lysander aircraft were to take off from Tangmere with agents and land in France. Agents going into the field were referred to by the pilots as 'Joes' and the Lysanders were affectionately called 'Lizzies'.

On duty that night were pilots Bunny Rymills and James McCairns, usually referred to as Mac. Rymills was flying Noor's Lysander. Her fellow passenger was Cecily Lefort, who was being landed in France as a courier. Cecily and Noor had trained together in Wanborough Manor. The second Lysander was flown by Mac and carried Diana Rowden (also a courier) and Charles Skepper, organiser of the Monk circuit, which operated in the south of France near Marseilles.

Noor had practised the drill many times before. After the briefest of greetings from Rymills (the pilots were not told the names of the agents), she climbed up the short ladder into the aircraft followed by Cecily. Rymills showed them where to put their bags below the wooden seat, how to plug their flying helmet into the intercom and how to switch their microphone on and off. He then climbed into his cockpit, slid the roof shut, primed the engine and started off.

The SOE circuits in France worked in threes – the organiser, the courier and the radio operator. The organiser was the head of the circuit, the courier was responsible for passing messages between the organiser and his contacts, and the radio operator sent their messages to head office. The radio operator was the only link between Baker Street and the circuit and all the crucial information would go through him. The Germans knew that if they caught the radio operator of a circuit, the others might easily fall into their hands.

Noor was the first woman radio operator to be flown into occupied France. Women agents dropped in previously had gone as couriers. The chronic shortage of radio operators meant that women had to be trained in this area as well. Women were considered to be skilled wireless operators because they were good at knitting and could master keying better than men. But clandestine radio work was very different from ordinary radio transmission. Radio operators had the most dangerous job in the field as chances of capture were high. Up till 1943, when Noor was sent to France, the SOE had trained only a handful of radio operators. Even at its peak, STS 52 at Thame Park was turning out only 16 to 18 trained operators a month.[1] Radio operators had a high chance of being arrested as they had to carry their wireless sets about with them most of the time and if stopped and questioned had to explain their incriminating evidence. Based in the Paris area, Noor would be specially vulnerable because she would have to use the Metro and the Gestapo frequently checked people at all the interchanges. The average survival time for a radio operator in the field was estimated by SOE to be six weeks. Despite this, the SOE had to carry on sending them out to France, as without them the agents could not communicate with London.

All the agents flying that night were doomed. Diana Rowden would later be executed at Natzweiler concentration camp. Cecily Lefort would die in Ravensbruck concentration camp, and Noor at Dachau. Charles Skepper would also die in Germany.

After the war, the pilots were shocked to learn of the fate of the three women they had flown that night. They could not believe that the jolly party that had left Tangmere after a hearty supper had all been flown to their deaths.[2] Vera Atkins recalled that they had all set out bravely, and the only sign of nervousness she detected was a slightly trembling cigarette in the dark (which could have belonged to any of the three girls).[3] But at that moment they were all charged up, waiting for the mission ahead.

Rymills remembered his passengers clearly. He remarked that Cecily Lefort looked like a vicar's wife whose French 'did not seem to be all that hot' and recalled Noor's green oilskin coat. It was also the time he forgot to switch off his transmitter during the flight. As the Lysanders took off in the clear moonlit sky, Mac remembered that Rymills' voice could be clearly heard on the next plane as he talked to his passengers.[4]

The moment they crossed the Channel, Mac heard Rymills say: 'Now Madame, we are approaching your beautiful country – isn't it lovely in the moonlight?' Back came the answer in a soft, accented voice, 'Yes, I think it is heavenly. What is that town over there?' Mac remembered thinking that the German listening service, which monitored the airwaves, would have heard the conversation as well. 'Black mark!', he thought.

In the tight confines of their Lysander, Noor and Cecily looked out at the country below. The flight to France usually took anything from two to six hours depending on the distance. Lysanders were the most popular aircraft by which agents were landed in France. RAF 161 Squadron was charged with the Lysander flights and took most of the agents to France during the war. The SOE had two airstrips at their disposal. The main one was the carefully camouflaged special-duties airfield at Tempsford, west of Cambridge. The second was at Tangmere, near Chichester, which was favoured by Lysander pilots as it was closer to the English Channel and they could secure a greater penetration into France from here.

The Lysanders were ideally suited for the dangerous job. The single-engined aircraft moved slowly at around 200 miles per hour, half the speed of the German fighter aircraft, which would fly by at double speed and not notice the Lizzy. It could also fly low, hedge-hopping before it landed. The Lysanders flew at a height of 8,000 feet. Since it was dangerous to fly them in the daylight when they could easily be seen, they were generally only used on full-moon night drops.[5] Initially the planes were painted black, but it was found that they were clearly visible when the sky was bathed in moonlight. So later versions had the top half of the aircraft painted blue and green. Lysanders were also particularly useful because they could land in muddy fields and on the smallest airstrips. To minimise the time the aircraft spent on the ground, the Lysanders were fitted with a small ladder on the side so agents could get in and out in the shortest time possible. Lysanders could carry two passengers easily, three at a pinch and four in a crisis, besides the pilot. If there was a third passenger he sat on the floor. Over 100 sorties were made by Lysanders during the war, setting down as many as 250 passengers and bringing out nearly 450.

Soon it was time to land. The familiar sign of the inverted L and the flashing Morse code guided the pilots to the landing strip. The landing code for the Lysander was a well-rehearsed one. Three

Amina Begum, née Ora Ray Baker, Noor's mother.

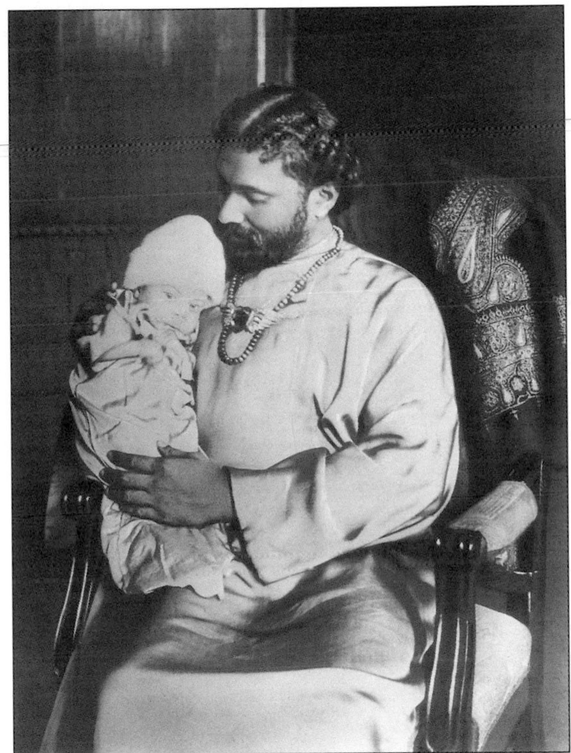

Inayat Khan with baby Noor.

The Inayat Khan children. From the left, Noor, Vilayat, Hidayat and Claire.

Fazal Manzil, the Inayat Khans' home in Suresnes.

Noor with her mother.

A family group. Two uncles are standing at the back.

A concert at Fazal Manzil. From the left, Hidayat, Claire, Noor and Vilayat.

Noor with her veena.

Noor on holiday in The Hague.

One of Noor's delicate illustrations for a handmade card.

The Inayat Khan children as young adults. From the left, Noor, Hidayat, Vilayat and Claire.

Beaulieu Manor, the training school for agents. (*Shrabani Basu*)

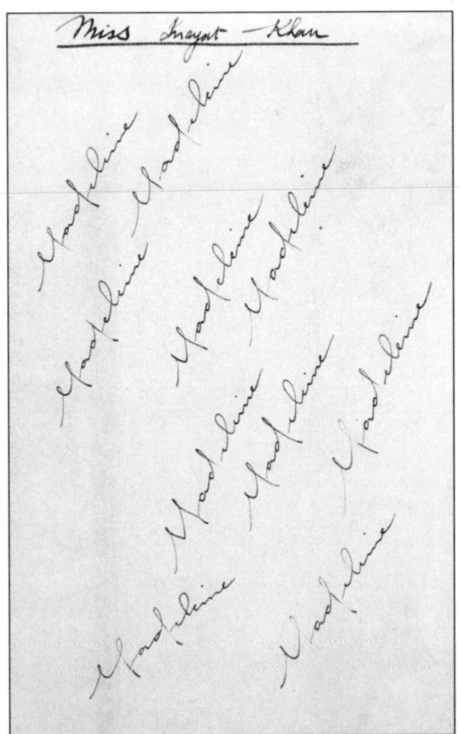

Some of Noor's practice signatures. (*National Archives HS9/836/5*)

Noor in WAAF uniform, 1940. (*Imperial War Museum HU 74868*)

Francis Suttill, code name Prosper, cover name François Alfred Desprez. (*Courtesy of Francis Suttill*)

France Antelme, code name Renaud, cover name Antoine Ratier. (*Courtesy of Alain Antelme*)

Gilbert Norman, code name Archambaud, cover name Gilbert Aubin. (*National Archives HS9/1110/5*)

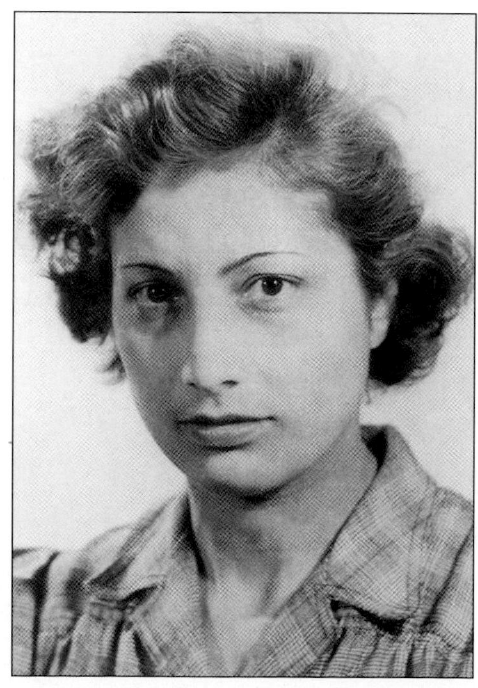

Noor's SOE file photograph. (*National Archives HS9/836/5*)

Mark III transmitters. (*Imperial War Museum HU 61098*)

No. 84 Avenue Foch, part of Gestapo HQ in Paris. (*Shrabani Basu*)

The gate at Dachau, with its cynical message. (*Shrabani Basu*)

The crematorium in Dachau. (*Shrabani Basu*)

The plaque to Noor's memory at Dachau. (*Shrabani Basu*)

The memorial stone for thousands of unknown victims killed at the camp. (*Shrabani Basu*)

torches – looking from the air like an inverted L – would make up the flare path which would guide the plane. Then the Morse code would be flashed, which had to be the special one the pilot was expecting. (If the prearranged Morse wasn't flashed the pilot's instructions were to turn around as quickly as he could and leave. In 'no circumstances'[6] was he to land.)

It was a particularly fine moonlit night in the Loir (not Loire) valley when Noor and her colleagues landed. The landing field was north-east of Angers, 5.25 kilometres south of Tierce, not far above the Loir's junction with the Sarthe and 3.5 km west-north-west of Villeveque.[7] The Lysander stopped and Cecily got off. Noor remained on board. It was her duty to pass the luggage down to Cecily, then take and store the luggage from the other passengers who were waiting to return. Only then did she clamber down the short ladder herself. It was a well-rehearsed drill aimed to take as little time as possible.

A double Lysander operation had to take no more than twenty minutes at the very most for both planes to load and unload passengers. Each plane usually took about three to four minutes, making it very difficult for the Germans to trace or intercept them. But the Germans probably knew about this flight. Noor and her colleagues were met by agent Henri Déricourt, F-section's air movements officer, who was later confirmed to be a double agent. He had five passengers waiting to be taken back to England. They were three French political figures, Madame Pierre Bloch, Pierre Lejeune and Vic Gerson, and two F-section returning agents – Jack Agazarian and his wife Francine. The returning passengers lost no time in boarding the aircraft, then the Lysander turned around and after a short run-up took off again. The last link with England had now gone. Noor and her colleagues stood alone on enemy territory.

The landing field had to be cleared as quickly as possible. Henri Déricourt and his assistant, Rémy Clément, had bicycles waiting for the arriving agents. Skepper and Cecily Lefort travelled south together, Diana Rowden headed for her address south-east of Dijon, near the Jura mountains. Noor hastily buried her pistol in the field, as she was not normally allowed to carry a pistol since it could incriminate her if she was searched. She got on her bike and rode in the direction of the nearest railway station, Angers. She had to head for Paris, the most dangerous area of all. Rémy Clément would travel separately and meet her at the station but the two of them would travel in different compartments as a precaution.

Noor had memorised her instructions from London. She was to go to 40 rue Erlanger, Paris 16e (8th floor opposite the lift door) to the house of Emile Henri Garry. Her password was '*Je viens de la part de votre ami Antoine pour des nouvelles au sujet de la Société en Bâtiment*' (I have come on behalf of your friend Antoine for news on the building society), to which the reply would be '*L'affaire est en cours*'[8] (The business is in hand).

Noor's instructions were to work as a wireless operator in the region of Le Mans. Her circuit would be Cinema, a sub-circuit of the famous Prosper circuit headed by Francis Suttill. Born in 1910 in Lille, the barrister Suttill was the son of an English father and a French mother. He spoke good French, and was an idealist with good leadership qualities. His job was to create an active circuit in and around Paris. On the night of 1/2 October 1942, Suttill (code name Prosper) had been parachuted in near Vendôme. He was preceded by his courier, the formidable Andrée Borrel (code name Denise), a young French girl, who had been parachuted in close to Paris on 24/25 September to prepare the way for him. A month later his wireless operator, Gilbert Norman (code name Archambaud) parachuted in near Tours. Suttill's Prosper circuit now consisted of himself as the organiser, Andrée Borrel as his courier, and his radio operator Gilbert Norman. The circuit expanded so rapidly that soon another radio operator, Jack Agazarian (code name Marcel), was parachuted to help him and landed in the Seine valley. Agazarian's wife Francine (code name Marguerite) acted as his courier. Suttill's extended circuit also included Jean Amps (code name Tomas), who became his lieutenant.

Suttill's first contact had been Germaine Tambour (code name Annette) who, along with her sister Madeleine, worked for the Carte circuit, which was notoriously insecure. Germaine introduced him to many people, including Professor Alfred Balachowsky[9] (code name Serge) of the College of Agriculture in Grignon, who became head of the Versailles/Grignon region, and Armel Guerne (code name Gaspard), who would also become Suttill's lieutenant. Suttill was very dependent on Andrée Borrel, who had worked with the French Resistance before leaving for England to be trained by F section and then returning to serve in France. She was a daring woman who travelled everywhere with Suttill, posing as his sister, to help him find his way around in the initial months. Suttill soon developed many contacts with the French Left and the circuit expanded rapidly, creating many sub-circuits. Contact with the Tambour sisters, however, endangered Suttill from the start.

Working closely with the Prosper circuit was the skilled F-section agent France Antelme (code name Renaud), who had been sent on a special mission to arrange money and food supplies for the Allied Expeditionary Force before the invasion of the mainland and to send back intelligence about the morale and organisational capabilities of the French. An important part of Antelme's brief was also to get in touch with non- or anti-Gaullist resistance groups and see if they could be of any importance. All the Prosper circuits and sub-circuits contacted Antelme for funds. It was he who had recruited Henri Garry to help Prosper and set up the sub-circuit Cinema, or Phono, to which Noor had to report.[10] Antelme would work with the Prosper and Cinema circuits and later with Noor.

Garry was a Frenchman who had not been trained by F-section in England. He had been given the circuit name Cinema by Suttill because of his resemblance to the actor Gary Cooper (F-section, not amused at this joke, later changed the circuit name to Phono). Garry was working for Prosper in the Eure-et-Loire and the Sarthe departments south-west of Paris, with headquarters at Le Mans. Noor had been sent to work as his much-needed radio operator.

The three members of the Prosper circuit lived in Paris but they used as their base the Ecole Nationale d'Agriculture at Grignon, the famous agriculture college to the north-west of Versailles. Another circuit that worked closely with Prosper was Satirist, headed by the 29-year-old sculptor Octave Simon, who had been active in the Resistance. Simon had been enlisted by Antelme and had gone on to set up a reception committee with some local farmers, their sons and the gamekeeper. Antelme also introduced him to Arthur de Montalambert, a count, who was prepared to have arms drops on his estates. Dutilleul, stationmaster at Le Mans, was drawn into the circuit and the three of them worked from the Le Mans region where they often coordinated arms drops for Suttill.

Another sub-circuit of Prosper was Juggler, headed by Jean Worms (code name Robin) who had also been with the Resistance. His assistants were Jacques Weil and Gaston Cohen (Justin) who was their wireless operator. They organised sabotage groups around Chalons and had had a few successes with derailments. Also in the Sarthe was the sub-circuit Butler headed by François Bouguennec (code name Max) with Marcel Rousset (code name Leopold) as his wireless operator and Marcel Fox (code name Ernest) as his courier. Another circuit that worked with Prosper was Chestnut, consisting of three racing drivers: Charles Grover Williams, Robert Benoist and Jean-Pierre Wimille. Benoist, a world motor racing champion in the late 1920s, was the director of Bugatti in Paris. He owned a large country estate in Auffargis and organised receptions in the nearby grounds in the Forêt de Rambouillet. Robert Benoist had access to a truck from Bugatti and permission to drive at night, which was helpful for carrying the arms which were then hidden on his country estate. Their wives helped with the receptions. Their radio operator was Robert Dowlen (code name Achille) who transmitted from a large house near Pontoise.

Other circuits working with Prosper included Privet, a sub-circuit in the Angers area with Ernest Wilkison (Alexandre) as organiser, a group in the Oise(West)/Eure(East) area organised by George Darling of Gisors, a group in the Orne area organised by Jean Michel Cauchi (Paul) of Falaise, a group in the Indre-et-Loire area run by Pierre Culioli (Adolph) and Yvonne Rudellat (Jaqueline) as courier, and a group in the Seine/Seine-et-Oise organised by Armel Guerne (Gaspard). Farrier, run by Henri Déricourt and his courier Julienne Aisner, and Scientist, run by Claude de Baissac (David) from the Bordeaux region also worked closely with Prosper.

By June 1943, when Noor arrived, the Prosper circuit and its sub-circuits had become one of the largest and most powerful forces around Paris extending as far as Le Mans, Orleans and Beauvais. Prosper had organised the sabotage of the Chaingy power station in March 1943 by which the power lines from Eguzon, Chevilly, Epines and Fortes were immobilised. It had also been responsible for the destruction of 1,000 litres of petrol and for successful attacks on enemy goods trains on the Orleans–Paris line. In April 1943, Suttill and his group had carried out 63 acts of sabotage: derailing trains, killing 43 Germans and wounding 110.[11] By June 1943 the circuit covered 12 departments, had 33 dropping grounds and had received 254 containers of stores.[12] They received 190 containers in June alone and further attacks were on the cards.[13]

It was at this time, when the Prosper circuit was at its peak, that Noor was asked to join the sub-circuit Cinema. Once she had established contact with Cinema, she had to send a post-box address back to Baker Street where she could be contacted personally if her wireless contact failed. She had to also send the SOE the address of a cachette (safe house). If she was in difficulty she would have to go to the cachette and advise London of the circumstances by coded letter or card. She would then be contacted in her cachette with a view to getting her out.

Before Noor left England she had been given detailed instructions about making contact with London if she ran into difficulties. If owing to unforeseen circumstances her circuit – Cinema – disappeared, she would have to advise London immediately and await further orders.[14]

She had to send headquarters the address of her cachette by code using Playfair.[15] If she could not use her radio for some reason she was to send a postcard to Lisbon with the word 'un' or 'une' in the text. She had to mention her name – Madeleine – somewhere in the text and refer to Madeleine as if she was in Portugal and not in France. The signature on the postcard should preferably be from someone who lived in the cachette. The postcard would be addressed to Senor Luis Alberto Peres, Rua da Libereade 220/20, Oporto.

If Noor changed her cachette she had to advise London again. If she needed to do this by postcard she would have to use the word 'deux' in it and the code name Madeleine. If she had to hide, she had to send a message saying 'Have gone to cachette'. If she had to send a postcard to Lisbon then she would have to use the word 'trois' in the text and also the code name Madeleine.

If an SOE agent went to see her in the cachette he was to ask the owner '*Puis-je voir Jeanne-Marie, la fille d'Ora?*' (Can I see Jeanne-Marie, the daughter of Ora?) The cachette owner should reply '*Vous voulez dire Babs?*' (Don't you mean Babs?)

Noor was also given an emergency address in Paris, that of a bookseller, Mme Rose, at 101 rue de Passy, Paris 16e. The password she was to use if she had to call on this address was '*Avez-vous des exemplaires neufs?*' (Have you got new copies?), to which the reply would be '*Non, que des exemplaires d'occasion*' (No, only second-hand).

If Noor was in trouble and there was no other way out, she would have to escape through Spain. In this case, she was to send a postcard to Lisbon with the word 'quatre' in it and the code name Madeleine. On arrival in Spain, she had to try and reach the British Consulate at Barcelona and there give her name as Inayat Khan. Her cover story would be that she was a BOAC officer who had got stranded in the Dieppe raid.

Along with these incredibly detailed instructions were Noor's radio transmission timings, other instructions and her codes. Instead of a poem, Noor had been given a phrase and the numbering had been done for her. She was given the worked-out key by which she would have to start at the top of her list of keys and work down. She would have to use the key on her left for her first transposition and the key on her right for her second. Decoding would be exactly the same. She would have to write her message first under the key on the left-hand side and then on the right-hand side. She was asked to remember to use each indicator in sequence and, in order to make the messages 100 per cent safe, to cut off each key after she had finished using it.[16]

On her first night in France, Noor was clearly nervous. Her escort Rémy Clément, who travelled with her to Paris, but on a different coach for security reasons, saw her at Angers station poring over maps and looking thoroughly lost. He said her nervousness affected him. However Noor made it to Paris and called that evening at 40 rue Erlanger.

For some reason Noor thought that her contact was an old lady and so she brought a posy of flowers for her. When the door of the flat was opened by the young and flamboyant Garry, she was surprised.[17]

Finally she managed to stammer, 'I think I am expected'. An equally surprised Garry, who was waiting for her to give the password, decided to ask her in. His fiancée, Marguerite Nadaud, was sitting in the living room. Not quite sure what to do, Garry introduced her to Noor. Noor had still not introduced herself as she was waiting for the old lady. Meanwhile Garry and his fiancée were puzzled as to whether Noor was the agent they were expecting from London. They could not understand why she was not saying the password. Since Garry's password was the reply to hers he could not use it first.

This farce carried on for a while. Garry asked Noor to sit down and offered her cigarettes, which she took and then he casually asked if she was his contact from London. Noor answered in a measured way trying to test Garry. But Noor was still waiting for the old lady to present herself, thinking that the young couple must be her friends with connections in the Resistance.

Finally Marguerite excused herself to make some coffee, thinking maybe it was her presence that was stopping Noor from giving her password. While she was in the kitchen, she heard a peal of laughter and realised that the passwords must have been exchanged.

Noor had studied Garry for a while, decided to trust him, and spoken the password. He had replied immediately, much to her relief. She now told him the reason for her hesitation: that she had been expecting to see an old lady. Garry laughed out loud, told his fiancée and said: 'And she bought these carnations to give to me.'

The amusing incident over, Marguerite was presented with the flowers and Noor began to relax. Marguerite soon discovered that she had not eaten for 24 hours, since she had left England. She had been given a ration book by London, but she wasn't sure how to use the coupons and so rather than arouse any suspicion she had simply gone without any food. Clearly, Beaulieu training had not taken into account the need to teach the agents how to actually use the ration books. All Noor had bought on the way was a bottle of Vichy water and the bunch of flowers for her contact.

Marguerite immediately got busy in the kitchen making Noor something to eat. Over dinner Garry told Noor about the circuit and how he was working for Francis Suttill, head of the whole region. Garry had a residential address in Paris and one in Sarthe, Le Mans. He travelled between both and had a false card describing him as an engineer in the Société Electro-Chimie of Paris. Marguerite was also active in the Resistance and helped F-section agents. She was secretary to Max Bonnafous, Minister of Food and Agriculture, and had helped Antelme to get a much-needed official 'Mission Order' on behalf of her ministry which gave him access to any train, at a time when it was nearly impossible to travel by rail.[18]

Noor gave Garry and Marguerite her code name – Madeleine – which they already knew. She also told them her cover name, which was Jeanne-Marie. This was the name that she would be using in France.

Both Garry and his fiancée took an immediate liking to Noor although they thought her too young and vulnerable to be on such a dangerous mission. She told them about how hard it had been to say goodbye to her mother, and said that her mother had no idea where she was. Since she had nowhere to stay, Garry and his fiancée invited her to stay at their apartment. Noor gratefully accepted the offer as by now she was completely exhausted.

The very next day she met Antelme, head of the Bricklayer circuit, who worked closely with Prosper. His code name was Renaud and his cover name was Antoine Ratier. He was a tall, sporty Mauritian officer in his forties who took an immediate paternal interest in Noor. He took her out for two days so she could get on her feet in occupied France and reported to London that 'Madeleine had arrived safely' and was 'happy and all right'.[19]

Noor was also contacted by Francis Suttill and his radio operator Gilbert Norman, and she now got to know the immediate ring of circuit members she would be working with. Norman turned out to have been to the same school as Noor and was two years her junior. On 20 June, two days after her arrival, Norman took her to Grignon and introduced her to Professor Alfred Balachowsky of the National College of Agriculture, a distinguished biologist, and his wife, Emily Balachowsky, as well as the Director of the National College, Dr Eugéne Vanderwynckt, his wife and two daughters.

Noor's radio set had not arrived yet, so Norman took her to see his transmitter, which was concealed in a greenhouse on the premises in Grignon. Noor immediately made her first transmission to London from there. It was less than 72 hours after her departure and was the fastest response from any agent in the field after landing. Poste Madeleine was in operation. The message was received with relief by Maurice Buckmaster and Vera Atkins, who had been nervous about how the shy Indian girl was getting on.

Since the German listening machines were constantly circling the streets listening for transmissions, for their own security radio operators were asked to go on air only when necessary and to keep their transmissions short (maximum 10–15 minutes). Noor, like other wireless operators, used an A Mark II, which was a transmitter and receiver in one. It weighed 30 pounds and fitted into an ordinary-looking suitcase about two feet long. Its frequency range was quite wide but its signal weak (20 watts at best). It also needed 70 feet of aerial, which was the dangerous bit, since it could attract the eye of a policeman. The frequency the set worked on was determined by removable crystals, of which each operator needed at least two, one for night-time and one for day transmission.

Crystals were extremely delicate and could be broken if dropped. They were also impossible to disguise as anything else. Their only advantage was that they were small enough to fit in the palm of the hand and could be concealed on the person. If an agent was discovered with crystals they were highly incriminating and it would take a lot of luck to explain away their presence.

If the wireless operator was running their sets off the mains, there was further chance of getting caught. The German intelligence service's wireless direction-finding (D/F) teams were ruthlessly efficient (far more so than their counterparts in Britain). In Britain it could take about an hour to trace a transmission. But in France, wireless operators found that if they had a long transmission from a large town, D/F vans could be at their doorstep within half an hour.[20] The Germans would camouflage the D/F vehicles as bakers' vans or laundry vans, and the soldiers wore plain clothes so they could not be spotted. They had also worked out a way of establishing what part of a town a clandestine operator was working in, by cutting off the electricity sub-district by sub-district and noting when the transmission was interrupted. They would then concentrate on the area which they had isolated and get to work finding the block from where the transmission was taking place. Once they had got close, one of the soldiers would get out of the van and walk round the neighbourhood to pinpoint a precise address. He would carry a hidden antenna and the wire would pass through his sleeve to his ear, and he would casually stroll through the area trying to pick up the transmission.[21]

The agents did their best to protect themselves by having someone keeping a lookout for D/F vans while they transmitted. Even a man sauntering up the street wearing a beret and with his collar turned up could be a Gestapo officer with a miniature listening set in his ear and the agent would have to be warned to hide the set and leave the building. Transmitting from an isolated place in a country was usually safer, but Noor's area of work was Paris, and so she had to be constantly on the alert. As events developed around her she never actually went to work in Le Mans as originally intended by F-section, but remained in the city.

Staying on air for a very short time, and changing crystals frequently during transmission in order to confuse the enemy were precautions agents could take. Another safeguard was constantly changing the place of transmission. The operator could also use the accumulator instead of the mains, but there was the problem of keeping the accumulator charged.

SOE laid out rules for its radio operators, including Noor, to 'do nothing but w/t (wireless telegraph) work, to see his organiser as little as possible, if at all, and to have contact with the fewest possible number of people in the circuit'.[22] In the field, however, this didn't always work.

In the early days of the SOE, wireless messages were received by MI6 at Bletchley Park. These were then decoded and passed on to the SOE country section. From mid-1942, the SOE managed to get their own listening post at Grendon Underwood, north-west of Aylesbury in Buckinghamshire. It was called Station 53a.

Messages sent by the operators were now received directly in Grendon, where 400 FANY women operators manned the radio sets. Before they left for the field all operators would be given their daily schedules or 'skeds' – details of the frequency and time they should come on air to transmit back home.

In Grendon, the 'skeds' were posted on big boards in the transmission room, along with the agents' code names. Noor's first transmission came in on Norman's radio and his frequency. Knowing that the agent was transmitting under very difficult circumstances, in hiding and with D/F vans circling around while he was on air, the operator taking down the message in Grendon wanted to be as fast as possible and try to get it down without asking the agent to repeat themselves too much.

Sometimes the operators would add a small personal line to the agent just to let them know there were people back home thinking about them. Noor was informed about Vilayat's commission by Vera Atkins while she was in Paris. Once the operator sent her a message and ended with the words: 'May God Keep You.' It moved her greatly knowing they thought of her as someone more than just an operator on the other end of a wireless line.[23]

When the signallers had taken down the code, they would then send it to the building next door where coders sat on long pine tables working in pairs to break the code. Once these messages were deciphered they would be passed to the section office at Baker Street. Sometimes the codes arrived badly garbled and it was the job of the coders' office to try and crack them. Because the agent in the field could be put at great risk if asked to repeat the code again the next day, Leo Marks had a policy that no code would go unbroken before the agent came on the air on his or her next 'sked', which could be in the next 48 hours. There was no greater failure for the code-breakers than to know that an agent had risked his life to come on the air and they had not been able to read his message. Marks developed a personal relationship with the wireless operators, meeting each one before they left so he would get to know the personal style of the operator and see if there was a certain pattern of errors from their training files. This would help him to crack the code accordingly. So if there was a person who spelt badly, or an agent who was particularly nervous or slow, he would know what had gone wrong in the message.

Marks made a rule: 'There shall be no such thing as an indecipherable message' and he got a team of operators to work round the clock if necessary to break an agent's muddled code and get it ready for the next 'sked'.[24]

The messages from the field needed to be brief, accurate and as watertight as possible. It was also important for the receivers in England to watch out for the security checks being sent by the agents. If caught, the agent was supposed to alert London by dropping their security check. However, this did not always work as there were many lapses in the London listening room, with disastrous consequences.

Agents also worked through 'safe houses' and 'cut-outs'. A safe house was a place the agents could stay as the owner was known to the circuit. They could also use the house as a letter box to receive messages from other agents. Safe houses were also used by escapees who could be hidden in twos or threes as they made their journey back to England. The cut-out was a means of communication between two agents which could effectively delude the enemy. So one agent would pass a message in code to a cut-out. He could be a bookseller and the message would be 'Have you any Anatole France in stock?' The cut-out might reply, 'Yes, two volumes have just come in.' The agent would gather from that that two escapees had to be collected from the safe house in Boulevard Anatole France. If the reply was 'Sorry Mademoiselle, we are out of stock' it meant there was no one to collect. Cut-outs were always called from public call boxes so the calls would take longer to be traced. After the call the agent had to walk away from the call box very quickly.

Passwords were always kept simple so they could be memorised and dropped casually into the conversation. There were also strict instructions for carrying messages. It was forbidden to carry notes, or details with contact addresses on it. Verbal messages were always given in veiled language which the courier could not understand. If a message could not be memorised it had to be written on thin tissue paper and inserted into a cigarette or carried in such a way that it could be easily eaten or dropped. People in safe houses were forbidden to go out. Anyone calling on a safe house had to first check the security of the house by telephone. Agents were strictly forbidden to meet in certain places. These included certain Metro stations, black-market restaurants or bars and cinemas.[25]

The instruction given at Beaulieu to all agents was that, if caught, they were to hold on and say nothing to the Gestapo for the first 48 hours. During this time all the people in their circuit would move house and cover their tracks. When the two days were over, and if the pressure became unbearable, they could say what they wanted.

Agents were also discouraged from communicating with agents from other circuits. Again, in the field, this rule was not strictly adhered to. The Prosper circuit in particular grew too large. It had many sub-circuits and a potential disaster was waiting to happen as it could be easily infiltrated.

Noor herself was taken to Grignon within two days to meet the sub-agents. As she was a friendly person by nature, she got on well with everyone and felt quite at home. She even went to the kitchen to help the women make tea and carried it back on a tray. But her colleagues observed her make a crucial mistake. Noor poured out the tea for everyone and began to toast some slices of bread by the fire. One of the women noticed that she poured the milk into the cups before the tea and pointed this out to Madame Balachowsky. It was a particularly English way of making tea.

Madame Balachowsky immediately warned Noor that in France they always put the milk in last while making tea and told her that this mistake could betray her in front of Vichy sympathisers. Noor thanked her for the information but was to be ticked off for another indiscretion soon afterwards. She had carelessly left her portfolio containing all her security codes lying in the entrance hall. It was brought in by Professor Balachowsky.[26] The professor told her that it could easily have fallen into the wrong hands. It was obvious that Noor had little idea about the reality of life in Gestapo-occupied France. She was now told that she must learn not to trust anybody but the closest in her circuit, and to be aware that the Gestapo were everywhere and had infiltrated the tightest of Resistance circuits. The Professor told Noor to conduct herself as if she were always surrounded by spies and gave her a few tips to ensure her safety in her daily life.

Noor would work at Grignon till her transmitter arrived. At the school, she would pass herself off as one of the students. Dr Vanderwynckt lived in the school with his wife and two daughters and his son-in-law, Robert Douillet, who helped with parachute receptions. The Balachowskys lived in Viroflay, a suburb of Paris, but they spent a lot of time in Grignon. Noor told them about her family: her mother and her brother who was in the Navy. She told them that her real name was Nora Baker. They already knew her code name was Madeleine and that her cover name was Jeanne-Marie. Vera Atkins had often asked Noor to use the name Nora Baker in Beaulieu as a cover name in order to hide her Indian origins. Baker was her mother's maiden name. Noor continued to use the same practice cover name from Beaulieu, not disclosing her identity even to close circuit members. Probably she was being extra cautious as she did not want anyone to know her second name was Inayat Khan, as she was afraid the Germans could trace her brother Hidayat who was still in France and torture him or his children if she was arrested. The Balachowskys could sense that Noor missed her mother very much and knew that it had hurt her terribly to have left without telling her where she was really going. They felt she was too young and inexperienced for such a dangerous job.

Noor was still clearly getting to grips with life in occupied France, which was so different from the France she had lived in. She began to realise the extent of the occupation and the effect it had had on the everyday lives of the people. From the outside, Paris still looked the same: the cafés were full of people, and the locals went to work as usual. The Paris fashion houses were still catering for the Parisian elite. They now also supplied the Germans as the wives of the German officers wanted to indulge in Dior and Chanel. Though food and clothes were rationed and there were fewer cars on the roads because of the scarcity of petrol, there was no dearth of black-market shops for the rich. People rode around on vélo-taxis, which were something like rickshaws. There were plenty of black-market restaurants and the Metros ran on time until the curfew began at midnight. But the Mercedes zooming round the streets carrying Nazi officials told the story of a city that had been occupied. By evening the streets would be empty as most people preferred to get home well before the curfew fell.

Paris had fallen without a struggle. The pre-war talk of *sales Boches* (dirty Germans) was quickly replaced by the German propaganda of *sales Anglais* (dirty English). Paris was also emptied of Jews. From June 1942, all Jews above the age of six were required to wear the yellow stars and were initially imprisoned in France, then sent to concentration camps in Germany and Poland. Their vacated apartments were seized by the Germans and locals at bargain prices. Many French people were quick to collude with the Germans. The Vichy government was so eager to please the occupiers that it began handing over Jewish children even before the Germans had asked for them. Collaborators pointed out Jewish families. By the end of the war, about 75,000 Jews including 10,000 children had been sent by the French to their deaths in concentration camps.[27] There was an atmosphere of fear and mistrust. The swastikas flying from government-occupied buildings and the German signs on the roads brought home the reality of the situation. It was very different from London or Beaulieu.

The same day that she went to Grignon, Noor finally met Suttill in person. He had been touring arms dumps in Normandy between 15 and 18 June and been working on preparing the new identity cards for arriving agents. He'd only spoken briefly to Noor before that. Suttill arrived at Grignon at lunchtime. It was a merry Sunday lunch since nearly all the members of the circuit and sub-circuit were present: the Balachowskys, Norman, Borrel, the Vanderwynckts and their son-in-law Robert Douillet, and the son-in-law of the Belgian minister. None of the people gathered there, including a happy and relaxed Noor, sensed that danger was just around the corner.

EIGHT

The Fall of Prosper

Noor had still not received her own wireless set so she continued to use the transmitter at Grignon. She worked side by side with Norman, who helped her get on her feet. Norman told her to be very careful of her security, to memorise her plans and then burn them, as the Germans were always on the lookout for wireless operators. They worked from the greenhouse while the gardener, Marius Maillard, kept guard. Maillard also helped with the reception of parachute equipment. Noor took Garry's messages to transmit from Grignon. She was also introduced by Antelme to Robert Gieules, an administrator at the Compagnie Générale des Conserves, who had been recruited to help F-section, and to Paul Arrighi, an advocate, who helped the French Resistance, with whom she would work closely later. She got on well with her colleagues and soon settled into her new role.

On the morning of 21 June, Suttill met Déricourt and Rémy Clément at Gare d'Austerlitz to plan the handover of SOE agent Richard Heslop of the Marksman circuit and an airman, Taylor, for return to England. He then waited with Norman, Borrel, the Guernes and Marcel Charbonnier at a café in the station for two agents from the Sologne, Pierre Culioli and Yvonne Rudellat, who were supposed to bring with them two recently arrived Canadian agents, John Macalister and Frank Pickersgill. None of them arrived, as they had fallen into the hands of the Germans. Later, Suttill lunched with Armel Guerne unaware that the destruction of the Prosper circuit had been set in motion.

That same night (21/22 June), Suttill, Professor Balachowsky and members of the reception committee had to go to a farmhouse at Roncey-aux-Alluets near Grignon to receive some parachute drops. One of these contained Noor's transmitter and a suitcase with her personal effects. Unfortunately the parachute came down on a tree, and the suitcase burst open spilling all her clothes on the branches. It was crucial to remove all the evidence, so the men had to work into the early hours carefully retrieving each item and repacking it in her suitcase. Several of the other containers had also been scattered around and could not be traced. The reception committee were also worried because they had not seen F-section agent George Connerade (Jacquot), who was to be dropped that night. Armel Guerne was left in charge of the committee to carry out further searches the next day and Norman returned to Grignon to receive an early morning transmission from London.[1]

Norman received the message giving him the number of parcels and confirming that Connerade had been parachuted. The reception committee set out immediately to search the grounds and at 10 a.m. Guerne found Connerade's parachute neatly folded on the ground and some distance from it, his suitcase. By noon Norman had also found two of Noor's radio sets. Everything was quickly removed and hidden at Grignon.

On the evening of 22 June Norman, Antelme, Borrel and Suttill gathered at Guerne's flat at 12 rue Lalande to discuss the final results of the parachute drop. Suttill asked Norman to inform London that Connerade had not been found and to ask for his contact address. He also asked Antelme to make arrangements for Noor's wireless sets to be picked up and brought to Le Mans. Antelme arranged with Guerne that on 29 June he would send a man by car at a road intersection (which Antelme would mark on a road map) near Grignon at 2.30 p.m. A password was arranged and it was decided that Yves, a French youth who worked with them, would be there with the sets. Later that evening Suttill called at Antelme's flat and collected one million francs from him. It was the last time they would meet.

Unknown to the circuit, the two Canadian agents John Macalister (Valentin) and Frank Pickersgill (Bertrand) had been arrested by the Gestapo the day after the Prosper circuit members had met for lunch in Paris. The two agents had been parachuted into the Cher valley on the night of 15/16 June to set up a sub-circuit called Archdeacon. Five days earlier – on the night of 10/11 June – a parachute drop in this area had gone wrong as the containers had exploded. This led the Germans to set up roadblocks in the area. Pierre Culioli, who lived in the region and received the parachute drops, had warned Suttill and asked him to tell London not to make any more drops there. But Suttill refused to stop the arms drops, possibly thinking the Allied invasion would soon be under way and all supplies were essential.[2]

Macalister and Pickersgill were consequently dropped and spent the night with Culioli. On 21 June the two men, along with Pierre Culioli and Yvonne Rudellat, were on their way to Paris when they ran into a roadblock and were taken to the town hall for interrogation. Culioli and Rudellat cleared the interrogation and went outside to wait in the car, but the Canadians were having trouble persuading the Germans that they were innocent Frenchmen. Pickersgill's French was excellent but Macalister spoke French with a marked Canadian accent. It was enough to arouse suspicion, and the SS officer shouted for Rudellat and Culioli to be brought back. Culioli decided to step on the accelerator and make a dash for it. A car chase followed, Rudellat was shot and injured, and eventually all four were arrested.

The arrest of the Canadians was a terrific coup for the Gestapo. In the boot of the car was Macalister's wireless set. Besides this, the Canadians were carrying several messages from London for other agents in Paris which had been sent without coding. They were clearly addressed to each agent by his field name including 'Prosper' and 'Archambaud'. There were also some new crystals and detailed instructions for their use by Gilbert Norman (Archambaud). All the letters had been put in a brown paper parcel addressed to a fictitious prisoner of war in Germany and left in the glove compartment of the car. In Gestapo hands they now proved fatal. Culioli's briefcase contained the addresses of Norman, Borrel, Amps, and the letter box at Avenue Suffren.[3] The Germans had been trying to smash the Prosper network and now they had been supplied with the contact details. They started to close in.

On the night of 23 June, two days after the Paris lunch, Norman and Borrel dined with Armel Guerne and his wife, in their flat in rue Lalande. They left separately – Norman by bike and Borrel by Metro – but reached the address near the Porte de la Muette at the edge of the 16th arrondissement where Norman had moved in recently as a lodger with Nicholas Laurent, his old schoolfriend from Paris, and his wife Maud, local members of the sub-circuit. Borrel joined him at the flat and they settled down, perhaps to prepare fresh bogus identity cards for their circuit. Identity cards had been changed at this time to include profile photos rather than full face and were attached to the ID cards with rivets instead of staples, so they all had to be changed. On the desk was a huge pile of ID cards. It may have contained a card for François Desprez, cover name for Suttill. It would have had his photograph and address.[4] Just after midnight, in the early hours of 24 June, there was a knock on the door. It was the Gestapo and the whole household was arrested.

Suttill was out of Paris that night. He had a meeting with a Normandy sub-organiser, George Darling, and had gone to Gisors by the 7.10 p.m. train. He spent the night at Trie-Château in the safe house of Madame Guépin, and she saw him off next morning on the 7 a.m. train for Paris. Between 9 and 9.30 a.m. Suttill had a meeting with Marc O'Neil, leader of a Giraudist faction of the Resistance called OCM (Organisation Civile et Militaire), at Gare St Lazare and then returned to his hotel room in the working-class area of Porte St Denis. But in the middle of the night, the Germans had entered his hotel room at 18 rue de Mazagran where he had booked under his cover name of François Desprez, an engineer. There they waited for him all night and arrested him between 10 and 11 a.m. on 24 June as he returned from Gisors. Since he had moved recently, his address was known to nobody apart from Norman and Borrel. They would not have given it to the Gestapo but it was probably printed on one of the new identity cards they were preparing. Nicholas Laurent said later that he was shown two identity photos by the Germans at Avenue Foch and asked which one was 'François'.[5]

By the night of 24 June the Gestapo had made a clean sweep. Suttill, Norman and Borrel – the three key players of the Prosper circuit – were in their custody. The Germans had been on the trail of Prosper for a while as it was one of the biggest, busiest and most hazardous of the SOE networks. The circuit, however, became a victim of its own success. It had grown too large, and it was inevitable that it would be infiltrated. Suttill, Borrel and Norman were careless of security and flouted the basic rule of not being seen together. Borrel and Norman were lovers and were often out together. All three regularly lunched together in a black-market restaurant near the Etoile and met in the evenings at a café in Montmartre. They were an inseparable trio and often met Suttill's second radio operator Jack Agazarian, a handsome and dashing young airman. Agazarian had been ordered not to contact members of any circuit apart from his own, but he had transmitted for no fewer than twenty-three different agents, because of the shortage of trained operators. It had made him extremely vulnerable to discovery by the Germans who were circling and waiting to swoop. Suttill had been concerned about Agazarian's security and sent him back to London with his wife. They left on the same Lysander that brought Noor in on 17 June.

Another factor that severely compromised the security of the agents on the circuit was that they had sent long reports home with the double agent Déricourt, either inadequately coded or in clear. Once the Canadian agents had been arrested, the Germans unravelled the rest of the Prosper circuit with ease.

Suttill himself was aware that his circuit had grown too large. His first contact in France, Germaine Tambour, and her sister Madeleine had been arrested in April. He then became engaged in a negotiation with the Germans to release the Tambour sisters from Fresnes prison in exchange for one million francs. Dangerously, several members of the Prosper circuit used the same postbox address of a friend of Germaine Tambour's, Madame Monet, at 38 Ave Suffren, Paris XVe. It was used by Suttill, Norman, Borrel, Agazarian, his wife Francine, Dowlen, Biéler and his radio operator Staggs.[6] They continued to use the same postbox after the Tambours' arrest. After the arrest of Madame Monet, the Gestapo tried to trap Biéler through the address, but he was warned just in time. Despite all these misgivings, Suttill asked Antelme for one million francs for the Tambour sisters and collected it from him on Tuesday 22 June. He had instructed Worms (code name Robin) of the Juggler circuit to get in touch with a German colonel in Paris to negotiate the release. Suttill tore the notes in half and left instructions that the colonel would get the other half only after the sisters were released. But the women released were not the Tambour sisters and Worms took back the half-notes. The Germans then demanded another half a million francs before they would release the sisters. The saga of the release of the Tambour sisters angered and worried Suttill, and Antelme advised him to cut off the negotiations as he was risking too many agents' lives in the process.[7]

The fall of Prosper was in many ways due to negligence in London as well. Suttill was worried by the fact that the security of safe letter boxes was not working. He was shocked to find that Noor had been sent to France supplied with a dangerous address he himself had cancelled. On 19 June, his last report to London, he wrote angrily: 'Madeleine was apparently given the Monet letter box in spite of the fact that it is cancelled since February (cancellation confirmed personally by me in May visit). Please take disciplinary action. Had Madeleine gone there yesterday afternoon she would have coincided with one of the Gestapo's periodic visits at that flat!'[8]

Suttill was also appalled that Lejeune (the Giraudist who returned to London on the Lysander that brought in Noor) had given out the same address to one of his friends, despite being instructed specifically by Borrel not to use the address and to use the one for Madame Rose instead. He was furious about this lapse by the SOE and cancelled all his current letter boxes and passwords. In the letter, a clearly exasperated Suttill told his chiefs at Baker Street: 'I hope I have made myself clear. It is now 0100 hours 19th June and I have slept 7 hours since 0500 hours 15th June.'[9] Five days later he was arrested and could not circulate new letter boxes.

It is unclear why Suttill's earlier instructions had been ignored and Noor supplied with a letter-box address that was not safe. Her mission could also be seen to have been doomed from the start, as she and her companions were received by Henri Déricourt, the very man accused of being a double agent. In the fog of war these lapses were to have fatal consequences.

On the morning of 24 June 1943, Antelme had left for Poitiers. The same day he had sent Octave Simon to the Le Mans area to arrange for the pick-up of Noor's wireless sets. Simon had to give instructions to Dutilleul, postmaster at Le Mans and part of the reception committee, to proceed with his car on 29 June to the road intersection near Grignon, which he was to reach at 2.30 p.m. There he would see a young French boy to whom he would give the password, which consisted of asking for a certain road. He would be given a parcel which he had to bring back to Le Mans.

Meanwhile on 24 June, Noor had a meeting with Norman at Grignon. They had planned to stay there till 26 June so Noor could practise her transmissions and send Norman's messages.[10] She went to Norman's friend's apartment where they usually met and waited, but he did not arrive. She remained in Grignon till the next day but there was no sign of him.

On Friday afternoon (25 June), while Noor was still waiting for Norman, Professor Balachowsky came to inform her that his wife had just received a phone call from Paris 'from the doctor's wife in whose house Germaine and her sister were to be removed in safety after being taken away from Fresnes'.[11] The message said that en route to the rendezvous at which Germaine and her sister were to be handed over to them, Suttill, Worms, Borrel and fifteen others had been arrested and Norman had escaped. The woman said this had happened on Wednesday night. In fact, Suttill had been arrested separately and Norman had not escaped, but this was the initial warning that Noor got.

Moving quickly, Noor immediately got rid of Norman's radio set and with Professor Balachowsky's assistance buried it under a bed of lettuce in the vegetable garden. She returned to Paris, where she contacted Garry.

Both Garry and Noor then went to Antelme's apartment to wait for him and it was here that Antelme found them when he returned on the 9.15 p.m. train from Poitiers. They informed him of the arrests. Antelme immediately ordered Garry to lie low and organised a safe house for Noor with his friend Raymond Andres at 1 Square Malherbe, Paris.[12] He was an engineer in the employment of La Société d'Electricité Chime d'Ugine. Antelme left his own flat as well and moved into another apartment with a friend, Germaine Aigrain, owner of a shop on the Champs Elysées, who lived at the same address at 1 Square Malherbe. Germaine Aigrain was a friend of Raymond Andres and they lived together in Aigrain's flat, but they had a separate bachelor flat in the same building in which Noor was accommodated.[13] The flat was fairly close to Garry's at 40 rue Erlanger. Antelme also contacted Robert Gieules to tell him about the arrests and told him to be careful and to alert William Savy, another member of this sub-circuit. Antelme, who kept moving his hiding place, stayed a night or two with Gieules.[14] He contacted Simon, who confirmed that all was well in Le Mans and said that he had contacted Dutilleul about Noor's wireless sets.

The secondary ring of the Prosper circuit were safe for the moment since they had all managed to move house and heed security warnings. With the head of such an important circuit arrested, they would have to lie low for a while and see what they could do.

On Sunday 27 June, Antelme sent Noor to Grignon to contact Professor Balachowsky and Norman's friends. He wanted her to find out more about the phone message referring to the arrests. Antelme wanted to know who had phoned Madame Balachowsky.[15] Professor Balachowsky told Noor that in view of what had happened, she should not come to Grignon again and suggested she ignore them in future.

Unable to get any information from Grignon, Antelme called the same day on the owners of Chez Touret, the café where Suttill and Borrel dined regularly and used as a postbox, and contacted Armel Guerne through them. Guerne had been warned of the arrests and had moved with his wife to a safe flat belonging to the parents of Suttill's friend, Alain Bussoz, a local recruit. They told Antelme that the mysterious lady caller was Madame Helmer, an elderly woman doctor resident at Auteuil, and he dismissed her as just another person involved with the messy release of the Tambour sisters. Madame Helmer was actually the letter box for Borrel. Guerne informed Antelme that he was in contact with Worms, Weil, Biéler and Trotobas, other F-section agents. He told Antelme that on Wednesday 23 June, Norman and Borrel had dined with him and then left at 11 p.m.

Antelme then contacted the concierge at Borrel's flat, who told him that she had not returned on Wednesday and that on Friday afternoon two men had walked straight up to her flat and left with a radio set and two suitcases. He then asked Alain Bussoz to check out Norman's flat, which he shared with Nicholas Laurent and his wife, Maud, at 75 Boulevard Lanne, Paris. They found Norman's room to be extremely tidy, with the sheets folded and a tie hanging in the wardrobe. A bicycle given to him on Wednesday was leaning against the wall. His clothes and other effects had been removed. The Laurents' rooms were very untidy. The drawers were half open, clothes had been removed in a hurry and there was half-cooked food on the stove. It looked as if they had left in a great rush.[16]

On 29 June, Dutilleul duly proceeded on his mission to collect Noor's wireless sets as arranged. Yves was there and handed over the parcel to him, which he brought back safely to Le Mans. The same day, despite the chaos all around, Garry and his fiancée Marguerite got married as they had planned. Noor attended the wedding but Antelme stayed away.

The summer of arrests continued. Though they had moved out of their apartment, Madame Guerne had the habit of going back to her old flat every day to check with the caretaker for any news that he might have. On 1 July, when she went to the flat with Bussoz, they were intercepted by the Gestapo. Bussoz was arrested but Madame Guerne managed a miraculous escape from the fourth-floor flat. She called Worms and told him that the Gestapo had been searching her place and he should warn her husband and Antelme. She gave him Antelme's address. Worms called on Antelme at Madame Aigrain's flat just after lunch. It was the first time Antelme met the head of the Juggler circuit. He told Antelme that Madame Guerne had said that the Gestapo had got hold of Antelme's food card and she had torn off the first page and eaten it to get rid of his name. But his previous address was marked at the back of the card. Worms told Antelme that he would like to see him later and left him a number where he was to call and ask for 'Yvonne'.

At 6.30 p.m. when Antelme rang the number Yvonne answered and passed the phone to Weil, who informed him that Worms was 'ill' (code for being arrested). Weil was anxious to meet him but when Antelme called back again at 8 p.m., Yvonne told him that he would not be able to see Weil. Antoine gathered that he too had been arrested. He was just left with a number for the circuit. Later Antelme discovered that Yvonne was Countess Yvonne de La Rochefoucauld, who lived at 4 rue de la Neva.[17]

The same day, the concierge at Antelme's building told him that the Gestapo had been to his old flat and had come looking for him. They did not have his correct name and asked for him by his code name 'Antoine'. They gave a fairly accurate description of him and said he was tall and often wore a Basque beret. The caretaker said there were many tall men in the building and she did not know whom they meant. They tried to bully her, producing a Gestapo badge, and said they would be back. Antelme kept his head down and advised Noor to do the same.

Later they heard that the Gestapo had been to the Gisors arms depot near Trie-Château, and the reception committee had fallen to the Germans. George Darling, the man Suttill had gone to meet before his arrest, had been killed and the others were arrested.

The network had fallen into complete disarray within ten days of Noor arriving in Paris. She was clearly shaken but took Antelme's advice and lay low at his friend's apartment. The Garrys left for Le Mans. Germaine Aigrain looked after both Noor and Antelme, who were hiding in the same building. The situation was even more dangerous as it was clear that the Gestapo had a full description of Antelme and were actively looking for him. It has been suggested by Noor's friend and biographer Jean Overton Fuller that a romantic attachment developed between Antelme and Noor. They were thrown together in hiding for long periods as the circuit collapsed around them and an attachment was almost inevitable. Mutual friends of the couple told Fuller that they had even planned to get married once they reached London. Antelme was full of admiration for Noor and had remarked to a fellow agent that there was no one like her. But Madame Aigrain has suggested that Antelme was 'paternalistic' towards Noor.[18] Antelme was divorced with two sons living in Durban. He had also had a romantic liaison in London with Penelope Torr, F-section's records officer. Noor, too, was engaged and planned to get married when she returned, so it was unlikely that any relationship between them would develop further.

Meanwhile, Gieules organised a meeting at his flat at 66 rue de Pontieu between Antelme, his friend William Savy, Paul Arrighi, Arthur de Montalambert and Noor. William Savy was a lawyer who helped Antelme raise money for F-section activities in Paris. He had a withered arm and it was therefore extra brave of him to go into the Resistance. Savy was hiding at Gieules' flat because the Gestapo had raided his apartment. Antelme informed the meeting that it was dangerous for him to stay on in Paris and that he would return to London and take Savy with him.[19] Once during this turbulent period Savy and Antelme spent the entire night sitting in armchairs at Savy's office in order to evade detection by the Gestapo.[20]

On 1 July, while the Gestapo was making further searches, Noor returned to Grignon. She wanted desperately to transmit to London and thought she could do so from there. But the moment she reached the school she realised the building had been occupied. She withdrew quietly, abandoned her bicycle and took a bus back to Paris. There are some reports that there was a clash with the Gestapo at Grignon, and Noor's French citation for the Croix de Guerre says that she shot and either wounded or killed some of the Germans who pursued her. But this is not corroborated. Noor filed a report about the incident to London but did not mention anything about firing on Germans. She sent the details of the arrests to London by the Lysander that left on the night of 19 September.[21] This was probably the detailed report that was submitted later, as her message about the arrests had been transmitted much earlier.

Noor reported that about sixty German plain-clothes policemen had arrived at Grignon and reproached the director for his anti-German sentiments. They asked him a lot of questions which he refuted. His son-in-law Robert Douillet was also interrogated. The Gestapo then arrested the director and six older students and the gardener Maillard.

After this the Germans staged a show of shooting in a forest close to the college. They rounded up the students and demanded to know everything, threatening to shoot them if they did not cooperate. They marched them in groups of ten and fired shots in the air and then came back for more students, telling them they would be shot like the rest. But this yielded no results. The shooting exercise was a sham and the next morning the director was brought back to his office. The Germans told him that they knew he was not a Germanophile but he was not to spread his ideas if he did not want any problems. The Germans had claimed that the English officers arrested in Paris had talked.

On 2 July, the day after the incident at Grignon, Professor Balachowsky was arrested at his flat in Viroflay. After breakfast, there was a knock on the door and the maid answered it. Madame Balachowsky saw a tall broad-shouldered man entering and asking for the professor. The professor was led away by the Gestapo but Madame Balachowsky, to her surprise, was not arrested. She and the maid were left behind in the flat. Madame Balachowsky immediately set out to warn other members of the circuit not to come to their house. Noor was told about the arrest by the maid when she telephoned the flat at 11 a.m.

On 10 July, at 5 p.m. the Germans returned to Grignon and arrested Vanderwynckt again. As he was leaving he told his wife, 'Don't worry about my fate. I want to serve my country.'[22] Meanwhile Professor Balachowsky must have told the Germans where Noor had buried the wireless set because they went straight to the lettuce patch and dug it out.[23] He was the only one who knew where she had buried it as they had done it together.

During the following week, hundreds of French agents were rounded up and arrested as the Germans infiltrated the circuits. Arthur de Montalambert, a friend of Antelme's who worked with Octave Simon and the Satirist circuit, was arrested along with other members of the circuit. He died in Germany.

While the few left in the Prosper sub-circuit – Antelme, Noor and Garry – tried to warn others and relocate, the Germans tried their best to extract as much information from their prisoners. Suttill was subjected to the harshest of Gestapo interrogations, being questioned for three days continuously without being allowed to eat, drink, sleep or even sit down.[24] Despite this, he infuriated the Germans by refusing to reveal anything. Suttill had apparently 'been very "English" and haughty under interrogation, and had just sat in a chair and smoked cigarettes'.[25] But there is evidence that Norman cracked and gave a full deposition. Later, Norman told a fellow agent, Marcel Rousset, at 3 bis Place États Unis prison, that the Gestapo knew everything and that Suttill and he had admitted everything to save their lives.[26] Through Norman and the documentary material available the Germans gained a clear insight into the French section.[27] It was also after Norman's arrest that they learnt of the existence of 'Madeleine'.[28] They now had a personal description of her and knew she was a radio operator in the Prosper circuit. Immediately they set up a wireless detection station to observe traffic for the French section.

It was probably through Norman that the Germans got to know about the Juggler sub-circuit and made their arrests. Worms was arrested on 1 July while eating at his regular black-market restaurant, Chez Tutulle, in the rue Pergolese. He never kept his appointment with Antelme. Guerne and his wife Jeanne were also arrested with him. His second-in-command, Jacques Weil, saw him being arrested and fled to Switzerland. Their radio operator, Gaston Cohen (Justin) fled to the countryside and made his way back to England via Spain. The courier to the Juggler circuit, Sonia Olschanezky, managed to survive till January but was then arrested and sent to Natzweiler concentration camp where Andrée Borrel and she were both executed by lethal injection in July 1944.

After a few days of torture, during which they beat him insensible and broke his arm, Suttill too is said to have caved in and accepted a bargain made by the Germans. The bargain was that Suttill's leaders would order their subordinates to reveal to the enemy all their dumps of parachuted weapons and explosives in return for a promise that nobody but themselves would be executed. The details of the pact are revealed in Vogt's account to Jean Overton Fuller.[29] But it is disputed in many quarters. It was Norman who visited the houses of the Resistance workers, carried out most of the bargaining with the sub-agents and asked them to surrender their arms. Suttill was taken away to Berlin almost immediately for further grilling and was not seen by any prisoners after the first three days. It is, therefore, unlikely that he signed or even knew about the pact. It is clear from the SOE files that the chiefs at Baker Street regarded Norman as the traitor and had little doubt that he had cracked under Gestapo interrogation.[30]

When Armel Guerne met Norman at Avenue Foch prison, Norman told him that the Gestapo knew everything about the Prosper organisation since they had arrived but had let it run on.[31]

In jail, Guerne was shown photocopies of SOE orders for the bombarding of workshops where engines were repaired at Nantes. He also saw 8–10 photos included with the order which had been sent in 1943. Guerne said he saw a letter from Prosper to his wife and three reports, one with Prosper's signature. He saw radio messages in code in English and German and a message in Antelme's own handwriting, all of which made him think that the Germans did indeed have a fair knowledge of SOE activities.

Norman also told Guerne that he had agreed to a proposal made by the commandant of the Paris Gestapo that if Norman and Guerne surrendered all the arms depots, the Germans would spare the lives of all members of the group except the chiefs, and would stop their files reaching a military court. Guerne confessed to giving out names of a few agents and also identifying some depots.

The skilful mind games played by the German police officers – Ernest Vogt and Josef Goetz – probably sapped Norman's resolution. The number of arrests following this alleged pact ran into hundreds. Members of the Resistance – mainly farmers on whose lands parachutes had been dropped – were told that they would be treated as soldiers, not as traitors who would be executed, if they cooperated. In the confusion many farmers and labourers, who thought they were going to be discovered anyway, cooperated. When the Gestapo had the information they needed, they predictably broke the pact. An unknown number of Resistance workers, estimated at between 400 and 1,500, were arrested. Their treatment left many French families very bitter. The smashing of one network led to the infiltration of another. To his horror, a jailed leader of a Prosper sub-circuit was shown a Michelin map belonging to the F-section with clearly marked dropping zones. The map was presented to him by SS Hauptscharführer Karl Langer, who followed this up with a file of photocopies of reports to London of sabotage operations. Langer recited the dates and locations of parachute drops and then added: 'We know that your network has just received someone called Madeleine. We have not found her yet. We will.'[32]

Once the Gestapo had visited his flat, Antelme knew he was in danger. He burnt any compromising papers that he had, contacted Robert Benoist and moved to Benoist's estate at Auffargis near Rambouillet at the beginning of July. Here he stayed at the house of Robert's brother, Maurice Benoist. We know from Robert Benoist's files[33] that Noor accompanied him to Auffargis but do not have definite dates – apart from 17 and 18 July – that she stayed there. Other circuit members hiding in Auffargis were Maurice Benoist, his wife Suzy Benoist and their maid and Grover Williams and his wife. It is possible that Noor was transmitting from there and making the final arrangements for Antelme's return to London. Antelme remained in Auffargis all of July and left with William Savy by Lysander on a flight organised by Déricourt and Noor on the night of 19/20 July. Before leaving he made sure that Noor had a safe address and enough money. He had already given her 6,000 francs for her current expenses when she first went into hiding on 25 June. Any money she had was with Garry at the time. Before leaving he gave her 40,000 francs and then sent her a further 1,000 francs through Déricourt.

He also left 30,000 francs with Raymond Andres, in whose safe house Noor was living when he left. The amount, he said, would cover her costs and any other expenses Andres may have to incur on behalf of the circuit. Antelme later reported to London that 'Madeleine proved very useful to me during this disturbed period'[34] and said he had suggested to her that she should be attached to Déricourt, who would need his own wireless operator. He arranged for Robert Dowlen, wireless operator to Grover Williams, who was based in Pontoise, to lend her a set (since Noor's own radio set was still in Le Mans) and told Noor to stand by pending confirmation from London.

It was Noor on Poste Madeleine who broke the disastrous news of the destruction of the Prosper circuit to Maurice Buckmaster. She had managed to get her radio set from Le Mans with the help of Dutilleul and Simon and returned to Paris to her safe house. Buckmaster also received reports about its demise from Cohen and Dowlen (before Cohen had to flee and Dowlen was arrested). All the leaders and their equipment had been captured. Circuits in Gisors, Grignon, Falaise, part of Le Mans and L'Eporcé (the estate of de Montalambert) were blown. Noor's circuit leader, Garry, had left for Le Mans. There was now only one transmitter in Paris. It was Noor's.

Buckmaster replied that it was too dangerous for her to work and she should return to England. He would arrange a plane to fly her back. But Noor refused and said she would rather stay if she could. As the last wireless operator left in Paris, she felt it was crucial for her to remain where she was so that London would know what was happening in Paris. She said she would slowly try to organise another circuit and rebuild the old one.[35]

Buckmaster was in a dilemma. He knew that Noor's life was in danger and it was only a matter of time before she was arrested. But Poste Madeleine was now the last link with Paris and it had a crucial role. He accepted her offer as the sacrifice of a soldier and allowed her to remain. Buckmaster told Noor that since all the listening apparatus of the Germans would now be trained on her, she should not transmit for a while. He warned her that since hers was the only wireless operating in Paris, it would be easy for the Germans to track her with their direction-finding vans.[36] She could however receive transmissions, which could not be detected.

Virtually alone now in Paris, Noor agreed to lie low and transmit with extreme caution. Poste Madeleine's dangerous game was about to begin.

NINE

Poste Madeleine

With Antelme gone, Noor felt terribly alone in Paris. She was still staying at Raymond Andres' flat at 1 Square Malherbe with Germaine Aigrain keeping a maternal eye on her. Noor had her radio set with her, though she was not transmitting from her flat at this time. Antelme had given her some assignments before he left and on 20 July she had a rendezvous with Robert Gieules at the RAC Place Vendome, where she handed him 400,000 francs.[1] Antelme had also asked Noor to report regularly on the progress of plans for the financing of invading troops.

Noor's clandestine work now involved keeping in touch with three French agents – Robert Gieules, Paul Arrighi and Charles Vaudevire. The four met several times a week through the summer at a bench in the Tuileries gardens. In this circle she was known by the code name Raymonde. Vaudevire was the peacetime director of the French Société Radio Electrique, who serviced her transmitter when it broke down. Arrighi was a barrister who lived on rue de Miromesnil, Paris. Vaudevire also introduced her to Viennot, a Paris businessman who had employed members of the Resistance on his staff to provide them with cover. Viennot played a dangerous double game. Outwardly he was friendly with the Germans and tried to get information from their headquarters at Avenue Foch. He often smuggled attractive women into the German ranks to attempt to find out vital secrets. He also used a regular 'gang' of criminals to counter the Germans. These gangs undertook daring rescue jobs when required.

On the night of 22/23 July, London sent French section's second-in-command, Major Nicholas Bodington, to Paris to ascertain the scale of the damage to the Prosper circuit. He was accompanied by Jack Agazarian and the two of them made the crossing by Hudson. Déricourt arranged the reception and settled Bodington at the flat of his courier, Julienne Aisner (Claire), in the Place des Ternes while Agazarian stayed in a more modest flat in a working-class area of Paris. At this time Norman's wireless was being worked back to London by the Germans, and F-section had their doubts about whether his messages were genuine. Nevertheless London asked Norman for a safe address where he could meet Bodington and Agazarian. The message came back asking them to meet Norman in the flat of a Madame Philipowski in the rue de Rome. This address was then passed on to Bodington and Agazarian. Both of them were convinced that the message was a trap, but felt they should check it out. Agazarian offered to go. Predictably, he was arrested as soon as he knocked on the door on 30 July.[2] His captor identified him by sight. Agazarian refused to divulge any details despite brutal torture and finally ended up in front of a firing squad at Flossenburg, just six weeks before the end of the war.

With his radio operator captured by the Germans, Bodington now relied on Noor. She often stayed overnight in the flat in the Place des Ternes and transmitted for him. At the time Noor was also working for Déricourt as well as coordinating with Robert Gieules. Through Noor, Bodington discovered that elements of the Prosper circuit had remained intact. One was Garry's Cinema/Phono circuit, as Garry had escaped capture, and the other was a fragment of the French Resistance: a Giraudist rather than a Gaullist faction called OCM. It worked closely with F-section agent Claude de Baissac's Scientist circuit in Bordeaux. Claude de Baissac knew Suttill and Antelme well and often came to Paris to meet them. The local Paris contacts of de Baissac consisted mainly of OCM members under the leadership of a French major with the unlikely name of Marc O'Neil. For logistical reasons it had been decided to transfer the group to Prosper, and Suttill had met O'Neil on 24 June, the day of his arrest, to discuss this. After Suttill's arrest, Claude de Baissac had to take responsibility for the group again and it was handed over to him by Bodington.

Noor also organised a rendezvous between Bodington and Robert Gieules at the Tuileries.[3] Antelme had asked Gieules to establish a list of contacts of people in the Ardennes who would help the SOE in that sector, and Gieules conveyed this list to Bodington.

Bodington helped Noor rent a flat at 3 Boulevard Richard Wallace, Neuilly-sur-Seine.[4] It was in a block of modern flats facing the Bois de Boulogne, and Noor occupied a small room on the ground floor. The suitability of the apartment was questionable however, since most of the apartments were occupied by SS officers. Noor now lived directly in their midst. Bodington himself moved to another flat in Avenue Malakoff to an address unknown to other organisations.[5]

Meanwhile the bad news continued on the arrests. On 29 July two men went to Madame Lethias's house in Pontoise looking for Benoist's radio operator, Robert Dowlen, but he was out. On 31 July, 18 men came to arrest Dowlen, who had been traced by direction-finding vans. On 2 August, the Gestapo arrested Madame Lethias and took 12 million francs from her desk. The same day they arrested Robert Benoist's brother, Maurice, at seven in the morning at his home at 75 Boulevard Berthier, Paris.

Barely ten days after Antelme had left Auffargis, the Gestapo now arrived there. Accompanied by two Gestapo officers, Vogt and Peters, Maurice Benoist was driven to the family estates at Auffargis, calling first at his father's property and then his own. Grover Williams was arrested at Maurice Benoist's house and beaten up. Along with him the Gestapo arrested Maurice's wife, Suzy Benoist, and Mrs Williams. Next they were driven to Robert's farm where they discovered a stack of arms behind a false plaster wall hidden by bales of straw.[6] Maurice had hidden these himself with the help of Antelme. Benoist's father was questioned for eight hours and his mother was beaten, and then they were both taken to Fresnes prison. Robert Benoist had evaded arrest because he was in Paris at the time. He now hid in a friend's room in the city. On 5 August, when Benoist stepped out to make a call from a call box to enquire about his parents, he was asked by two Germans to get into their car. He made a dramatic escape from the car, hid in a friend's flat, contacted Déricourt on 7 August, moved to another safe house and escaped to London on a flight arranged by Noor on 19/20 August.

The capture and disappearance of F-section radio operators – Norman, Agazarian, Robert Dowlen, Macalister, Dubois and Cohen – left Noor as the only operator in and around Paris and though she had been warned by Buckmaster to lie low, she started transmitting cautiously. Single-handedly she did the work of six radio operators. She went on air and exchanged messages with Antelme (now in London), who wanted her to keep in touch with Octave Simon and send him information about the financing of troops during the invasion.[7] On 28 July he sent a message saying Noor should contact Simon to ask his brother-in-law about the matter. Through Simon, Noor was to arrange direct contact with the people who would be connected with the scheme. Noor sent him a message on 31 July that the goods depots were now ready at Amiens. She reported that there were 3,000 gearboxes for Tiger tanks in the factory at present and gave its exact location. On 3 August Antelme replied that he assumed the Amiens goods depots were connected with Dutilleul (Champagne) and asked Noor to get the latest news from Garry and to collect 150,000 francs from Grover Williams for Dutilleul. (Unknown to him, Grover Williams had already been arrested.)

Antelme had complete faith in Noor and knew that she would rise to the occasion despite the difficulty of working in Paris at that time. The work was dangerous as Noor had to carry her wireless set around with her most of the time. In the early days this was still in the form of a bulky suitcase, weighing about 30lb, and could attract the attention of the Gestapo. It was only later, by 1944, that the wireless sets were hidden in smaller briefcases which were lighter to carry and less noticeable. Some time in early August, Noor was involved in a scrape with the Gestapo when she went to meet Octave Simon. After they had lunch she accompanied him to his home, but the Gestapo were shadowing them.[8] Noor was a fast runner, however, and so she managed to outrun the Gestapo. She later met Déricourt's courier Julienne on a Metro platform and told her what had happened.

Noor had been warned by Buckmaster that the German listening apparatus would be tuned in on her. In order to evade detection she transmitted from various places and under different conditions. Sometimes she would drive out with Arrighi or Vaudevire, and transmit from the suburbs of Montrouge, Levallois and Noisy-le-Grand. They would stop the car in a quiet lane where Noor could let out the aerial and transmit. Arrighi had lost both his wireless operators, so he asked Noor if she could send messages for him as well. He worked for General de Gaulle and needed to send messages to the headquarters in London. Noor readily agreed and she was now sending messages not only to French section, but also directly to De Gaulle's office in England. She would go out with Arrighi every Wednesday and Friday and transmit between 5 and 5.30 p.m. She arranged for a drop of one million francs to be flown in and delivered to him. All the while she kept in touch with Gieules, who liaised between the F-section and important French civilians.

Meanwhile Bodington decided to buy a café in Place St Michel to be run by Julienne. It was to be used as a contact point for agents seeking to escape from France and also to evacuate RAF pilots or French Resistance workers who needed to go to England. Once he had done this, he returned to London on Déricourt's aircraft on 16/17 August. Noor received the messages organising Bodington's flight. With him went F-section agents Claude and Lise de Baissac, the brother and sister duo. Claude was the leader of the Scientist circuit in Bordeaux and Lise often acted as a courier for Antelme. On 19/20 August, Noor organised the flights and escape routes by Hudson for ten more people returning to London. They included Octave Simon, Robert Benoist and Vic Gerson. Noor remained the only British agent in the field (the others were mainly local recruits) and she must have felt increasingly isolated, but she carried on undaunted.

Noor needed safe places to transmit, so she turned her attention to old schoolfriends. This period of her life in Paris has been pieced together to a large extent by her friend Jean Overton Fuller, who went to Paris after the war and traced Noor's friends and the surviving people in her circuit. Noor first called on her music teacher Henriette Rénie, whom she had not seen for nine years.[9] Noor asked her if she knew of a room to let.

Henriette Rénie asked Noor to stay with her, but Noor told her she could not do that. Noor told her that she had come to establish a wireless post for transmission to England. She knew she could not compromise her teacher's safety. Henriette Rénie was alarmed at the risks Noor was taking. She had known Noor as a quiet girl and was amazed at how much she had changed. Yet on one level Noor was still very much the same person that her teacher had known: shy, earnest and friendly.

When Henriette exclaimed that if she was discovered she would be shot, Noor simply said she knew. She said her predecessor had been shot by the Germans and she had volunteered to come when London needed a person with language skills to do the job. Noor left quickly after that and it was the last time her teacher saw her.

Noor now moved around with her radio set most of the time. She desperately needed to find different houses, preferably with trees outside where she could hang up the aerial, in order to transmit. So far she had transmitted mainly from country roads with Arrighi and Vaudevire and occasionally from Julienne's flat. She also dyed her hair in an attempt to disguise herself. The Germans had put out her description at all stations. They were also trying to detect her transmissions. The wireless detection stations often caught her on the airwaves but they could not close in on her as she constantly changed the place of transmission.[10]

One day, probably around the end of August, Noor was spotted cycling up the Champs Elysées by Madame Salmon, one of her neighbours from Fazal Manzil.[11] Madame Salmon called out, 'Noor!' Startled at hearing her real name shouted out loud, Noor stopped and quickly led the other woman into a side street. She told Madame Salmon the reason why she was in Paris and said she was known here as Jeanne-Marie and no one knew her real name.

Noor was wearing dark glasses and had dyed her hair red, which made her look very different and somewhat odd. She was wearing a simple summer frock. Noor was hoping to throw the Germans off her track in case they were looking for a lady with dark hair. Madame Salmon, who had known her for a long time, still managed to recognise her despite the disguise.

They agreed to keep in touch by meeting in cafés. By now Noor had clearly become much more security-conscious and they did not exchange addresses. They arranged to meet again at a café and decide at each meeting a rendezvous for the next. The next time they met Noor had dyed her hair blonde, which Madame Salmon thought suited her much more than the red hair.[12]

Still on the lookout for a room to broadcast from, Noor paid a visit to her old family doctor, Dr Jourdan, and his wife.[13] The Inayat Khans' family physician had always been very fond of little Noor, whom he had operated on for an inflamed appendix as a child. On being cured, she had presented the Jourdans with a small potted rose tree. They had planted it in their country house in Marly-le-Roi and called it the 'Noor Inayat'.

Seeing Noor now on such a dangerous mission moved the Jourdans and they told her that she could occasionally use the garden of the house at Marly-le-Roi to transmit. Here she could put up her aerial in the trees. Noor went to Marly, where she found that the rose tree had grown luxuriantly and covered the house in pink blossoms. It filled her with nostalgia. Noor transmitted about four or five times from the house in Marly.

She visited the Jourdans at their Paris flat quite often and Madame Jourdan thought that she managed to relax in their company. The strain of constantly escaping from the Gestapo and carrying her wireless around with her was clearly taking its toll. Madame Jourdan noticed that Noor kept changing her hairstyle. Despite all the stress of the job, she would always bring Madame Jourdan flowers when she visited.

Though she was tense and exhausted, Noor sent back cheery letters to her family in mailbags that went in the August Lysander. She wrote to Vera Atkins that her little bird had cheered her up and things were going well. She hoped they would be celebrating soon.[14] She told Vilayat in a letter that she had missed being with him on his birthday, and looked forward to seeing him in uniform. (She had learnt via Vera Atkins that he had got his commission.) She wondered when they would meet again and said they would have so much to say to each other.[15] Noor also wrote to her mother. All her letters were photocopied by Déricourt and handed over to the Germans. These copies were shown to her when she was arrested.

Noor used her flat at Boulevard Richard Wallace extensively as a letterbox to pick up and drop off messages. Sometimes she transmitted from there. The concierge of the building, Madame Jourdois, later told Jean Overton Fuller that Noor always seemed to be in a rush. Her husband and she realised that Noor was leading a double life as she hardly ever stayed at the flat and strange men came and collected or left parcels for her. They knew, however, that she was a 'nice girl' and were aware that she was working for the Resistance.

Despite the enormous risks she was taking, Noor transmitted throughout August. One night she had a particularly narrow escape. She needed to send an urgent message to London and decided to hang her aerial from the tree on the pavement outside her flat. It was dusk and she hoped no one would notice. She dropped the aerial out of the window and went outside to pick it up. As she was struggling to hook it up on the tree, she heard a voice and spun around.

It was a German officer from one of the flats. 'May I help you?' he asked. Noor coolly replied that she would be grateful if he would. The officer helped her put up the aerial, no doubt thinking she was an innocent French lady who probably wanted to listen to some music on the wireless![16]

Noor now took another risk. Desperate to find new places to transmit, she went to Suresnes to visit her old friends. It was a risky thing to do since she would be instantly recognised in the suburb in which she had grown up. But she trusted her instinct that her childhood friends and neighbours would not let her down. She climbed up the hill to Suresnes and almost walked up to the gate of Fazal Manzil, but good sense prevailed and she knocked instead on the door of Madame Pinchon, a few houses away.

Madame Pinchon was amazed to see Noor standing outside and even more stunned to learn about Noor's mission. Noor told her she needed a house with a garden where she could set up a regular post. Madame Pinchon told her the house was surrounded by Germans. Even Fazal Manzil had been occupied by German soldiers. The news horrified Noor. From Madame Pinchon's house she could see the gardens of Fazal Manzil and it broke her heart to see her childhood home now being used by the Germans.

Next she knocked on the door of her childhood friend Raymonde Prénat. Madame Prénat, like the others, was shocked to see Noor, but agreed to let her use a room in the house for transmission. They decided the front living-room would be most suitable.[17] Noor immediately climbed up on the roof to find a suitable spot to put up the aerial. Raymonde remembered that Noor moved sure-footedly like a cat. Trusting her instinct, Noor felt it was safe to transmit from Suresnes. From the living room window she could clearly see the gate and anyone who was approaching. Madame Prénat had told her that in case of any emergency Noor was simply to run out of the back door and not worry about anything. Madame Prénat would hide her wireless somewhere. Although there were Germans around, Noor did not think she was putting Raymonde's family at any great risk and she set herself up in her friend's house for regular transmission.

She would arrive around noon and spend the rest of the day with the Prénats. In some ways it felt like old times and she was happiest there. She told Raymonde about her life over the past three years since she had left Fazal Manzil, how she had trained in England and the sort of work she did. She told Madame Prénat about the Gestapo and their methods and wondered what would happen if they arrested her. 'It doesn't matter! They can do what they like with me. I don't mind. I shan't tell them anything,' she said.[18]

Carrying her transmitter around in a place where so many people could recognise her was dangerous, but Noor carried on. Meanwhile, London received her messages loud and clear. They would listen out for her at 1500 hrs GMT every day.[19] She would receive messages from London at around 1730 hrs. Leo Marks noted with satisfaction and pride that Noor had 'astonished all who believed they knew her' by surviving and working in Paris where others had been arrested.[20] He noted that her transmissions were flawless, with all their security checks intact.

Noor was working with French Resistance workers and saboteurs, and trying to rebuild the Prosper circuit with local contacts. The group had traced underground sewers in which the Germans stored torpedoes to be shipped to the U-boat pens at Brest, and Noor passed on their request to London to be sent the new explosive known as 'marzipan' because its sweet smell resembled that of almonds.

A message from Poste Madeleine to operators in London in her own handwriting was probably carried back by the August Lysander. In it she writes:

> Please arrange everyday scheds, also using 3407.
>
> If sched is missed, possible contact at 1800 GMT same day.
>
> Please send another 3408 crystal, one already u/s.
>
> Suggest when message is sent blind, A1310 is repeated after message.
>
> Have not yet found suitable operational site for night work.
>
> Someday if possible, please send white mac, FANY style.
>
> Thanks a lot, its grand working [with] you. The best moment I have had yet.
>
> Kindly send one more Mark II as one is u/s – am trying to repair.
>
> Madeleine

Noor was clearly determined to keep her spirits up and carry on working. After her initial shakiness, she had taken like a natural to the field. She even managed to talk her way through another close encounter with the Gestapo.[21] One day while carrying her wireless on the Metro, she saw two German soldiers looking at her. There was no way she could get off, so she had no choice but to wait. They walked up to her and asked her what she was carrying.

'A cinematographic apparatus,' Noor replied, cool as a cucumber. They asked to see it and Noor opened up the briefcase slightly. She saw that they had no idea what was inside so she continued bluffing. 'Well you can see what it is,' she told them. 'You can see all the little bulbs.' The soldiers, apparently not wishing to display their ignorance of what a cinematographic apparatus might be, let her go, saying, 'We thought it was something else.'

Poste Madeleine was now crucial to the war effort. Between July and October Noor sent over twenty messages in extremely difficult circumstances. She managed to facilitate the escape of thirty Allied airmen shot down in France and ensured that arms and money were delivered to the French Resistance. She also pinpointed positions for parachute drops of arms and arranged for other agents to escape back to England. In September she arranged false papers for four agents and saw that these were delivered from London. The agents needed identity cards, ration cards and textile cards. Her transmissions became the only link between the agents around the Paris area and London.

Occupied Paris was more dangerous than ever for the agents. The Gestapo were quite literally everywhere. As they were often not in uniform, it was difficult to spot them. Noor simply relied on her sixth sense to keep out of their way. Later Josef Kieffer, a German officer, acknowledged that Noor's careful evasion tactics had made it very difficult to track her.[22]

Some time at the end of August, the Garrys moved back to Paris and took a flat in Neuilly. This would have made Noor feel less isolated. Garry's sister Renée sometimes stayed with them. Noor began transmitting Garry's messages to London: usually requests for arms, explosives and other commodities needed by the French Resistance. London would send details about parachute drops. Noor sometimes used their flat in Neuilly to transmit and receive messages, but knowing that the German listening machines were all trained on her, she needed to keep changing locations. Vaudevire introduced her to Madame Peineau, who agreed to let her transmit from her house in Bondy, an industrial suburb of Paris. She also said Noor could sleep in the front bedroom there.

Noor worked regularly from this address, arriving in the afternoon, transmitting and deciphering till late and leaving early the next morning. One day she was told off by Madame Peineau for leaving her notebook open on the kitchen table with all her codes in it. Once again she was told that she must not trust anyone, even people who had been introduced to her by members of the circuit.[23]

Noor was now moving between her flat in the Boulevard Richard Wallace, Garry's flat in Neuilly, the house in Bondy and Raymonde's house in Suresnes, carrying her transmitter with her all day. She was transmitting from at least five flats and houses in and around Paris. In between she had to meet her contacts and collect messages. Madame Peineau noticed that she looked exhausted.

A message from Noor carried back by Lysander on 19 September listed motor companies like BMW and Renault along with other companies that seemed to be working for Germany in violation of the terms of the Armistice. She also added that she would give the complete information on Orly (presumably targets for air strikes or sabotage) in the next eight days. A hastily handwritten note at the end of the message said that the information had been provided by Verlaine and Noor added that she would confirm the identity by wireless. She was following SOE security procedures of breaking up the message into two components to avoid revealing unnecessary details if it was intercepted.

By that same September Lysander she received a letter and a tin of sardines from her mother. Madame Peineau noticed her reading it over and over again and saw how delighted she was. She could not bring herself to eat the sardines as she regarded them as too precious, having been sent all the way from London.

In September several members of Garry's organisation were arrested. Garry moved out of his flat in Neuilly once again and rented a studio in Porte d'Orleans. At the same time he found another room for Noor for occasional transmissions. It belonged to a friend, Solange, and was at 98 rue de la Faisanderie, not very far from the Avenue Foch, headquarters of the Gestapo. The address could also work as a letter box.

In mid-September Noor sent London a brief summary of the agents who had survived the double downfall of the Prosper and

Chestnut circuits and were still available for work. She was in regular wireless contact with London and arranged for an arms drop. She had successfully, and at great risk, managed to keep in touch with agents and Resistance workers, and sent back crucial information to London. Arthur de Montalambert, who had worked with Octave Simon, had been arrested. Simon himself had returned to London in August and Noor's contacts were slowly dying out. Liaising with Gieules and the French agents Vaudevire and Arrighi, among others, she kept up the flow of information to London for which she earned a mention in dispatches.

Noor now received instructions from London to go to the Café Colisée on the Champs Elysées, meet the cloakroom attendant and give a password, which would get her in touch with two Canadian agents of the French section. Noor did as instructed and met the two men who gave their code names as Bertrand and Valentin. What London and Noor did not know was that the real Canadian agents – Pickersgill and Macalister – had been arrested and these were Germans posing as the Canadian agents. The Germans had done their homework well. One of the agents was Karl-Horst Holdorf, an ex-steward with a US shipping line who had lived in America and spoke fluent English with an American accent. The other was Joseph Placke, who spoke poor French. Noor had no reason to suspect them. The Germans had seized the radios and codes of Pickersgill and Macalister when they arrested them and had been regularly playing back their messages to London. Not realising the deception, London had willingly provided them with a contact when they asked for it. They had sent Noor straight to the Germans.

But the Germans were wanting to make a clean sweep and wanted to get more from Noor. The two men told her they wanted to organise a network in the north of France – le Nord – but needed to contact a Monsieur Desprez, with whom London needed them to work. Noor knew that Robert Gieules was in touch with Desprez for the operation in the north.[24] This had been discussed by Antelme, Gieules and later Bodington. Desprez was the director of a factory in St-Michel, Hirson. Noor told the German agents that she could put them in touch with someone who could help.

On 20 September Noor rang Gieules and told him London wanted her to put an agent in touch with Desprez.[25] They arranged to establish contact on 25 September at 2.30 p.m. at the Place de l'Etoile and then have the meeting at 3 p.m. at the Société Générale de Fonderies at rue Cambaceres in Paris. Noor introduced Gieules to the two agents at the Etoile and then Gieules walked with them to the Société Générale, where they had a short meeting. The two agents told Gieules that they would meet again the following week. Gieules noted that one of them spoke French and the other 'only Canadian'. The second agent was blond with blue eyes and was wearing a large hat. Gieules later asked Noor if she knew the two men and Noor told him she had been put in touch with them by London.

A day before the meeting with the German agents, Gieules had a call from Dutilleul who had come from Le Mans to Paris. Dutilleul told Gieules that he wanted to get in touch with Antelme about matters in the north. He also asked Gieules if he had heard any news of a 'traveller' (code for agent from London). Meanwhile, at the meeting of 25 September, the German agents had told Gieules that a British agent called Jacques had arrived from London and wanted to know if Gieules would like to meet him. Gieules immediately connected this with the 'traveller' spoken of by Dutilleul and asked the Germans if he could bring a fellow agent to their next meeting. In fact, Jacques Michel had been arrested by the Gestapo on 23 September – the very day he had arrived from London. He had been given a contact in a café near the Gare de l'Est and given a password and even met an 'agent'. After lunch he was driven to a hotel on the Avenue de la Grande Armée and, suspecting nothing, was immediately arrested. He had also been sent a message on a wireless set worked by the Germans.

Completely unaware of this, Noor rang Gieules on 28 September to arrange a meeting with the British officer. The next day she rang him again and gave him the place. He was to go to the middle of the rue Tronchet behind the Madeleine church. Gieules met one of the agents there and set up a meeting for 2 p.m. at the Place du Trocadero, near the Palais de Chaillot. There he would have to meet the agent who would put him in touch with the British officer. He said he would be wearing a tailcoat, a beige khaki raincoat and a maroon trilby hat, with a morning newspaper in his hand.

Gieules found Dutilleul waiting for him at 2 p.m. in front of the Trocadero. They waited for some time near the Palais de Chaillot and then a person corresponding to the description approached them, asking if one of them was Dutilleul. They had barely exchanged a few words when they were surrounded by eight policemen armed with revolvers. The police handcuffed them and drove them separately in two cars to the Avenue Foch.

At Avenue Foch, Gieules told his interrogators that he was simply a friend of William Savy and was doing a few errands for him while he was away in London. He said he knew nothing more. The Germans pressed him for Noor's number, but although Gieules knew both her number and her address he insisted it was always she who called him, and did not give it away.

The Gestapo now used Gieules to set a trap for Noor on 30 September. Noor was worried that she had not heard from Gieules after 28 September. She confided in Viennot that she suspected he had been arrested. He advised her to ring the house and find out. Unknown to Noor, Gieules was sitting in front of two armed Gestapo officers when she called. He had been told to arrange a meeting with Noor. He deliberately tried to sound vague but asked her to meet him on 1 October at 10 a.m. at the Etoile, on the corner of Avenue MacMahon and rue Tilsit.

Noor had her misgivings, and Viennot advised her not to wait at the meeting place. He left Noor near the Arc de Triomphe and went to check out the site near the Etoile. Sure enough he saw Gieules there, but at a discreet distance there were six tall men guarding him from all angles. He returned to Noor and told her it was definitely a trap. At 10.40 a.m. Noor and Viennot saw the six agents bundle Gieules into a car and drive away. Noor had had a narrow escape. Gieules realised that she had sensed the trap and given the meeting a miss.[26]

Viennot realised that Noor was now in very real danger since the Gestapo had seen her and talked to her. He took her to a good hairdresser in Paris and asked for her hair to be dyed brunette. Noor had dyed her hair so many times now that it had become coarse and stiff. He also got rid of her English-style macintosh and grey dress and bought her a blue suit, a grey polo-necked jumper and a navy-blue hat. He remarked that she looked more French now.

Viennot noticed that Noor always carried her notebook with her in which she had written her codes and a full record of all the messages that she had sent to London. He reminded her that it was a dangerous document and if found on her would incriminate her at once. It would also reveal many useful things to the enemy. But Noor said she carried it on her precisely because it was so important, and she did not like to leave it anywhere. He also asked her why she did not destroy her past messages, as these were dangerous too, but Noor told him that London had told her to be particularly careful in 'filing' her messages.[27]

London had indeed said that all agents were to be very careful about filing their messages. They had, however, meant the use of the term 'filing' in a journalistic sense (as in sending a story). Noor had taken it literally as 'filing' in the bureaucratic sense and preserved the messages neatly and in order. This simple mix-up could have been avoided if agents had been told in clear terms to destroy all their messages after they had been sent.

Viennot found that Noor would not listen to him, and she insisted on obeying what she thought were orders from London, even though in the wrong hands the notebook could reveal a considerable amount to the Germans.

Noor was very shaken at the way she had nearly been betrayed by Gieules, a person she had worked so closely with for the past few months. She knew now that the Germans were closing in on her. They had actually seen her face to face. The strain of it all became too much for her and she broke down at Madame Prénat's house, burying her face in her hands and crying: 'I wish I was with my mother.'[28]

Some time around the end of September Noor was spotted in Paris by her old friend and acquaintance Alexis Danan, the journalist from *Paris Soir* with whom she had planned to set up a children's paper.[29] Danan saw her on one of the avenues that converge on the Etoile. Their glances crossed and there was a look of surprise and recognition on Noor's face. They instinctively started moving towards each other when Danan noticed her hesitate. Her dark eyes told Danan that he was to avoid her. Noor was carrying a small black case with her (probably her transmitter). Danan then strolled in front of the window of a bookseller allowing her the opportunity to approach him if she wanted to. Noor clearly wanted to talk to her old friend, but she restrained herself. She returned twice to the bookshop and walked close to Danan. He saw her 'magnificent surprised eyes' but she did not smile at him. Her eyes told the story. It was their last meeting.

The Gestapo had been trying to track Noor down since the beginning of July. Their wireless-detection system was trained on her and they had often heard her transmissions, but despite their best efforts they had not yet managed to capture her as Noor was following strict SOE guidelines of short transmissions from different locations.

Once the German listening machine intercepted a phone call from Sablons 88.04 that told them an agent was at work. It was the telephone number of Noor's address at the Boulevard Richard Wallace. They raided the flat some time in early October. But here too they found nothing. Immediately after the Gestapo had tried to trap her, Noor had collected her things, paid Madame Jourdois the rent and left the flat. She had told her it was unsafe for her to stay there any longer.

Throughout September, Noor had become like a hunted animal and on two occasions she told Madame Jourdan that she had been followed by the Gestapo and nearly got caught. One night she came to their house at nine, trembling like a leaf and said she had done her job, but that time she had felt she would not make it.[30] The Jourdans knew that Noor had been on a particularly dangerous job that night. She had called in before the job, entrusted them with her transmitter and told them to bury it if she did not come back. They had been waiting tensely for her return, and were greatly relieved when she did walk in. Already Noor was living on borrowed time.

Seeing the state that Noor was in, Madame Jourdan begged her to stay with them. But Noor would not be persuaded. She told Madame Jourdan that she had obligations in Paris and there were some people she had to meet every day to exchange notes. And she stepped out in the night again.

Viennot and Vaudevire now decided that Noor should lie low for a while and they arranged for her to go to Le Havre in Normandy. She put up a stubborn resistance but they said her arrest could compromise the others, so she was forced to agree. Vaudevire took her to the station at St Lazare and put her on the train himself. This was around 5 October.

Noor, however, returned in two days saying she could not vegetate in a farm in Normandy when she was needed in Paris. But Garry was away and Noor found that she was isolated again as both Arrighi and Vaudevire told her that she should not work from Paris any more. They advised her to return to England as it was clearly unsafe for her to stay there any longer.

Noor meanwhile told London that she would be going off the air for a while. Since she refused to leave her post till a replacement had been sent, Buckmaster advised Noor that he had found somebody to fill her position and she should return by the mid-October Lysander, to which she agreed.[31]

Noor now made a quick dash to Suresnes to say goodbye to Raymonde and Madame Prénat. She told Raymonde she was leaving for England and that she would see her again after the war. She gave Raymonde a parting gift of a gold compact (this was probably the one given to her by Maurice Buckmaster before she left for the field).

Vaudevire went with Noor to a rendezvous at Porte Maillot to meet a contact who would arrange her passage to England. When they got there they saw the agent, but felt something was not quite right and walked away. They had escaped another Gestapo trap.

On 9 October Viennot got a frantic call from Noor asking him to meet her at the Pont Levallois. He was not sure if this was a genuine call but went there anyway. Noor was not there. Neither did she come for an important meeting that night in which the Resistance were discussing how to blow up a building that housed the instruments for submarine warfare. They thought she had been arrested.

But Noor was still safe. She visited the Jourdans and told them that she was leaving for England on 14 October, and that she would see them on the day. They begged her to stay with them but once again she said she had other obligations.

On 10 October she did not go for her usual transmission to Madame Peineau's flat but rang her the next day. On 11 October she visited Madame Aigrain and told her she was leaving on the 14th. The next day, she rang Madame Aigrain again and asked her if she could come and see her. She sounded frantic.

Madame Aigrain had some visitors who were not sympathetic to the Resistance and she told Noor that she should not come just then. It was the last she heard from her. Within half an hour the Gestapo had entered Madame Aigrain's flat at 1 Square Malherbe and arrested her and her friend Raymond Andres.

Noor had told everyone about her planned departure. It seems she would have successfully outwitted the Germans, as she had done for the past three months, and managed to return to England, if she had not been betrayed by a person named 'Renée'. This was probably Renée Garry, sister of Henri Garry, her first contact in Paris. Noor knew Renée well and had often stayed in the Garrys' flat with her.

Renée, according to the German officer who met her, was a Frenchwoman, about '30 years old with dark hair and fairly corpulent'. She came to the Gestapo headquarters at Avenue Foch and told the head, Josef Kieffer, that she was prepared to betray a British agent if she was paid a certain amount of money. It was arranged that the arrest would not take place at the flat and that the other agent (Solange, Garry's friend) would not be arrested. She gave a personal description of Noor and the full address of the house in which she was staying.[32] The description matched the one the Germans had of Noor, and they now had the address they so badly needed. Renée was promised 100,000 francs for supplying the details about Noor (one-tenth of the amount that the Germans usually gave for the capture of British agents).

The house that Noor was staying at was on the rue de la Faisanderie, a corner house on a street parallel to the Avenue du General Serrail, which led off the Avenue Foch. The street was right opposite 84 Avenue Foch, headquarters of the Gestapo, who were distributed in small groups to watch her house. On the morning of 13 October Noor came out of the main entrance and walked into the baker's shop which was situated in the same building. Within minutes she came out again and walked away.

The German officers sent out to arrest her, Werner Ruehl and Haug, were sure the girl was Noor. She was wearing a blue tailored dress trimmed with white, and a dark hat. It was the dress Viennot had bought her a few days earlier. They started following her. Suddenly Noor turned around and saw them. Instinctively she knew she was being followed and quickly disappeared around a corner. They did not see her again though they searched the area thoroughly. Once again Noor's Beaulieu training had come in handy as she managed to shake off her followers and disappear.

After a lengthy search Ruehl and Haug returned to the station. Two hours later they heard that Madeleine had been arrested. The man who made the arrest was Pierre Cartaud, a French officer working for the Gestapo.

After she had shaken off the German officers, Noor had at some time returned to her flat in rue de la Faisanderie. She turned the key in her lock and went in. Standing behind the door was Pierre Cartaud. He had let himself into the flat and was waiting for her. A violent struggle followed. Cartaud seized Noor by her hands, but she fought back savagely and bit his wrists. As Cartaud tried to free himself, Noor continued to struggle and bit him harder, drawing blood. Eventually he was forced to release her hands. Cartaud tried to push her on the sofa and handcuff her, but he could not subdue Noor, who was attacking him ferociously. Finally, he drew his gun from his pocket, told her to keep still or he would shoot. Then with one hand training the gun on her, he used his second hand to make a telephone call to Kieffer at Avenue Foch and asked for assistance.

Kieffer immediately sent Ernest Vogt and told him to take two or three men with him. Vogt described the scene later: 'Pierre was standing covering her from the farthest possible corner of the room and Madeleine, sitting bolt upright on the couch, was clawing the air in her frustrated desire to get at him, and looked exactly like a tigress.'[33]

Noor's eyes were flashing with rage and she unleashed a stream of insults on her captors, calling them *sales Boches* (dirty Germans). Vogt said he had never seen such fury. Noor was also cursing her luck. She exclaimed that this would have to happen at the last moment, just before she was going to leave for England. Outnumbered by the Gestapo, she sank back on the couch.

Cartaud's wrists were bleeding heavily. Vogt and the other officers led Noor down the steps. Trying not to attract the attention of the other residents of the building, they bundled her into the waiting car for the short drive to 84 Avenue Foch.

The Gestapo had finally caught up with Noor. At Avenue Foch, Kieffer was delighted with the news of her arrest. Ruehl remembered thinking that she must have been a very important agent indeed.[34]

TEN

Prisoner of the Gestapo

The wide tree-lined Avenue Foch is one of the most exclusive boulevards of Paris, running from the Arc de Triomphe to the Bois de Boulogne. Named after the French general Marshal Foch, to whom the Germans had surrendered in November 1918, it was ironic that the Gestapo chose this boulevard for their headquarters. The symbolism was not unintentional. It was just outside Paris in the forests of Rethondes that the Germans had surrendered to Marshal Foch after the First World War. On 21 June 1940, four days after the Armistice had been agreed by Marshal Pétain, Hitler chose to visit this very spot to reinforce the fact that the Armistice was a *diktat* rather than a diplomatic agreement.

Accompanied by Goering, Ribbentrop and Hess, the Führer surveyed the scene in the forest. The site included a statue of Marshal Foch, a wagon-lit that had been there during the surrender, and an inscription condemning 'the criminal pride of the German Empire'. These Hitler looked at with an expression of 'hate, scorn, revenge, triumph'.[1] He stayed only a few minutes to hear the preamble to Pétain's armistice read out and left after the German national anthem had been played triumphantly on the spot. His troops then blew up the slab with the inscription, razed the entire site and towed away the wagon-lit to Berlin.[2] To Hitler, it symbolised the victory of the Third Reich and revenge for the defeat in 1918. The Gestapo then chose to have their headquarters on Avenue Foch to rub further salt into the wounds.

The German word 'Gestapo' was the abbreviation for Geheime Staats Polizei or Secret State Police, the organisation founded in 1933 by Goering and controlled by Himmler. The Gestapo was the most hated branch of the German forces, notorious for arresting people who were never seen again. Such was the fear of the Gestapo that Parisians would say that a person had been taken to the Avenue

Foch rather than mention that they had been picked up by the Gestapo. The job of arresting agents was the responsibility of the Gestapo. It overlapped with the Sicherheitsdienst (SD), the party security service, as both were divisions of the Reichssicherheitshauptamt or RHSA, the SS-controlled security service. There was little difference in practice between the two departments and in Allied eyes they worked as one.[3] Both their officers and non-commissioned officers were all members of the SS, Hitler's crack bodyguards. At the Nuremberg trials the two bodies were indicted jointly.

The three buildings of numbers 82, 84 and 86 Avenue Foch were occupied by the SD and the Gestapo. It was to no. 84 that captured F-section agents were sent. Heading the Gestapo team at no. 84 was Sturmbannführer Josef Kieffer.

Number 84 was a magnificent building with high ceilings and a wide marble staircase leading to the upper floors. On the fourth floor were Kieffer's office and residential quarters. One of the large rooms with a grand chandelier was used as the office while at the back of the house were the bedroom and kitchen and a hall with a white wooden staircase running up to the fifth floor. Here there were a few small dark rooms originally meant to be servants' quarters. The Gestapo had converted them into seven mini prison cells. Two slightly larger rooms to the front of the house on this floor were used by the guard and the interpreter, Ernest Vogt. There was a bathroom and two lavatories, one of which was used by the prisoners.

Escorted by four guards, Noor was taken straight up to the office of Ernest Vogt on the fifth floor. When they had arrested her, Cartaud and Vogt had collected a notebook with her codes and messages in it from her bedside table. It was the one that Viennot had asked her to destroy. They had also seized her radio set. It was a prize haul for the Gestapo.

Noor was still shaking with rage when she was led to her room. She faced Vogt's questions with fierce resistance, telling him over and over again that she would say nothing, no matter what. Vogt, however, continued to fire questions at her. Who was she working with, who did she meet every day, who were the people that provided her with safe houses? Noor remained stubbornly silent, and Vogt finally decided to send her to her room. Noor asked if she could have a bath.

This was an unusual request, but thinking it was better to go along with her, they agreed. But the guards left the door slightly ajar so they could keep an eye on her. At this Noor let loose another temper tantrum, saying she wanted to undress and have a full bath and she would not tolerate the guards looking at her. Vogt, thinking all the while that it was better to humour a feisty prisoner like Noor, agreed and asked the guard to shut the door.

Within seconds, Noor had climbed out of the bathroom window and was standing on a narrow gutter which ran underneath the attic windows. She walked like a cat, holding on to the tiles for support. Noor had always been sure-footed, clambering on to roofs in the past to hook up her aerial. She had wasted no time in making a bid to escape.

Vogt, not entirely comfortable with having to leave Noor alone, went to the lavatory next door and looked out of the window. He was shocked to see Noor standing on the gutter. She was making her way towards his window, unaware that he was there.

He didn't want to distract her and make her lose her footing. A fall from here meant certain death. Instead he waited till she reached the window and then said quietly 'Madeleine, don't be silly. You will kill yourself. Think of your mother! Give me your hand.'[4]

She looked shocked to see him, hesitated and then grasped his extended hand. Vogt pulled her in by her shoulders, head first, and marched her to her cell. Defeated, Noor sat down on the narrow bed and broke down. She cursed herself, crying that she had been a coward and should have allowed herself to fall and die rather than be captured. She was almost hysterical with anger and frustration. Finally Vogt decided to bring her colleague Gilbert Norman to see her. Ever since his arrest with Andrée Borrel and the Laurents in June, Norman had been kept a prisoner at Avenue Foch. Noor was surprised to see him. Vogt asked Norman to try to calm Noor down and tell her there was no need to commit suicide. Norman did his bit, telling her, as he had told other agents he had met at Avenue Foch, that the Germans knew everything and there was no point in trying to hide anything.[5] It did not make the slightest difference.

Seeing Norman apparently quite comfortable in Avenue Foch made Noor even more angry. She refused to cooperate with Vogt and remained silent. After a few hours had passed, a guard brought

Noor lunch, but she refused to eat it and later refused dinner as well. Vogt was trying hard to placate her. He ordered her to come for dinner to his room and offered her English tea and cigarettes. She accepted the tea and smoked the cigarettes furiously, but hardly touched the food.

Vogt now started playing the psychological games which he used to demoralise prisoners. He showed Noor that they had managed to decipher her codes from her notebook. He also showed her copies of the letters she had sent to her mother by the August Lysander, along with copies of her reports and letters to F-section. Vogt tried to give her the impression that the Germans already knew a lot, so it was pointless trying to hide anything. Vogt tried to make Noor believe that the Germans had an informer in Baker Street so she would feel even more vulnerable. He told her that he knew Maurice Buckmaster was their head, that they trained at Beaulieu in Hampshire (he even pronounced it correctly as 'Bewley') and that she had done her parachute training in Ringway in Manchester, and showed her aerial photographs of some of the schools. Noor had not done parachute training so this bit of information was wrong. Nevertheless, Noor was shocked to learn that the Germans knew the details of their training schools. It had the desired effect.

'You must have an agent in London!' she gasped. Vogt let her think they did.[6] He questioned her till midnight but got nothing out of her. Finally he decided to call it a day.

The next morning the interrogation began again. Vogt showed Noor the copy of her messages and demanded to know who the people mentioned in them were and what they did. Once again Noor remained silent. He then told Noor that some of the people may have helped her in small ways by providing a room for the night. If she didn't give the names, these innocent people too would be arrested, as they would eventually round up and arrest everyone. Vogt was a skilful interrogator who had mastered the tactics. While at Avenue Foch he wore civilian clothes so as not to appear too threatening. But there is a photograph of him in full SD uniform standing at Avenue Foch with the rest of the staff. On one hand he talked tough; on the other hand he tried to confuse Noor and hoped his gentle persuasion would make her open up. But Noor gave out nothing. Her stubborn streak matched Vogt's persistence and the German repeatedly drew a blank.[7]

Kieffer had the help of a radio specialist, Josef Goetz, who played a dangerous radio game with London called *Englandspiel*. Once the Germans had captured the wireless sets they could easily use them to transmit back to London. All the sets came with their own special crystals which were tuned to a certain frequency to contact London for incoming and outgoing messages. Goetz studied the style of transmission of the operators and successfully imitated it, coming on the airwaves on the same frequency and giving London the impression that the agent was transmitting from the field. Initially Goetz worked on his own, then as the game got larger he was assisted by Joseph Placke, Von Kapri and Werner Ruehl. Each had three or four decoy transmissions on hand during the time when the radio game was running.[8] Together they sent false messages to Baker Street and demanded equipment and reinforcements, which the Germans seized. They could also use the radio game to find out the location of SOE agents and set traps to capture others. Goetz had successfully played back the wireless sets of the two Canadian agents, Macalister and Pickersgill, and later that of Norman. These had led to the arrests of Jack Agazarian and Robert Gieules. Goetz now tried to work on Noor. He took Noor down to his office trying to get her to reveal her security checks and some of the technical side of her work. Once again he faced a wall of silence. True to her word, Noor said nothing.

Goetz, however, had Noor's past codes from her diary and her radio set and crystals. He used this to transmit to London and started a radio game called Operation Diana. He even imitated her particular style of transmission. On 17 October, the Germans sent a message on Poste Madeleine: 'My Cachette unsafe. New address Belliard. Hundred and Fifty Seven rue Vercingetorix, Paris, Password de la part de monsieur de Rual. This perfectly safe. Good bye.'[9]

At the receiving station at Grendon, the signals operator noted that the true security check was present but the bluff check had been omitted. Though Noor had not returned on the full-moon mid-October Lysander, London was not alarmed. They replied that they had received the new cachette address. Leo Marks had always taken a special interest in Noor, and followed her messages closely. Up till the end of September he had noticed that her transmissions were flawless, with all the security checks intact, and was secretly very proud of her. He had told the operators at Grendon that he had given Noor a special security check and they should watch her wireless traffic very closely and look out for it. But the girls at Station 53a had not noticed.

Noor, however, had remembered her extended briefing with Marks in London and what he had told her about her special security check. He had told her not to use a key phrase containing eighteen letters. If she ever did so, he would know she had been captured. In her first message through Goetz, Noor had sent a transposition-key eighteen letters long. Later, Marks saw the message and noticed Noor's cry for help. He immediately took it to Buckmaster and said he thought Noor was a prisoner, but Buckmaster did not believe him. He said he intended to continue the two-way traffic.[10] This decision would lead to further fatalities for F-section agents. Marks prayed that Noor's coding had just been a lapse, but in his heart he knew that she had sent him her special security check and he feared the worst.

London was, however, slightly guarded from now on. Goetz asked for twelve containers of supplies and received only one. The Germans knew that without the security check, the messages were not foolproof and they would soon be discovered.

Vogt now adopted a different tactic. He tried to make Noor relax, talking to her about unrelated things, sometimes about her family. But all he learnt was that her name was Nora Baker. Noor once again gave out the name she had told the Balachowskys and others in the Prosper sub-circuit who thought that Nora Baker was her real name and Jeanne-Marie her cover name. Noor had concealed her real identity even from those she was closest to in the circuit. She did not want to reveal that her real name was Inayat Khan, because she did not want the Gestapo to catch up with Hidayat who was still in France and use him or his children as hostages to make her speak.

As time went on without Noor being tortured, she slowly lost her fierce attitude to her captors at Avenue Foch. Vogt in particular played up to her, trying to be the friendly face of the Gestapo. He would talk to her every day trying to learn anything he could. Noor spoke about her mother and Vogt could gather that she was very close to her.

Sometimes he called her for dinner to his room to extract information. But Noor never dropped her guard, and though they discussed many things, she never let slip any details about her operations or the people she worked with. Sometimes she chose her words carefully and revealed a trivial fact which she knew he would know already and which was of no use to anybody. Later in their sworn statements, Goetz and Kieffer both said that no arrests were made as a result of Noor's capture as she revealed nothing.

Vogt later told Jean Overton Fuller that he had never met anyone like Noor and he admired her courage, bravery and kindness. He once asked her whether she sometimes felt that she had wasted her life by joining the service and that her sacrifice had been in vain since they had mopped up three-quarters of the French section. But she replied that it did not matter. She had served her country and that was her recompense.[11]

Noor was not an easy prisoner. She demanded things. She asked for fresh clothes, toiletries and paper and requested that someone go to her residence at the rue de la Faisenderie to collect them. She thought Solange would know that she had been arrested and sent a note asking for the things to be given to the 'bearer'. Solange, however, did not know that Noor was a prisoner. Taking advantage of this, Vogt sent Pierre Cartaud to collect the items, pretending to be a member of the French Resistance so that he could gather some more information and possibly trace other agents. Sure enough, Cartaud saw Garry and his wife at Solange's flat on 17 October and came back and reported this to Vogt. The Garrys had moved out of their own flat after they heard of the arrest of Madame Aigrain and were trying to get a flight to England. They had come to stay at Solange's flat hoping to get a message about their flights on 16 October. The very next day they were spotted by Cartaud, who had called with one of Noor's notes. Cartaud, Vogt and three other Gestapo officers now returned to the apartment where the Garrys had just finished breakfast and arrested them. They were taken to Avenue Foch. Noor had no idea about these arrests. Neither did Solange, because she had left the flat earlier. She thought the Garrys had left suddenly, as they often did.

On 30 October Charles Vaudevire, Paul Arrighi and their associate Emmanuel de Sieyes were also arrested, but Vogt and Kieffer had no idea that Noor knew them and had worked with them, because she had said nothing to give anyone away. Now 84 Avenue Foch housed several agents who had worked together. Noor had met Norman on the first day. Henri Garry was also there. She was to establish contact with two others.

One night, Noor tapped out a message in Morse on her wall to the prisoner next door. She got a reply almost immediately. The prisoner identified himself as a Frenchman, Colonel Léon Faye, former head of the Alliance circuit which worked with MI6. She told him she was a British agent and that they should help each other and try to escape.

The second agent she established contact with was Captain John A.R. Starr (code name Bob), an F-section agent of the Acrobat circuit active in the Dijon area, who was arrested on 18 July after being betrayed by a double agent. Starr was sent to prison in Dijon, then Fresnes and finally to Avenue Foch. The three of them now made a bold plan to escape, which if it had succeeded would have gone down in the history books as one of the most daring and dramatic escapes of the Second World War.

Starr was a poster artist by profession. Kieffer recognised that he was a good draughtsman and had an excellent talent for drawing, and gave him quite a lot of work to do.[12] Starr's experience at Dijon and Fresnes prisons had been dreadful and he found Avenue Foch far more congenial. He decided to cooperate with the Germans and do what they asked: copy maps and even produce portraits and greeting cards. He was in a cell directly next to the guards' room where a four-man guard was permanently present. Soon Kieffer was asking Starr to do drawings of subjects that had to be kept secret. If he escaped, Kieffer's office could be compromised so he asked the guards to be extra vigilant in guarding Starr.

Starr was also used by the Germans in their radio games. He would be taken down to the room where Placke played the captured wireless sets back to London and asked to check that the wording of the false messages being sent by the Germans was in the typical English style. Starr cooperated and soon got to know a great deal about German counter-espionage work, their wireless operators, arrested agents and organisers of hostile intelligence services. It was at this time that Noor was arrested and brought to Avenue Foch.

Starr had heard about Noor from the German officers, who had told him she had fought fiercely and been very difficult to arrest. One of them had even shown Starr a bite on his finger which Noor had inflicted. Starr was told that she had made an attempt to escape within minutes of being brought into Avenue Foch.

Since Starr was usually taken to the guard room to do his map work and drawing, he could see Noor being taken down to Kieffer's office. She usually wore a light grey polo-necked jumper, navy-blue slacks and plimsolls – the clothes she had been arrested in. Once she had ordered fresh clothes from Solange, she had other things to change into. Prisoners at Avenue Foch were allowed to choose a book from the library in the guards' room and Starr had seen Noor at close quarters when she had come in to select one. Noor had already asked the guards for writing paper and spent her time writing in her cell when she was not being interrogated.

At night Starr heard her crying in her room. Her cell was opposite his. He wanted to console her but could not think how he could do this. The only common place they used was the lavatory. One day he pretended to drop a pencil and while bending to pick it up managed to slip a note under Noor's door. It told her to cheer up as she was not alone, and maybe they could find a way to escape. He told her to check under the basin in the lavatory for further notes.

The next day there was a reply from Noor. She said she had already established contact with another prisoner who shared the adjoining cell, Colonel Faye. He would now join them and an escape plan could be hatched. On tiny notes that went back and forth between the three prisoners, a daring plan was worked out. Starr reported that his room had a small window in the ceiling with three iron bars. These were fixed to the window on a wooden frame. A simple screwdriver would be enough to unscrew the frame. He would need a screwdriver and a stool to stand on.

The others told him that their skylight windows had the iron bars screwed into the wall so they would be a little more difficult to remove. The problem now was getting a screwdriver. This problem was solved unexpectedly. One day the cleaning woman entered the guard room complaining that the carpet sweeper was not working. Starr jumped up and volunteered to help, saying he knew all about carpet sweepers. He asked for tools to repair the sweeper. But the Germans were watching him closely and he could not conceal a screwdriver under their noses. So he mended the carpet sweeper badly, knowing it would break down again soon.

Sure enough the cleaner soon brought the faulty machine to him again, helpfully supplying the tool box once more. This time the Germans weren't watching so closely and Starr managed to retain a screwdriver. He left it at the lavatory for Noor and Faye. They were to keep it on alternate nights, passing it between them until they had managed to loosen the bars on their windows. As Starr's window bars were much easier to remove, he would be given the screwdriver when they had nearly finished.

Starr had to devise a way of reaching his skylight. If he moved the bed to the centre of the room, the guard would immediately be suspicious. So one day he moved the bed to the other side of the room. When the guard asked him why, he said he wanted to change the view. Though they were not pleased with this explanation, they did not take the matter any further. Starr next moved the bed to a new side of the room every few days till the guard lost interest in him. He then moved the bed to the centre of the room. He still needed a chair to reach the skylight, so he brought one from the guard room. Again a round of questions followed, but Starr said he needed to put his clothes on something and so had borrowed a chair. Once again the guards let this pass.

Meanwhile Noor was also having problems reaching the window in her room. Her bed was a pull-out iron bed which folded back into the wall. There was no way she could move it at all. She had to stand on the iron cot and lean over to reach the skylight. She was small in build, which didn't help either. One night Starr heard a loud thud. Noor had simply fallen over while leaning from the edge of the bed and trying to work the iron bars in her skylight. The guards rushed into the room, but a flustered Noor told them that she had been trying to commit suicide by hanging herself from the bars. They did not suspect her and soon she managed to get rid of them. They had not noticed the window bars half hanging out, or the screwdriver.

As Faye and Noor continued to work at their iron bars, the holes were getting conspicuous. Noor asked Starr whether he could get something to fill the holes. He suggested face powder. So Noor sent out for one more of her famous parcels from Solange, asking for face powder, eau de cologne and scent. When this arrived she shared it with Faye, passing it to him through their postbox in the lavatory. Solange still had no idea that Noor was in prison and presented the items to Cartaud, who was pretending to be a friend of Noor's.

Noor had also asked for more clothes. She had some Metro tickets in her pocket which the guards had not discovered. These she shared with the others as they would help them make a quick getaway. Faye was the first to loosen his bars. The screwdriver was then passed to Starr and he unscrewed his. Noor's was going to take some more time. Finally she gave the signal that she was ready.

They decided that they would hang their shoes around their necks before climbing out of the window, and they would take blankets with them so that once on the roof they could knot the blankets together and let themselves down to the ground with them.

On the night of 25 November, Starr sat up late in the guard room finishing Kieffer's portrait. At about midnight the guards went to the other rooms and switched off the lights. Starr knew there would be some noise from Noor and Faye's rooms as they scraped their bars. He went noisily to the bathroom whistling loudly to distract the guards. Finally he told them he was going to bed, so a guard came and locked him in. He let himself out from the window and stood on the roof. Faye was already there, but Noor was missing. She was still struggling with the last bit of her bar. They tried to help her but it was difficult. They were painfully aware that time was passing and that the scraping noise could be heard by the guards. Finally Faye was able to remove the bar. He pulled Noor out, kissing her in sheer delight.

Slowly they started to walk across the length of the rooftop. It was a cold night and they could feel the biting wind. They had to try to reach a neighbouring house with a flat roof to the rear of no. 84. This house was slightly lower down. They started walking precariously, carrying their blankets, Noor the most sure-footed of the three. Finally they reached the house on the other side and started tearing their blankets to make a rope for the first jump. But luck was against them. They had barely managed to make one jump when the air-raid siren went off. The RAF were attacking!

Stuck on the roof, the three prisoners were desperate. They knew that their absence would be discovered immediately as the guards came to check the cells whenever there was an air-raid warning. Their only hope was to try to move quickly. But already anti-aircraft fire was going up and the searchlights were sweeping the roofs. They lay flat on the roof trying to blend into the shadows.

Down below the guards had raised the alarm. At 3 a.m., just after the air-raid warning signal, Kieffer was woken up with the news that the prisoners had escaped. He immediately ordered a cordon to be placed around the area.

The three fugitives now had to climb down on to a roof one storey below them. But the roof below was slanting with no flat spacc on which to stand. They used another blanket to make a rope and decided to take their chances. They swung down, broke the window of the house below and clambered in. They crept down the stairs to the front door, opened it and looked out. To their dismay it was a close and one side of the road was blocked. The side that opened up to the road already had a cordon around it. They could see the Gestapo walking around. They were trapped.

Faye decided they should make a dash for it. The alternative, in any case, was recapture. Noor agreed. When they reached the corner, Faye ran. Immediately, there was a volley of gunfire and the guards fell on him and seized him.

Starr pulled Noor back towards the house. They went in almost aimlessly, walked up the stairs and into the living room. They noticed a woman looking down at them from an upper landing. But before any of them could react, the Gestapo burst in and captured Noor and Starr. Both were kicked and beaten and marched back to no. 84.

Kieffer was livid. He threatened to shoot all three of them and lined them up against a wall. But something cracked in him as he looked at their faces and he ordered them to be taken up.

Later that night Kieffer went to Noor's cell upstairs. In her room, Noor had drawn a V sign on the wall and an RAF symbol. He chose to ignore it. Kieffer told Noor to sign a declaration that she would not try to escape again. Only then would he be able to keep her in Avenue Foch under the same conditions. But she refused, saying it was her bounden duty to try to escape if she could. Once again, Noor could not tell a lie. Faye refused to sign either. Only Starr signed the declaration and was permitted to stay.

Kieffer now hammered off a telegram to Berlin saying he could not take responsibility for these dangerous prisoners in Avenue Foch since it did not have the regular security of a prison. He wanted them transferred to Germany.

The authorisation came immediately by return telegram from Horst Kopkow, the head of the Berlin Gestapo. Kieffer was a Karlsruhe man and his mother and brother still lived there. He decided to send Noor to Karlsruhe, hoping that his brother would be able to keep him updated on news about her and he himself would have an excuse to travel to Karlsruhe if he ever wanted to reinterrogate her. But the prison at Karlsruhe was overcrowded and Noor was sent to Pforzheim prison, about 20 miles away.

Noor and Faye were transferred from Avenue Foch on the day they were recaptured, 26 November 1943. Noor became the first British woman agent to be sent to Germany. Jean Overton Fuller thinks she may have attempted another escape while being taken to the station en route to Pforzheim prison, because her friend Raymonde Prénat claimed she saw her again in November, breathless and harassed, and asking if she could come in at night to transmit. Noor never returned and was obviously recaptured. Later Noor told the governor of Pforzheim prison that she had nearly managed to escape the Gestapo a third time but had been caught. Possibly the Gestapo did not report this escape attempt out of embarrassment, as they had seized her swiftly and were soon on their way to Germany as planned.[13]

Faye was sent to Bruchsal prison (he was executed on 30 January 1945 at Sonnenburg). In Kieffer's sworn testimony after the war he said that it was very difficult for Starr to re-establish the trust he had developed with the Germans. Kieffer declined to use Starr's help for some time because he had disappointed him. Kieffer asked him why he had tried to escape and Starr replied that Noor had approached him with an escape plan and that if, as a woman, she had the courage to escape and had succeeded in doing so, she would have made life impossible for him in England had he not displayed the same courage.[14]

After signing his declaration not to escape, Kieffer said Starr behaved in an exceptionally correct manner and was called upon again to monitor wireless messages. This monitoring was less dangerous than his previous assignments and he was watched constantly. He did not deceive the Germans again and was one of the last prisoners to be kept at 84 Avenue Foch, where he remained till July 1944. Shortly before the German withdrawal from Paris, he was sent to Sachsenhausen concentration camp and then to Mauthausen extermination camp, where he was rescued when the camp was overrun by the advancing Allies.

According to the prison records, Noor spent the night of 26 November in Karlsruhe and arrived in Pforzheim prison the next day. She had spent nearly one and a half months at Avenue Foch. Pforzheim prison, on the north of the Black Forest, about 20 miles from Karlsruhe, was a civilian prison. Noor's admission to Pforzheim is recorded in the prison register. She was brought in at 2.30 p.m., and the type of detention was described as 'protective custody'. Noor also became the first political prisoner to go to Pforzheim.

On direct instructions from Berlin, Noor was classified as a 'highly dangerous prisoner' and 'to be treated in accordance with regulations for "*Nacht und Nebel*" prisoners.'[15] The full term *Nacht und Nebel – Rückkehr Unerwünscht* meant Night and Fog – Return Not Required. It was the expression used for people who 'disappeared'. No reply of any kind was ever given to any inquiry from friends or relatives of the person arrested under this category.

Noor was to be kept on the lowest rations, in solitary confinement and had to be chained hand and foot. A third chain connected her hands to her feet. No one was allowed to talk to her. She was kept in a cell on the ground floor, separated from the other cells by two wire fences with heavily locked gates. Between the two rows of cells, after the wire fences, was a corridor which led into a small inner courtyard. Since she was handcuffed she could not feed or clean herself. This was done by a woman attendant who was also instructed not to speak to her. Isolated in the cell, Noor had no idea of the time and made out the approximate time of day by the times breakfast, lunch and dinner were brought to her. Warders walked the passage outside night and day keeping an eye on the cells.[16] Her door was never opened except when the warden visited.

The cells on either side of Noor's were kept empty. After a few weeks had passed, the governor of the prison, 72-year-old Wilhelm Krauss, took pity on the English girl and decided to remove the chains from her hands.[17] But shortly afterwards Josef Gmeiner, the head of the Karlsruhe Gestapo, telephoned him and reprimanded him for not observing the regulations about chains, which had to be strictly adhered to. Noor was shackled once again.

The only people allowed to visit Noor's cell were Anton Guiller, at that time the Hauptwachtmeister or chief warden, and the woman attendant who cleaned her and brought in a change of clothes once a week. It was Guiller who brought her drinking and washing water and meals. Every Saturday, the woman attendant gave her a change of clothes and dressed her. Her used clothes were taken away. Though she lived on a meagre diet of potato peel or cabbage soup and was weak and hungry, Noor would not let them break her spirit. She exercised in her cell, walking slowly in her shackles, and tried to keep her mind active.

The elderly Krauss felt sorry for Noor. He had never seen a prisoner kept in such harsh conditions. He would sometimes go to her cell, sit on her bed and talk to her. Noor told him that she was half-Indian, that her father had been a sort of priest and that she had studied Indian literature and philosophy. He realised she was an educated and cultured person and developed a great respect for her.[18] All the time during her lonely incarceration in Pforzheim, Noor thought about her father and drew strength from his Sufi philosophy. It helped her to meditate and get through the ordeal. She was not allowed any writing material and had nothing to help her pass the time. The small window in her cell was high up and she could not look outside. By seven in the evening the lights were switched off and she had to sit in the dark or sleep.

Back in England, her family had no idea that she was a prisoner. Despite some initial doubts F-section still believed that she was free and were responding to the messages being sent on her wireless set by Goetz and Placke. In October 1943, F-section had received reports that Noor and Garry had been arrested[19] but when the Germans came on air using her radio, they thought she was free. By Christmas, under cover of seasonal messages, they had put a few trick questions to Noor about her family, which they knew only she could answer, to test if her messages were genuine. But after a little delay they received answers to these. Vogt had learnt some facts about Noor's family during his conversations with her at Avenue Foch. He had seen Noor's letter to her mother and gathered she was close to her. Noor had mentioned her casually, never thinking this information could be of any importance to the Gestapo. But Vogt used these facts to reply to F-section and soon they were confident that Noor was still transmitting. Even Antelme, who got to know her well in Paris, was taken into their confidence by SOE chiefs and shown her correspondence to decide whether it looked as though it had been sent by the Germans. Marks told him about

Noor's special security check and how he was sure she had sent him a warning, but Antelme too did not believe it and said he thought she may have used it by accident.[20] London continued to play into the hands of the Germans by sending supplies of arms and cash as requested by Operation Nurse.

The weeks passed by in the cold German cell and Noor knew that the new year had begun. She spent a lonely birthday in her cell and hoped that 1944 would bring news of the invasion and Allied victories. Unknown to her, Baker Street had promoted her to the rank of Ensign with effect from 1 January 1944.

That month, a group of French women political prisoners was sent to Pforzheim prison. One of them was Yolande Lagrave from Bordeaux. She was repatriated on 1 May 1945. All the others in her group were murdered. After the war Yolande went looking for Noor. She wrote to the commanding officer of the Service Officers in order to find out whether 'Nora Baker' had returned from deportation but the letter was returned marked 'not known at this address'. She then contacted the War Office and informed them about her association with Noor in Pforzheim prison.

Yolande was in Cell Number 12 with two other prisoners, Rosy Storcke and Suzy Chireiz. Noor was in Cell Number 1, which was across the corridor with the two wire fences in between. Yolande described how she managed to establish contact with an 'English parachutist who was interned and very unhappy'.[21]

The French women prisoners were put through a rigorous regime at Pforzheim. They were woken up at 6.30 a.m. and had to clean their cells before the guard came. At 7.30 they were given some breakfast consisting of weak coffee and bread. They were then allowed to walk in the courtyard in a circle as the guards watched over them. At lunchtime they were given a bowl of soup, and a main course usually unfit for consumption made from sour cabbage, crushed peas and swedes. The evening meal was soup again. They had to be in bed by 7 p.m., after which the cells would be dark. Noor's conditions of captivity were worse as she was in chains and kept on the lowest rations.

Yolande and her colleagues noticed that Cell 1 was never opened even though they knew there was a prisoner inside. One day Yolande's cellmate, 27-year-old Rosy Storcke, had an idea. The prisoners were given the job of threading tickets through knitting needles to keep them occupied. Rosy thought they could use these knitting needles to scratch a message on their food bowls to establish contact with other prisoners. So they scratched on their bowls – 'There are three French girls here'.[22]

The bowls were taken away after lunch to be washed and returned after 5 p.m. with the evening meals. The girls searched eagerly for a response. They were not disappointed. On the back of the bowl was a reply from Noor: 'You are not alone, you have a friend in Cell 1'. It was the start of their written conversation.

Through these exchanges they learnt that Noor was desperately unhappy, that she never went out, that her hands and feet were in chains. Her cell door was never opened, unlike those of the other prisoners, nor was she given her meal through the small opening in the door at the same time as the other prisoners. Instead she was given her food only when there was no one in the passage and the people who carried the saucepans had passed. While the other prisoners were taken out for short walks, Noor was never allowed outside.

They asked her what her name was, but Noor replied: 'I cannot, it would be too dangerous.' She relented, however, and scratched on her bowl:

> Nora Baker,
> Radio Centre Officer,
> Service RAF,
> 4 Taviton Street,
> London

This was the name Nora had used in Paris. Yolande wrote the address down and sewed up the paper carefully in the hem of her skirt, promising herself that she would look for Noor after the war was over. Noor also gave the address of a friend, the head of the school at the Porte de Lilas in Paris. It was from this address that Yolande traced her family later. The messages now became Noor's only contact with the outside world. There was no prisoner next to her, so she was not able to tap a Morse code on the wall as she had done at Avenue Foch. She was not allowed to write letters so was completely isolated. The notes from the other prisoners cheered her up and kept her going.

The messages exchanged could take days to get through as the bowls were common property and sometimes went to other prisoners. However the steady stream of information carried on. Noor asked her friends if they belonged to the Alliance or to the French section. She told them she was an English agent. 'Think of me, I am very unhappy,' Noor wrote to the girls.

One afternoon Yolande and her friends heard a noise in the yard outside and thought it might be Noor coming out. They scrambled on to their beds and looked out of the window. Noor raised her eyes to their cell and the girls exchanged a smile. She was not wearing prison clothes. It was the first time they had seen Noor. From February, as it became clear that Noor was going to be there for a while, Guiller allowed her to walk under supervision in the courtyard for about 45 minutes. Noor would walk around doing gymnastic exercises. She spoke good German and was polite to the officer who let her out.[23]

Noor was eager for news about the progress of the war. 'Give me news if you know,' she scratched on her pot. They told her what they had heard, keeping up her morale.

Noor's condition in the prison was also reported after the war by Marcel Schubert, who was a prisoner in Pforzheim and was used as an interpreter by the Germans. He related that Noor's hands and feet were bound nearly all the time, even during meals, for months on end. While the other prisoners could go out for a walk together in the morning, Noor was allowed out only for a very short time in the afternoon and was always heavily guarded. Schubert said the prisoners believed Noor was a Russian countess, but she had told him she was British.[24]

Kieffer had sent Noor to Pforzheim so he would have an excuse to travel to the area to visit his family. He never came to see her, however. Meanwhile, the Germans continued their radio games on Noor's wireless sets and deceived Baker Street into sending money and agents. Goetz was delighted to receive half a million francs by Mosquito, which was sent to the Cinema circuit and fell straight into German hands. In the early months of 1944, the Germans started asking for more money and arms supplies.[25]

London was still completely unaware of Noor's arrest. On 24 February 1944, Buckmaster wrote a personal recommendation for Noor to be given the George Medal, an award for gallantry. He wrote:

> This officer's devotion to duty enabled contact with this country to be maintained and as a result it was possible to reinforce and reconstruct the group. It is unique in the annals of this organisation that a Circuit which was so completely disintegrated should be able to be rebuilt and this must be attributed to the conduct of this young woman, who, regardless of all personal danger, remained at her post – often alone – and always under the threat of arrest.
>
> It was considered at the time that the risks she was taking were unjustified as the Gestapo knew enough to make her capture only a matter of days. She was therefore, instructed to return to England, but pleaded to be allowed to remain and lie low for a month. This was agreed to and a month later she reported that she felt her security re-established as a result of arrangements she had made. Subsequent events have fully justified this course of action and ever since the reorganising of her circuit Ensign Inayat Khan's work and example has been beyond praise.

By now Noor had spent nearly four months in prison, and her circuit was blown.

In February 1944, seven agents were parachuted by F-section to two receptions manned by the Gestapo. Four agents were dropped near Poitiers – R.E.J. Alexandre, a 22-year-old French aircraft fitter who was carrying 300,000 francs for Garry who, unknown to F-section, had been imprisoned long ago; Robert Byerly, an American secret service man who had come as a radio operator; Fred Deniset, a Canadian who was to be an arms instructor to Garry, and the Anglo-French Jacques Ledoux, who was going to start a fresh circuit around Le Mans. All four were arrested. The next flight out was on 28/29 February. Despite bad weather, Antelme set out for a second trip to France with Madeleine Damerment as his courier, and Lionel Lee as his radio operator, to set up a circuit called Bricklayer. The instructions about his landing were transmitted to Noor on Operation Nurse. Again, unknown to London, the message had gone straight to the Germans. The three were arrested as they approached Paris and driven to Avenue Foch. Antelme was furious when he realised the deception. He however stuck to his cover story and said he had come to work with Garry and knew nothing. Incarcerated in her cell in Pforzheim, Noor had no idea that Antelme had returned and been arrested. From Avenue Foch, he was sent to Gross Rosen concentration camp where he was killed. Madeleine Damerment was sent to Karlsruhe, from where she would join Noor on the journey to Dachau. Lionel Lee was executed at Gross Rosen. Noor had no knowledge that her radio post had been used to lure agents to their death.

After the arrests, the Germans sent London a message on Operation Nurse that Antelme had injured his skull on a container when he landed. They continued to send false medical bulletins about him finally reporting his 'death' without regaining consciousness at the end of April. The Germans also played back Lee's set to London and it took Baker Street three weeks to notice that the security checks were wrong. It was finally by March that London realised that the wireless messages were false and the agents, including Noor and Antelme, were in German hands. Leo Marks heard the news in his office in Malvern Court while briefing another agent. He found it hard to hide his emotion and found himself saying a silent prayer: 'Please God, can anything be done to help Noor, who knows you by another name? I can feel her pain from here, and know how much worse it must be for you.'[26]

The months crawled by, the harsh winter of 1943/4 changing into spring. Alone in her cell Noor became weaker, and the girls thought she looked very frail and sad. Noor felt particularly low in the months of May and June as the birthdays of her mother and Vilayat passed. She missed not being able to write her usual birthday poem to her mother and cried silently to herself in her cell. She had told Vera Atkins to say nothing to her family if she was missing, so she knew they had no idea she was in prison. She hoped that Claire was managing the house well. When the sympathetic Krauss visited her cell she told him how much she missed her mother and her family. Once again she meditated and thought about her father, drawing strength from his philosophy. Yolande and her friends tried to keep up her morale as they knew Noor was having the hardest time of all of them. Once she told her friends never to tell her mother that she was in prison and that she was so unhappy.

If the girls were feeling low, Noor would try to cheer them up. As the French girls gave her news of the progress of the war, she felt happier. On 4 July, American Independence Day, Noor wrote

'*Vive le 4 juillet*' (Long live 4 July) on her bowl and passed it round. On 14 July, Bastille Day, she wrote '*Vive la France libre*' (Long live free France) and drew two small flags – one British and one French – on the mugs. This rallied the French girls and so the time went by at Pforzheim.

They could hear the roar of RAF jets go over the prison and hear the bombing. The French girls, who were probably allowed to write letters or receive parcels, were somehow able to keep up to date with news of the outside world. They passed this information to Noor and kept her posted on the Allied victories. They told her to have courage as the war would soon be over and they would celebrate and drink champagne together.

Two women prisoners in Cell Number 3, Alice Coudel and Clara Machtou, also communicated with Noor. They sang the news to her when they were passing her cell. Yolande heard the singing and heard a prison warden called Trupp raising his voice angrily. She heard him open Noor's cell door and strike her and take her down to the basement, from where they could hear her cries. The girls were appalled by the treatment but could not help Noor. After he had beaten her, Trupp returned to the cell where Alice and Clara were imprisoned, shouted at them in German and left.[27] Everyone noticed that Noor was singled out for the worst treatment.

One day the chief warden, Guiller, noticed that the spy hole in Noor's cell was open. He went into the cell and shouted at Noor. Yolande and the other prisoners heard him screaming at her, then they heard Noor replying with great dignity in German. Rosy Storcke told them that Noor spoke to Guiller in very good German and held her head high even as he insulted her. Then they heard him slap her on the face and heard Noor reply defiantly. Later they heard her sobbing in her cell.

'That day again all of us felt deeply for Nora,' said Yolande,[28] who had become very attached to the frail and gentle young woman who bore all her torture and abuse with tremendous spirit.

A few days after the incident, they saw Noor walking in the courtyard dressed in a sackcloth. That night they received a message from Noor on their food bowl that the prison wardens had taken away her clothes. In the middle of September came her final message, 'I am leaving', written in a nervous, trembling hand. It was her last note. The girls did not know where she had gone.

The Pforzheim prison register shows that Noor was discharged from the prison at 6.15 p.m. on 11 September and driven 20 miles to Karlsruhe. Orders had come directly from Berlin to move Noor. She was now summoned to the office of Josef Gmeiner, head of the Karlsruhe Gestapo.

Just after 2 a.m., in Gmeiner's office Noor met three other SOE agents, Eliane Plewman, Madeleine Damerment and Yolande Beekman. She had known Yolande from her training days at Wanborough Manor. All four agents were given their orders to leave for Dachau. They were escorted by Gestapo officer Christian Ott and driven to the station in Gmeiner's car. At Bruchsal Junction they were joined by their second German escort, Max Wassmer, and together they caught the express train for Stuttgart. At Stuttgart they had to wait on the platform for about an hour for the train to Munich. The women stood on the platform and talked. On the train to Munich they were given window seats and allowed to relax. They exchanged news about how they had been arrested and what had happened to their colleagues. Eliane Plewman, 25, was the daughter of an Englishman, Albert Browne-Bartroli and a Spanish-French mother. After many years in Marseilles, the family returned to England in the 1930s and Eliane married a young engineer, Tom Plewman, in 1942. Eliane joined the SOE with her brother Albert, who parachuted into France with Robert Benoist, the racing-car driver, in whose chateau Antelme and Noor had hidden in July. In August 1943, Eliane parachuted in near Lons-le-Saunier and made her way south to join Charles Skepper's Monk network in Marseilles where she worked as a radio operator. Skepper had flown in by Lysander to start his circuit on the same day as Noor in June 1943.

In the spring of 1944, Skepper's Monk network was infiltrated and he was arrested. Eliane and another colleague, Arthur Steele, a twenty-year-old London music student, tried to rescue him but were captured. Skepper was taken to Hamburg where he was executed. Steele was hanged at Buchenwald and Eliane was taken to Fresnes prison, then to Karlsruhe with the other two girls.

Madeleine Damerment's fate had been sealed by the chain of events after the fall of the Prosper and Cinema circuits, and the subsequent wireless games of the Gestapo. The 26-year-old was the daughter of the head postmaster of Lille and had became a postal clerk just before the war. The Damerment family joined the Resistance after the fall of France and Madeleine worked with a Belgian doctor, Dr Albert Guérisse, who organised escape routes for Allied airmen and Resistance workers under the name of Pat O'Leary. [29] Madeleine eventually reached England where she was trained by SOE and returned to France with Antelme and Lionel Lee on the night of 28/29 February 1944, parachuting in near Sainville, 31 kilometres south-east of Chartres. All three were arrested almost immediately and taken to the Avenue Foch, from where Madeleine was taken to Fresnes and then Karlsruhe. Antelme and Lee were tortured and sent to Gross Rosen where both were executed. Noor now learnt that Antelme had returned to Paris and had been arrested.

Yolande Beekman had also been arrested as a result of the collapse of the Prosper and Cinema circuits. Beekman was the radio operator for the circuit Musician which had been established by Gustave Biéler in the St Quentin area of northern France. Yolande Beekman joined him in the late summer of 1943. Yolande's father, Jacob Unternaehrer, was of Swiss/French origin. Yolande went to finishing school in Switzerland and was fluent in German and French. She married a young officer, joined the WAAF and was given wireless training like Noor. Later she joined the SOE and was parachuted in near Tours from where she made her way to St Quentin to work with Biéler. The circuit successfully destroyed the lock gates at St Quentin, which was at the heart of the canal system of north-east France through which the Germans transported arms, troops and materials.

On 13 December 1943, the Gestapo pounced on Biéler and Yolande as they met at a café at St Quentin. Biéler was tortured and killed within weeks at Flossenburg and Yolande was taken to Avenue Foch, and then on the familiar route via Fresnes to Karlsruhe. Eliane, Yolande and Madeleine had all been sent to Karlsruhe in May 1944 by Kieffer. By September 1944, the tide had turned in the war. With Paris liberated and the first US army at the German frontier and the Nazi troops in western Russia routed, the end of the Third Reich clearly lay ahead and the Nazi leaders turned their fury on the captives, exterminating nearly 200,000 French men and women in concentration camps and forced labour camps.

Josef Gmeiner said later that the orders to move Noor and her colleagues had come by teleprinter from Berlin. One was addressed to his office at Karlsruhe and the other to the Commandant of the concentration camp. Gmeiner's instructions were to transfer the prisoners to the camp at Dachau. The instruction to the Camp Commandant of Dachau ordered the execution itself.[30]

Though they did not know it, the four women were making their final journey together. Both Wassmer and Ott knew about the orders but did not tell the women anything. Wassmer told Madeleine Damerment that they were being taken to a camp where farming was done. After a few hours, they had their lunch; they also smoked English cigarettes. It was a happy reunion for the agents and they savoured the little freedom they were given. They admired the scenery during the train trip, particularly the beautiful Swabian mountains. At Geisslingen there was an air raid which held them up for two hours. The women remained calm. At Munich Central, they changed trains again for Dachau. It was midnight when they reached Dachau and they walked up to the concentration camp, where they were locked in separate cells.

The end came in the early hours of the morning. Madeleine Damerment, Eliane Plewman and Yolande Beekman were dragged out of their cells, marched past the barracks and shot near the crematorium.

For Noor it would be a long, tortuous night. According to two letters received by Jean Overton Fuller's publishers after her book appeared in 1952, Noor was stripped, abused and kicked all night by her German captors. One of the letter writers was a Lieutenant Colonel Wickey, who worked for Canadian intelligence during the war and was Military Governor in Wuppertal in the British zone after the war. Here he met a German officer who had spent time in Dachau. This officer had been told by some camp officials that four women had been brought to Dachau from Karlsruhe. He described the women as French but added that one had a darker complexion and 'looked much like a Creole'. The officers told the German officer that she (Noor) was considered to be a very 'dangerous person' and to be given the 'full treatment'. Wickey then traced the German camp officer who had given the account and was told by him that Noor was tortured and abused in her cell by the Germans. She was stripped, kicked and finally left lying on the floor battered and bruised. Then in the early hours of the following morning she was shot in her cell.

Wickey identified the 'Creole woman' as Noor Inayat Khan.

The second letter received by Jean Overton Fuller through her publishers was from a man in Gibraltar who said he had been a prisoner in Dachau. His account matched that of Wickey. He said he had been told by another camp officer, Yoop, how Noor had been killed and described it as 'terrible'. Noor he said, had been stripped, kicked and abused all night by an officer called Ruppert. When Ruppert got tired and the girl was a 'bloody mess', he told her that he would shoot her. He ordered her to kneel and put his pistol against her head. The only word she said before dying was '*Liberté*'. Both accounts confirmed that Noor had been tortured before her death.

When Vera Atkins interrogated Ott, he told her that he had been told by Wassmer, who Ott said had been present at the time, that some time between eight and ten on the morning of 13 September 1944, the four agents were taken to the crematorium, made to kneel in pairs and shot through the back of the neck. Ott had recalled that Wassmer had told him that before she was shot, Madeleine Damerment, whom he described as the woman who spoke German, had asked to see a priest. But the Commandant said there was no priest in the camp. Three of the girls had died with a single shot but Damerment had to be shot twice as they were not sure she was dead. All the bodies were then burnt in the crematorium ovens.[31] But Ott had been constantly changing his story. In his first interrogation, he had given the wrong dates and said he took the girls to Dachau on 23 August 1944. Later he changed his version and amended the dates. However, Wassmer denied that he had been present at the execution and said he had slept the night at the camp, simply collected the receipt of their deaths at 10 in the morning and set out for Karlsruhe.

When Ott was reinterrogated by Vera Atkins, he too said he never believed Wassmer's version, and Atkins is known to have rejected it herself.[32] Vera privately believed and had told her niece, Zenna Atkins, that Noor had been raped and tortured before her death. However, Noor's personal files carry the official line given out by Wassmer and Ott. The letters from the eyewitnesses lie with the family and with Jean Overton Fuller's publishers at The Hague.

Further evidence that Wassmer had lied was recorded by Alexander Nicholson, the war crimes investigator, who had taken over the Karlsruhe investigation from Vera Atkins. When Nicholson reinterrogated Ott, he was told that when Ott had asked Wassmer what really happened, he had replied: 'Do you want to know what *really* happened?'[33] And he had left it at that. Which meant, according to Ott, that Wassmer did not want to reveal the real details of the execution and he had made it all up. Ott further said that he had mentioned this fact during his interview in May 1946, but the secretary, Hirth, had said it wasn't of any interest to him and did not put it down on record.

'I was in prison in Dachau for six months and was convinced that Wassmer's story wasn't the truth,' said Ott. Whatever did happen on the night of 12/13 September 1944, the only truth was that Noor and her colleagues died a horrible death in Dachau.

Berlin wanted no secret agents to survive the war and reveal the inner workings of the Nazis. Nor did they want the Allies to discover what happened to agents who had fallen into enemy hands. They knew too much about double agents, Nazi methods, and the radio game. Nearly all captured agents were deliberately killed as a matter of secret service policy.

Orders to do so came directly from Himmler in Berlin. Himmler's decree was that the Führer's enemies should die, but only after torture, indignity and interrogation 'had drained from them that last shred and scintilla of evidence which should lead to the arrest of others'.[34] Of the more than 200 captured agents of the two French sections of the SOE, only 26 lived to tell their tale. Radio operators were particular Nazi targets and very few survived. Two who did were Jack Starr, who was rescued by the Allies in Mauthausen, and Marcel Rousset, who escaped from a Gestapo prison in Paris.

Barely seven months after the execution of Noor and her colleagues, in April 1945, Dachau was liberated.

Aftermath

When the war ended, Vera Atkins took upon herself the task of finding out what had happened to the women agents she had sent to the field. Atkins had developed a bond with each of them, getting to know about their personal lives, their families and their commitments. She travelled to Europe to unravel the story of the missing agents and interview the German officers who had captured them.

By July 1944, Noor was recorded as 'captured' in the SOE Battle Casualty form.[1] At this time nothing definite was known except that her circuit had been blown and she had been reported as being a prisoner at 3 bis Place des États Unis, Paris. In fact, Noor was imprisoned at 84 Avenue Foch and had been moved to Pforzheim by November.

On 15 October 1944, the War Office wrote to Noor's mother, Mrs O.R. Baker-Inayat at 4 Taviton Street, London, informing her that they had recently been out of touch with her daughter and she must be considered 'missing'. They hoped they would soon get to know her whereabouts, and hoped to hear that she was a prisoner of war.[2]

The news brought complete devastation to the Inayat Khan household. Amina Begum, always frail, and with no idea that Noor had gone on a dangerous mission, was inconsolable. It was left to Vilayat and Claire to try to comfort her as best they could.

Nine months later, by July 1945, the family still knew nothing. Vilayat wrote to Vera Atkins apologising for worrying her for news of his sister: 'So much time has now passed since the time of the collapse of Germany that I have lost in my own mind any hope of ever seeing my sister again,' wrote Vilayat.

He continued in the same desperate vein: 'But surely, is there so far no clue at all as to her past whereabouts? I don't suppose there is any chance that she should still be in a D.P. [Displaced Persons] camp, since I understand that all the British have been retrieved.'

Vilayat had been asked not to make any enquiries about his sister for security reasons. He now asked: 'Is it not possible at this stage to know something of the circumstances of her capture and the work she was doing?'[3] Vera Atkins replied immediately that they were still waiting for news and the family was now free to make their own enquiries as well.

On 4 October 1945, Major General Colin Gubbins, head of the SOE, recommended that Noor Inayat Khan be appointed a Member of the Order of the British Empire (MBE) for her bravery and devotion to duty despite the collapse of her circuit and the arrest of her organiser. At this stage the SOE also knew that Noor had had some narrow escapes from the Gestapo.

The recommendation mentioned that she was instrumental in the escape of thirty Allied airmen shot down in France and that she had not returned to England despite instructions to do so and had pleaded to be allowed to remain. She maintained communication with London till October when she was arrested and deported to Germany. At the time of this recommendation, the SOE files still had Noor as 'missing'.

Meanwhile on 20 December 1945 the offices of the SOE were closed down. Vera Atkins wrote to Amina Begum on 22 December giving her the details of what Noor had been doing in the war.

She told Amina Begum that Noor had gone to France in June 1943 as a wireless operator for a British officer who was working with the Resistance movement in the Paris area. She said Noor had been very keen on her work and had sent her a personal note from the field. 'The one thing that worried her at the time of her departure was the fact that you might long remain without news of her and she particularly asked that we should continue to write to you even if we did lose touch with her,' Vera Atkins told Amina Begum.

'Unfortunately after months of magnificent work she was captured. It was only in the late spring of 1944 that we became aware of this, but in view of her special request and the imminent invasion we continued our letters to you. We hoped that we might find her in France after the liberation.'

Vera Atkins told Amina Begum that after her imprisonment, Noor had managed to make a gallant attempt at escape which was unsuccessful. She had even excited the admiration of her German captors and she was not ill-treated.

In December 1945 Atkins was under the impression that Noor had been sent to Karlsruhe prison in May 1944 in the company of other British women and they had remained there till 25 July 1944, after which they were transferred to another prison. At this time she still did not have details about what had happened to Noor. But the War Office had practically abandoned all hope of finding her alive.

It was in April 1946, nearly a year after the war ended, that Vera Atkins learned about the fate of four British agents who had been executed at Natzweiler concentration camp in June 1944. She believed that Noor was one of the four young women who had been killed by lethal injection at the camp. The others were Andrée Borrel, Vera Leigh and Diana Rowden. The mystery fourth girl had been identified as having dark hair and being petite and Russian-born (as Noor was), and the SOE thought it was Noor. Actually it was Sonia Olschanezky, a Russian Jew and a professional dancer, who had been a courier to Jacques Weil and worked with Juggler, a Prosper sub-circuit.

Vera Atkins reported back to the War Ministry that all four girls had been kept in prisons in Paris until May 1944. On 12 May, eight women agents left Fresnes prison near Paris and travelled to Karlsruhe where they were placed in the civilian jail for women. They were Andrée Borrel, Vera Leigh, Diana Rowden, Odette Sansom, Madeleine Damerment, Yolande Beekman, Eliane Plewman and Sonia Olschanezky. However, the eighth girl was thought to be Noor.

It was Odette Sansom, the only SOE agent of those eight who had survived and returned from Ravensbruck concentration camp after the war, who told Atkins that the eighth girl was Noor. Odette seemed to remember the eighth girl on the train resembled Noor when she was shown her photographs. They had never met previously so she did not know her personally. Vera Atkins now listed the eight girls who left Fresnes prison as Odette Sansom, Diana Rowden, Noor Inayat Khan, Vera Leigh, Andrée Borrel, Eliane Plewman, Madeleine Damerment and Yolande Unternaehrer. The last three were at this stage still untraced as they had left Karlsruhe on the night of 11/12 September 1944.

In Karlsruhe the girls were placed in separate cells which they shared with German women who were political prisoners or criminals. They were not ill-treated and managed to communicate with each other though they were not allowed to meet. The women wardens had identified the prisoners by looking at their photographs.

Another German political prisoner in Karlsruhe told Vera Atkins that he remembered seven women passing him in the corridor in July 1944, between 4 and 5 a.m. They included the British agents he had seen before. The Gestapo officers now took them to a strange-looking grey car and took them away.

Four of the girls, thought Vera Atkins, were taken to Natzweiler, a camp in France about 100 miles from Karlsruhe. On 6 July the girls were seen by many of the inmates as they walked in. They were identified by Brian Stonehouse, an SOE agent, R.M. Sheppard and Albert Guérisse, the Belgian doctor who ran an escape line. Stonehouse described the fourth girl as having black hair, aged between twenty and twenty-five and being short. This girl was thought to be Noor.

Photographs of Andrée Borrel, Vera Leigh and Noor Inayat Khan were identified by fellow inmates and the story pieced together with eyewitness accounts.

The girls were brought in to the camp between 1 and 3 a.m. and taken to separate cells. Andrée Borrel managed to communicate with Dr Georges Boogaerts, who was in the next cell. He threw her some cigarettes and she threw him her money bag. Vera Leigh got into conversation with a prisoner working in the Zellenbau (cells close to the crematorium) and asked him for a pillow. Guérisse exchanged a few words with Diana Rowden or Noor Inayat Khan.

That night a curfew was imposed in the prison at 8 p.m. and the blackouts drawn. One prisoner saw that between 9 and 10 p.m. two SS men went to the Zellenbau and came away with one of the women who was led to the crematorium. One by one the same men came and took away the others. The next day the prisoners went to the crematorium and saw the charred bodies of the women and one unburnt woman's shoe.

The prisoner in charge of the crematorium, a German criminal, stated that he was instructed to light the furnaces and have them up to maximum heat by 9.30 p.m. At the same time the SS officer in charge came into the crematorium with the SS doctor and the former camp doctor. The prisoners working in the crematorium were locked up in their cells and the prisoner on the top bunk could see from the fan window into the room next door. He saw the women prisoners being taken one by one to the doctor's room, which adjoined the men's dormitory. A few minutes later they were dragged out unconscious and taken towards the furnaces. The fourth resisted in the corridor and started to scream. She was overpowered and a few minutes later she too was dragged out unconscious. The prisoners heard the doors of the crematorium open and assumed that the women were immediately cremated.[4]

The War Office now sent a formal letter to the already shattered Inayat Khan family giving the circumstances of what they thought was the death of Noor Inayat Khan. Vilayat received the news and rushed in a frenzy to Jean Overton Fuller's house. Ashen-faced he told her, 'I've found out what happened to my sister. She was burned alive . . .'[5]

Since his mother was in poor health and already shattered by the news that Noor was missing, presumed dead, Vilayat and Claire did not tell her about the latest letter they had received about Noor's death. He also sought power of attorney so that he could handle Noor's affairs since his mother was heartbroken and the doctor had warned him that any shock could be fatal for her. He wrote these details to the War Office asking them to communicate with him and not with his mother who 'becomes hysterical at the mention of my sister's name. She has been so deeply grieved.'

On 24 May 1946, the War Office informed Amina Begum that the officials of Natzweiler concentration camp were to be tried as war criminals. The trial began at Wuppertal on 29 May 1946. Though her name was there as one of the victims, Noor had not been one of the unfortunate girls to have died at Natzweiler.

But soon Vilayat was to hear more. He received a letter from Yolande Lagrave, a Frenchwoman, who said she had been with his sister at Pforzheim prison in Germany. Vilayat wrote again to the War Office on 12 February 1947 saying that the notification of Noor's death on the 6 July 1944 at Natzweiler did not tally with the information given by the Frenchwoman, explaining that Lagrave had seen Noor in Pforzheim. They had exchanged addresses on bowls without giving names and so she had traced the family. The girl had told him that his sister had left Pforzheim in September 1944 for an unknown destination.

Another informant was a German woman by the name of Elsa Findling, who communicated the message through D. McFarlin of the United Nations Refugee Association, who was based at Pforzheim.

From this source Vilayat had learnt that at the time when Strasbourg was taken by the Allies, all internees were taken to be executed. 'My sister is buried in the local cemetery. The jail keeper who is said to have beaten my sister, has remained in his post to this day,' wrote Vilayat in obvious despair.[6]

His letters to the War Office, all held in Noor's personal file, reveal the deep anguish Vilayat was suffering. On one hand, he had to come to terms with his sister's death, details of which seemed to be continually changing; on the other, he had to remain strong to support his mother, who had taken it very badly.

Vera Atkins now concentrated on discovering when Noor went to Pforzheim and where she was taken from there. Captain A. Nicholson of the War Crimes Group of North West Europe was given the task of obtaining photocopies of the Pforzheim prison register. He reported to Major N.G. Mott at the War Office. From the sworn statement of the prison director, they learnt that Noor was removed from Pforzheim to Dachau in September. Major Mott then reported to Vera Atkins that Noor, along with three other specially employed women, were removed to Dachau, where they were executed the following morning, 13 September. The long and tortuous path to investigate the death of Noor had come to an end.

The news was broken to a devastated Vilayat, who was told that there was little room for doubt that his sister had met her end in Dachau. It had taken two years after the end of the war to discover her fate.

On 16 November 1949, Vilayat had to go through the painful experience of meeting face to face the person who had allegedly betrayed his sister to the Germans. Renée Garry was tried before a French military court at the Reuilly Barracks on charges of betrayal. He had to appear as a witness for the prosecution. Other witnesses were Vogt (who at that time was a prisoner of the French), Madame Garry and Madame Aigrain.

Vogt was asked to identify the woman who stood before him in court as the 'Renée' he had mentioned in his sworn statement. He admitted she looked a little different and had put on some weight. He said he had met her once more after Noor's arrest as she had called the office and demanded the rest of the payment that was due to her. He said he had told her that she would have to come to the office of the treasurer and show her identity card before she could collect the money. Though she was reluctant to undertake the formalities she did so and he read the name on her identity card. It said 'Renée Garry'.[7]

Renée Garry denied it was she who had made the call that betrayed Noor. Marguerite Garry, who had known Noor well, and who was now a widow, said Renée was a possessive sister and did not like the attention being shown to Noor. She said Renée was also jealous of Noor because she, Renée, was in love with Antelme but Antelme had no time for her after he met Noor.

Renée Garry was asked if she would have liked to have sent her brother to his death. She replied, 'No'.

The sole witness for the defence was Gieules, who had unknowingly been sent by Noor on the orders of London to meet the Gestapo. Still holding a grudge against her for something that was no fault of hers, he said Noor was in touch with double agents and was not conscious of security. The defence also produced a letter in court written to Renée Garry by Maurice Buckmaster after the war, thanking her for her support of members of the organisation.

On the basis that her brother too had been captured by the Gestapo after Noor's arrest, and that the only witness against her was a Nazi, Renée was acquitted. Vilayat said he could never bring himself to forgive her, though his Sufi faith demanded that he do so. He said he could forgive the German soldiers who carried out orders but not the person who betrayed his sister. The conflict always remained with him.[8]

On the German side, Sturmbannführer Hans Josef Kieffer was tried before a British military court at Wuppertal on the charge of having passed on an order (which had come from Berlin) for the execution of a party of uniformed soldiers captured in Normandy in August 1944. Kieffer called John Starr as a witness to say whether he had seen any prisoners at Avenue Foch being tortured. Starr said he hadn't seen any himself. But when he was asked whether he had seen all the prisoners brought to Avenue Foch, Starr had to say no. He could also not speak for other prisoners held elsewhere. Kieffer was executed.

For some time after the war the SOE was kept under wraps. Little was revealed about its organisation and methods, which were all kept strictly classified under the Official Secrets Act. SOE itself was closed after the war and much of its material lost in a fire that broke out in the Baker Street office. It was only when the war crimes tribunals of Wuppertal began in May 1946, that the first wave of publicity began. The trial of the prison officers of Natzweiler brought out the stories of the agents who had been killed by lethal injection. Though the victims were not named, there were reports that the girls were not quite dead when they were put in the crematorium ovens. It caused an outrage. Newspapers carried headlines saying that British women had been burnt alive.

It was the first time the British public became aware that women agents had been sent into the field on dangerous missions. Some asked what the justification for it was. In 1958, the journalist Elizabeth Nicholas investigated what had happened to her friend Diana Rowden, whose name she read in the papers as one of the thirteen women agents who had died in France. Their names were mentioned (for the first time) in a plaque dedicated in their honour at St Paul's Church in Knightsbridge in 1948. Nicholas went on to publish her book *Death Be Not Proud* about seven SOE agents in the war. It was she who revealed the identity of the fourth victim at Natzweiler, Sonia Olschanezky. Without Nicholas's pioneering work, the fourth victim may have gone unnoticed and her family would never have known what happened to her.

By 1952 Jean Overton Fuller's *Madeleine* had been published. Fuller went to Paris to trace what had happened to her friend Noor and met her friends and the Germans who held her in captivity. Noor's story led her to research other books about the SOE in France. Both *Double Webs* and *The Starr Affair* caused a stir. In these Fuller spoke for the first time about the radio game played by the Germans on the captured wireless sets which led to agents, arms and money being dropped straight into the hands of the Gestapo. She also claimed that England was aware of the games and wilfully carried on the deception so as to distract the Germans. Both Nicholas's and Fuller's books led to the impression that innocent girls had been sent to their deaths in France by the SOE. They had allowed the radio game to go on and sacrificed agents. While it was true that England did play the radio game back to the Germans, it was not till the spring of 1944 that this started, when Baker Street realised that the Germans were deceiving them.

Why London continued to send agents when there were doubts that a circuit may have been blown is hard to explain. Once again, the reason was that in the fog of war, they sometimes did not stick to the strict rules of security checks, thinking the agent may have dropped the check in a moment of carelessness or hurry. Buckmaster himself said it was not possible to be watertight in imposing these rules as agents could forget to give their security checks if they were transmitting under very difficult conditions. Yet there is no denying that there were serious mistakes, for which Noor and her colleagues paid a heavy price.

When Gilbert Norman had been captured and the Germans forced him to send radio messages, he used only his bluff security check to warn London that he had been captured. Not only did London ignore the dropping of the security check, but Maurice Buckmaster himself actually replied to Norman telling him that he had forgotten his security check and to be more careful next time.[9] This was a crucial lapse of security which was to prove disastrous. How Buckmaster could have sent such a note when the very purpose of the bluff security check was to establish whether an agent had been captured, showed fundamental flaws at the highest level in F-section. The note revealed to the Germans that there were two security checks and they put further pressure on captured agents. Since Norman's arrest had been reported by Noor, as well as by Cohen and Dowlen, it was incredible that such a message should have been sent at all. It also showed poor lack of coordination in Baker Street. Norman was said to have been so distressed at the way his message was received that he started cooperating with the Germans. They successfully continued to play back Norman's set and that of Macalister, sending Agazarian, Gieules and Dutilleul straight to the Gestapo.

Noor too, had been sent by her chiefs straight to the Germans, when they had told her to meet two agents at Café Colisée. She had had a narrow escape, but had come face to face with the Gestapo who from then could identify her physically. For ten months from July 1943, the Germans ran four *Funkspiele* (wireless games) with captured F-section transmitters. Later, in February 1944, they played Noor's set and captured France Antelme, Madeleine Damerment and Lionel Lee. Once again Buckmaster had ignored Leo Marks' warning that Noor may be in German hands, with fatal consequences.

Buckmaster had also been sent a telegram from Berne on 1 October 1943 from 'Jacques' saying:

> Sonja returned from Paris 25th reports Ernest Maurice and Madeleine had serious accident and in hospital. Maurice is Barde. Madeleine is w/t operator. If you go ahead on pick up plan I could tell on receipt of photograph whether genuine or Gestapo Maurice. Am trying to get further information via Sonja.

Buckmaster replied:

> Have had apparently genuine messages from Madeleine since 25th therefore regard Sonja's news with some doubt. Can you give us estimate of Sonja's reliability?

The original message was sent by Jacques Weil of the Juggler circuit, who had escaped to Berne after the Prosper debacle. The 'Sonja' in the message is clearly Sonia Olschanezky, his courier and fiancée, who was lying low in Paris, and who was later killed at Natzweiler. Though the warning was wrong as Noor was never hospitalised and was not caught till mid-October, it nevertheless should have put London on guard and made them examine her messages more carefully. This, again, Buckmaster did not do, despite Noor sending out her distress special security check after capture.

It took F-section six weeks to realise that Norman had been arrested and the messages coming from his wireless were false. When London realised the game the Germans were playing they started playing the same game back to them. They continued to drop arms and cash to the Germans, giving them the impression that they had not tumbled to their deception. This gave the SOE time to build new circuits which the Germans did not get to know about. It also gave the Gestapo a false sense of security. Besides, London could find out where the Gestapo had their local reception committees organised.

Goetz and his assistant, Joseph Placke, were delighted at the large amounts of cash they received (about 8,572,000 francs or nearly £43,000),[10] but SOE felt it was a loss worth incurring. By distracting the Germans, Maurice Buckmaster hoped to build new circuits in south Normandy of which the Germans knew nothing. These were the Headmaster and Scientist circuits which played a crucial role in the area before D-Day. But by then many of his top agents had been captured.

In April and May, Himmler, Goering and Hitler are said to have discussed the radio game. They had been wondering when they should tell London that they had captured some of their best agents. Hitler thought this blow should be delivered to them at such a time that it disarmed them completely. But by then Baker Street, too, was in on the act. Resistance had been planted firmly on French soil. The sacrifice of the wireless operators, who suffered the highest casualties in the field, would be simply remembered as their contribution to the war.

Apart from the controversy over the radio games, there was also the belief that the SOE had protected double agents like Déricourt for their own ends, exposing their own agents to the Gestapo. Jean Overton Fuller, was, however prepared to give Déricourt the benefit of the doubt, saying he had carried on a deliberate deception of the Germans and given them some secrets to win their trust. In exchange, he had managed to secure the evacuation of many agents back to England. Déricourt managed to charm and convince Jean Overton Fuller that he was not just a double agent but a triple agent reporting to someone else as well as Buckmaster. The third group, he implied, was MI6.

In June 1948, Déricourt faced a military tribunal in France accused of betrayal of agents. But F-section's Nicholas Bodington appeared as a witness in his favour saying he not only knew that Déricourt was friendly with the Germans but 'also how and why'. He claimed he was doing it for a reason and he would trust his life to Déricourt. When Bodington visited Paris in July 1943, Déricourt had arranged his safe passage. This could be the reason Bodington had infinite trust in him. But according to the Germans (Hugo Bleicher of the Abwehr), Déricourt had arranged for Bodington's stay and safe passage with German help, precisely so that Déricourt would get the full support and trust of the SOE. The extensive SOE files on Déricourt reveal that they mistrusted him, had him watched and even tried to bug him, but in the end they let him get away. The files reveal that the SOE also mistrusted Bodington, but again did little about it.

Goetz had said that Déricourt had dined with him and Karl Boemelburg (the head of the Paris Gestapo based at 82 Avenue Foch), the last night before he left Paris. He also said that Déricourt made copies of all the letters that went on his Lysanders and passed them on to Boemelburg.[11] Déricourt had informed Goetz about the place of transmission of his own radio operator, so that the German wireless-detection squads would not arrest him. He suggested Déricourt was Boemelburg's agent, and the latter had 'complete confidence' in him.

Déricourt's photocopies of the letters no doubt demoralised British agents, including Noor, by giving the impression that there was a traitor in London. Both Kieffer and Goetz said they had got information from Déricourt. Other agents in the field, like Henri Frager of the Donkeyman circuit, had had their suspicions about him,[12] but in the end it was the word of Bodington, an F-section chief, versus a Nazi, and Déricourt was acquitted. One of F-section's most controversial double agents walked free. He died in a plane crash in 1962.

There were strong allegations that each one of Déricourt's flights was watched by the Germans and the arriving agents were followed. Despite all these suspicions, Déricourt had been retained by F-section, leading to questions in many minds about the SOE's game plan. Since it was Déricourt who had greeted the Lysander flight of 16 June carrying Noor and her colleagues, could it be a surprise that all four agents would die on their mission? Many of these questions remain unanswered.

What was beyond a doubt, however, was that though the SOE made many costly slip-ups back home, their agents in the field had done exemplary work. According to General Dwight D. Eisenhower, Supreme Commander of the Allied Forces, the contributions of the SOE had shortened the war in Europe by six months.

According to SOE historian M.R.D. Foot, it was the necessity of war that led to the radio game and the greater goal of deceiving the Germans and securing the Normandy landings. It was unfortunate that by the time London started playing the game back, they had already lost many top agents. The need to fight a force like Hitler had led to unusual methods. Mistakes were made in the heat of the moment, but the ultimate victory had been achieved.

Foot thought it questionable that agents like Noor were sent into the field without finishing their training, but the exigencies of the hour demanded a radio operator and she had to leave. 'To the question why people with so little training were sent to do such important work, the only reply is: the work had to be done, and there was no one else to send,' wrote Foot.[13]

Sixty years after the war it is easier to assess the role of the SOE. According to Foot, the sacrifice made by the sappers (three-quarters of whom were killed or badly wounded) when they went to clear the minefields before the Normandy invasions was on a par with those demanded from Suttill, Noor and the other SOE agents. Both jobs had to be done to prepare for the invasion, and both jobs were absolutely invaluable.

Noor's courage and performance in the field were exemplary and except for misunderstanding her instructions about carefully filing her stories (instructions which were in any event not at all clear), there would have been nothing to fault her with. If she had not been betrayed, Noor would have actually beaten the Gestapo at their own game. Her courage and strength led her to hold on till the end without giving in, and she stood proud till thc last. When Vogt put it to her that her sacrifice had been in vain, she told him: 'I have served my country. That is my recompense.'[14]

In the end, Noor was able to justify the faith that Maurice Buckmaster, Vera Atkins and Selwyn Jepson had put in her. She successfully used her training and wit to keep the Germans from arresting her for over three months by changing locations, changing her looks and using her circuit of loyal friends to help her. She would have returned to England if she had not been betrayed. Unlike other radio operators (like Brian Stonehouse or Robert Dowlen), who were caught by direction-finding vans while on the air because they transmitted from the same place, Noor was arrested through no fault of her own. Even her German captors admitted that she had evaded arrest for months despite their best efforts to trap her.

'I had first learnt of the existence of Madeleine at the time of Archambaud's arrest,' said Goetz in his interrogation after the war.

> We had a personal description of her and knew she was a W.T. operator of the *reseau* Prosper. It was, naturally, of the greatest interest to us to arrest her as we suspected she carried on W.T. traffic with London . . . The wireless detection station had such a sender under observation but could not close in on it as the place of transmission was constantly changing. In October or about this time it was thought that one was closing in on it, but again it was impossible to effect an arrest.[15]

And Josef Kieffer confirmed this: 'We were pursuing her for months and as we had a personal description of her we arranged for all stations to be watched. She had several addresses and worked very carefully.'[16]

After Noor's arrest, her behaviour was exemplary. Though the toughest of SOE agents cracked under interrogation and torture (Gilbert Norman and Dowlen, to name just two), Noor stood firm – revealing nothing despite torture and hardship. Even her captors could not help but be impressed by her. Kieffer apparently broke down before Vera Atkins at his interrogation when told that Noor had been sent to Dachau from Pforzheim and executed.

On 5 April 1949, Noor was posthumously awarded the George Cross, the highest civilian honour in Britain.

The citation said:

> The King has been graciously pleased to approve the posthumous award of the George Cross to Assistant Section Officer Nora Inayat Khan (9901), Women's Auxiliary Air Force.
>
> Assistant section Officer Nora Inayat Khan was the first woman operator to be infiltrated into enemy-occupied France, and was landed by Lysander aircraft on June 16th, 1943. During the weeks immediately following her arrival, the Gestapo made mass arrests in the Paris Resistance groups to which she had been detailed. She refused, however, to abandon what had become the principal and most dangerous post in France, although given the opportunity to return to England, because she did not wish to leave her French comrades without communications, and she hoped also to rebuild her group. She remained at her post therefore and did the excellent work which earned her a posthumous Mention in Despatches.

The Gestapo had a full description of her, but knew only her code name Madeleine. They deployed considerable forces in their effort to catch her and so break the last remaining link with London. After three and a half months she was betrayed to the Gestapo and taken to their HQ in the Avenue Foch. The Gestapo had found her codes and messages and were not in a position to work back to London. They asked her to co-operate but she refused and gave them no information of any kind. She was imprisoned in one of the cells on the fifth floor of the Gestapo HQ, and remained there for several weeks, during which time she made two unsuccessful attempts at escape. She was asked to sign a declaration that she would make no further attempts but she refused, and the Chief of the Gestapo obtained permission from Berlin to send her to Germany for 'safe custody'. She was the first agent to be sent to Germany.

Assistant Section Officer Inayat Khan was sent to Karlsruhe in November 1943 and then to Pforzheim, where her cell was apart from the main prison. She was considered to be a particularly dangerous and uncooperative prisoner. The Director of the prison has been interrogated and has confirmed that Assistant Section Officer Inayat Khan, when interrogated by the Karlsruhe Gestapo, refused to give any information whatsoever either as to her work or her colleagues.

She was taken with three others to Dachau camp on September 12, 1944. On arrival she was taken to the crematorium and shot.

Assistant Section Officer Inayat Khan displayed the most conspicuous courage, both moral and physical, over a period of more than twelve months.

The French had presented Noor with their highest civilian award, the Croix de Guerre with Gold Star, three years earlier on 16 January 1946. The citation said:

On the proposition of the Minister of the Armies, the President of the Provisional Government of the Republic, Chief of the Armies, Minister of National Defence, cites to the order of the army corps.

A/S/O Nora Inayat Khan, WAAF

Sent into France by Lysander on June 16th 1943, as a wireless operator with the mission of assuring transmissions between

> London and an organisation of the Resistance in the Paris area. Shortly after her arrival a series of arrests broke up the organisation. Obliged to flee, she nevertheless continued to fulfil her mission under the most difficult conditions. Falling into an ambush at Grignon, in July 1943, her comrades and she managed to escape after having killed or wounded the Germans who were trying to stop them. She was finally arrested in October 1943 and deported to Germany.
>
> This citation carries the award of the Croix de Guerre with Gold Star.
>
> Signed – General Charles De Gaulle

At a memorial service in Paris for Noor, Madame de Gaulle-Anthonioz, the General's niece, President of l'Association Nationale des Anciennes Déportées et Internées de la Résistance, said:

> Nothing, neither her nationality, nor the traditions of her family, none of these obliged her to take her position in the war. However she chose it. It is our fight that she chose, that she pursued with an admirable, an invincible courage.
>
> No, we will never forget Noor Inayat Khan, auxiliary officer of the English army who was also a fighter of the French Liberation Forces. She returned to France, gave up her marriage, left her training to replace the lives of ours that the Gestapo had decimated. She never gave up the fight, struggling up till the end against all natural prudence till her arrest . . . For all of us, for the children of our country, what a marvellous example.

Her chiefs at SOE remembered the petite Indian girl, who had caused such controversy at Beaulieu, with fondness. Buckmaster had always had a paternal attitude to Noor and admired her courage greatly. He, along with Vera Atkins, had recommended that Noor's George Medal be converted into the George Cross after they learnt the full extent of her courage both in the field and, later, in prison.

In a final comment Buckmaster added: 'A most brave and touchingly keen girl. She was determined to do her bit to hit the Germans and, poor girl, she has.'

A plaque at the crematorium in Dachau pays tribute to Noor Inayat Khan and her three colleagues who were killed there. There is another plaque in her memory in the Remembrance Hall of the Museum in Dachau.

A plaque at St Paul's Church, Knightsbridge, London, dedicated to the thirteen SOE agents who never returned from France, bears the name of N. Inayat Khan – GC.

Her name is included in the RAF Memorial in Runnymede in Surrey dedicated to the RAF personnel with no known graves and is inscribed on the Memorial Gates to the Commonwealth soldiers near Hyde Park Corner in London.

There is a plaque in her honour at the agricultural school in Grignon where she first began transmission.

A plaque outside her childhood home in Suresnes says:

> Here lived Noor Inayat Khan 1914–44
> Called Madeleine in the Resistance
> Shot at Dachau
> Radio Operator for the Buckmaster network

A leafy square in Suresnes has been named 'Cours Madeleine' after her and every year on Bastille Day – 14 July – a military band plays outside Fazal Manzil on the rue de la Tuilerie, remembering the sacrifice of the young Indian woman who gave her life for France and freedom.

Ten days after the announcement of Noor's George Cross in April 1949, Amina Begum died. She had never quite recovered from the news of Noor's death. It had weakened her physically and mentally. Vilayat, carrying the burden of the family on his young shoulders, had brought Amina back to Paris. It was as if she had clung to life just to hear the posthumous honour of her daughter and to return to the house she had set up with Inayat Khan all those years ago.

Fazal Manzil was the same when they returned, nearly seven years after they had left it. The war had taken its toll but it was still home. It had been preserved by their friends and neighbours and the uncles who had stayed back in France. Noor's harp was returned to Fazal Manzil, where it joined Inayat Khan's memorabilia.

Noor's achievements become even more important today, sixty years after the war, when we see her as a Muslim woman of Indian origin who was prepared to make the highest sacrifice for Britain.

Though committed to Indian independence, she had no doubts about supporting the Allied war effort against Germany. At a time when the Indian freedom struggle was reaching its peak with the Quit India movement of 1942, she was applying for a commission at the RAF, giving her frank views about India, her support for the freedom struggle and the reasons she was keen to support England in the war. She would back England during the war and back the freedom struggle after the war. Her brother Hidayat was convinced that if she had lived, her next cause would have been Indian independence.[17]

In prison Noor stuck to her story of being Nora Baker. There are reports that the Germans treated her worse than others because of her dark skin, but she bore it all with dignity, never betraying her colleagues or giving out any information about her organisation.

In the end, Noor's monkeys did cross the bridge. They escaped from the wicked king and found the road to freedom. On a slightly chilly September morning in a bleak death camp in Germany, Noor knelt down and made the ultimate sacrifice. Today on the site, just near the crematorium at Dachau, where the ashes of over 30,000 victims lie buried, the simple flower garden symbolises her gift to the free world.

APPENDIX I

Circuits linked to Prosper

Name	Code Name	Cover Name
Cinema/Phono		
Noor Inayat Khan	Madeleine	Jeanne-Marie Renier
Henri Garry	Cinema	
Prosper		
Francis Suttill	Prosper	François Alfred Desprez
Andrée Borrel	Denise	
Gilbert Norman	Archambaud	Gilbert Aubin
Jack Agazarian	Marcel	
Lise de Baissac	Odile	
Armel Guerne	Gaspard	
Alfred Balachowsky	Serge	
Pierre Culioli	Adolfe	
Yvonne Rudellat	Jacqueline	
Francine Agazarian	Marguerite	
Jean Amps	Tomas	
Bricklayer		
France Antelme	Renaud	Antoine Ratier
Lise de Baissac	Odile	
William Savy	Alcide	
Farrier		
Henri Déricourt	Gilbert	
Rémy Clément	Marc	
Julienne Aisner	Claire	
Satirist		
Octave Simon	Badois	
Dutilleul	Champagne	
Arthur de Montalambert	Bistouri	
William Savy	Alcide	
Chestnut		
Charles Grover Williams	Sebastien	
Robert Benoist	Lionel	

Name	Code Name	Cover Name
J.P. Wimille		
Robert Dowlen	Achille	
Juggler		
Jean Worms	Robin	
Gaston Cohen	Justin	
Jacques Weil	Jacques Atin	
Butler		
François Bouguennec	Max Garel	
Marcel Rousset	Leopold	
Marcel Fox	Ernest	
Musician		
Gustave Biéler	Guy	
Yolande Beekman	Mariette	Yvonne de Chauvigny
Farmer		
Staggs	Guy	
Michael Trotobas	Sylvestre	
Archdeacon		
John Macalister	Bertrand	
Frank Pickersgill	Valentin	
Scientist		
Claude de Baissac	David	
Lise de Baissac	Odile	
Acrobat		
Diana Rowden	Paulette	
John Starr	Bob	
Carte		
Peter Churchill	Raoul	
Henri Frager	Paul/Louba	
Germaine Tambour	Annette	
Madeleine Tambour		
Frager		
André Dubois	Hercule	
Peter Churchill	Raoul	
Donkeyman		
Henri Frager	Paul/Louba	

APPENDIX II

Agents and Resistance members who worked with Noor and the Prosper Circuit

Though the tangled web of the SOE circuits often overlapped, it is beyond the scope of this book to cover the stories of the other agents. However, here is a brief look at the fate of the agents and Resistance workers who were linked to Noor and the Prosper circuit and who we have described in the previous chapters. Most were killed in concentration camps. Only a few lucky survivors lived to tell their stories.

Francis Suttill – killed at Sachsenhausen
Gilbert Norman – executed in Mauthausen, 6 September 1944
Andrée Borrel – executed at Natzweiler
Jack Agazarian – killed by firing squad at Flossenburg
France Antelme – executed at Gross Rosen
Henri Garry – executed at Buchenwald, September 1944
Marguerite Garry – sent to Ravensbruck, returned 1945
Charles Vaudevire – executed at Buchenwald
Viennot – sent to Mauthausen, returned in 1945
Paul Arrighi – sent to Mauthausen, returned in 1945
Robert Gieules – deported to Germany, survived the war
Arthur de Montalambert – executed at Mauthausen
Octave Simon – executed at Gross Rosen
William Savy – reached England safely, survived the war
Germaine Aigrain – returned from prison, survived the war
Raymond Andres – died in Avenue Foch in a mine accident after the Gestapo had left in August 1944
Armel Guerne – escaped while being transported to Germany, survived the war
Alfred Balachowsky – deported to Buchenwald, returned in 1945
Eugène Vanderwynckt (Head of Grignon Agricultural College) – executed in Germany
Marius Maillard (gardener at Grignon) – killed at Dora
Robert Benoist – executed at Buchenwald
Charles Grover Williams – died at Sachsenhausen
John Macalister – executed at Buchenwald
Frank Pickersgill – executed at Buchenwald
Henri Frager – hung by a meat hook at Buchenwald
Madeleine Damerment – executed at Dachau

Yolande Beekman – executed at Dachau
Diana Rowden – executed at Natzweiler
Eliane Plewman – executed at Dachau
Sonia Olschanezky – executed at Natzweiler
Vera Leigh – executed at Natzweiler
Cecily Lefort – died at Ravensbruck
John Starr – escaped from Mauthausen
Leon Faye – executed at Sonnenburg
Brian Stonehouse – returned from Dachau
Gustave Biéler – executed at Flossenburg
Yvonne Rudellat – died in Belsen
Jean Worms – executed at Flossenburg
Julienne Aisner (Déricourt's courier) – returned to London 5/6 April 1944
Henri Déricourt – returned to London 8/9 February 1944

APPENDIX III

Chronology

Date	Events in Noor's life	Events in Europe	Events in India
1 January 1914	Birth of Noor	Unrest in Russia	
May 1914	Inayat Khan leaves Moscow	Tension in Europe	
28 July 1914		First World War begins	
August 1914	Inayat Khan moves to London		
January 1915		Europe at war	Gandhi returns to India from South Africa
13 April 1919			Jallianwala Bagh massacre
28 June 1919		Treaty of Versailles signed	
Spring 1920	Inayat Khan moves back to France		Gandhi begins Satyagraha resistance campaign
5 February 1927	Inayat Khan dies		
April 1930			Gandhi goes on Salt March
April 1931	Noor joins Ecole Normale de Musique		
Autumn 1931			Gandhi attends Second Round Table Conference in London
30 January 1933		Hitler becomes Chancellor of Germany	
11–12 March 1938		The Reich annexes Austria in the Anschluss	

Date	Events in Noor's life	Events in Europe	Events in India
9/10 November 1938	Noor publishing stories in *Le Figaro*	Kristallnacht (Night of Broken Glass, when German Jews were attacked by the Nazis)	
15 March 1939		Germany invades Czechoslovakia	
Summer 1939	Noor's *Twenty Jataka Tales* published	Germany and Italy announce formal alliance; Germany and USSR sign non-aggression pact	
1 September 1939		Germany invades Poland	
3 September 1939		Britain, New Zealand, Australia and France declare war on Germany	
10 May 1940		Winston Churchill forms coalition government in Britain. Germany begins aggression against Belgium, Holland and Luxembourg	
28 May 1940		Belgium surrenders to Germany	
5 June 1940	Noor and family leave Paris		
9 June 1940		Norway surrenders	
17 June 1940		Pétain declares armistice; De Gaulle leaves for Britain	
18 June 1940	Noor wants to help war effort	De Gaulle broadcasts from London rallying Free French	
28 June 1940		British government recognises De Gaulle as leader of Free French	
10 July 1940		Battle of Britain begins	

Date	Events in Noor's life	Events in Europe	Events in India
16 July 1940		SOE is born	
19 November 1940	Noor enlists in WAAF		
2 March 1941		Germany attacks Bulgaria	
6 April 1941		Germany attacks Yugoslavia and Greece	
5/6 May 1941		First SOE agent George Bégué drops into France	
Summer 1941			Subhas Bose begins recruiting Indian prisoners of war in Germany to join his Indian National Army in the fight for independence from the British. Meets Ribbentrop.
7 December 1941		Japan attacks Pearl Harbor	
8 December 1941		USA, Britain declare war on Japan	
14 June 1942	Noor's 'The Fairy and the Hare' broadcast on BBC Children's Hour		
8 August 1942			Congress leaders launch Quit India movement
28 August 1942	Noor attends RAF interview for Commission		All top Indian leaders in jail
November 1942	Noor attends interview for SOE	Prosper circuit building up in Paris	
February 1943	Noor signs Official Secrets Act	Bose's movements watched closely by SIS and IPI (Indian Political Intelligence) at Bletchley. His submarine journey	Gandhi begins three-week fast against British violence against demonstrators. On 8 February

Date	Events in Noor's life	Events in Europe	Events in India
		monitored by British intelligence	Bose sails in a submarine organised by the Germans to reach Japan.
February 1943			Bengal famine caused by diversion of food to feed troops leads to three millions dead over three years (1942–44)
June16/17 1943	Noor flown in by Lysander		
21 June 1943		Cullioli, Rudellat, Macalister and Pickersgill arrested	
23 June 1943		Norman, Borrel arrested	
24 June 1943		Suttill arrested	
1 July 1943		Worms and Guerne arrested, Grignon staff arrested	
2 July 1943		Prof. Balachowsky arrested	
19 July 1943		Antelme leaves	
22/23 July 1943		Bodington and Agazarian return to Paris	
30 July 1943		Agazarian arrested	
31 July 1943		Robert Dowlen arrested	
2 August 1943		Maurice Benoist, Grover Williams arrested	
16/17 August 1943		Bodington returns to London	
19/20 August 1943		Robert Benoist returns to London	
7 September 1943		Rousset arrested	
29 September 1943		Gieules arrested	
13 October 1943	Noor arrested		
26 November 1943	Noor sent to Pforzheim		

Date	Events in Noor's life	Events in Europe	Events in India
29 February 1944		Antelme, Madeleine Damerment and Lionel Lee arrested	
6 June 1944		Normandy Invasions	
6 July 1944		Diana Rowden, Sonia Olschanezky, Andrée Borrel, Vera Leigh executed at Natzweiler camp	
17 August 1944		Gestapo move out of Avenue Foch. Last trainload of Jews leaves France for Auschwitz	
26 August 1944		De Gaulle heads parade from Arc de Triomphe to Notre Dame	
13 September 1944	Noor, Eliane Plewman, Madeleine Damerment, Yolande Beekman executed at Dachau		
26 January 1945		Soviet troops enter Auschwitz	
29 April 1945		Dachau liberated	
8 May 1945		VE Day. Germans surrender	Subhas Bose's Indian National Army surrenders in Rangoon
15 August 1945		VJ Day. Japan surrenders after bombs on Hiroshima (6 Aug) and Nagasaki (8 Aug)	
18 August 1945			Subhas Bose dies in air crash
November 1945			Trial of INAofficers begins in Delhi leading to an outcry
16 January 1946	Noor posthumously awarded the Croix de Guerre		

Date	Events in Noor's life	Events in Europe	Events in India
18 February 1946			Royal Navy Mutiny in India
April 1946		Stewart Menzies, head of SIS, and heads of Indian intelligence agree to continue cooperation	
2 June 1946			Governor General Lord Wavell takes direct control over Indian intelligence – IB and IPI
15 July 1947		Britain in financial crisis. Hugh Dalton, former head of SOE, now Chancellor of the Exchequer, tries to control it	
8–9 August 1947			Plans for partition of India revealed leading to riots
13 August 1947		Hugh Dalton retires ill to Wiltshire as currency crisis continues	
15 August 1947			India wins independence
5 April 1949	Noor posthumously awarded the George Cross		

APPENDIX IV

Indians awarded the Victoria Cross and the George Cross 1939–1945

Two and a half million Indian soldiers volunteered for the Second World War. It was the largest volunteer army in recorded history and suffered the greatest casualties. They served in fields far away from the sub-continent in Italy, Africa and the Far East and 28 VCs were awarded to members of the Indian army during the course of the war. There follows a list, plus a brief outline of the reason for the award.

A) Recipients of the Victoria Cross for services in the Second World War

1. **Jemadar Abdul Hafiz – 9th Jat Infantry – 1944, Imphal, India**
   Led an attack up a bare slope with no cover. Though the Japanese fired at him from the top and injured him, he continued his assault killing the enemy one by one till he had chased all the Japanese from the top of the hill. A final bullet in his chest finally grounded him, but he was still trying to give cover fire to his colleagues when he died.

2. **Naik Agansing Rai – 5th Royal Gurkha Rifles – 1944, Bishenpur, Burma**
   Securing the crucial post of Mortar Bluff and Water Picquet in the face of devastating enemy fire.

3. **Sepoy Ali Haidar – 13th Frontier Force Rifles – 1945, Fusignano, Italy**
   Destroyed enemy post in face of heavy gunfire, killing many Germans. Battalion could enter after he cleared the way, took 220 of the enemy and secured the post.

4. **Rifleman Bhanbhagta Gurung – 2nd Gurkha Rifles – 1945, Tamandu, Burma**
   Took five positions single-handedly using his bayonet, grenades and his kukri to kill the Japanese in fox-holes and bunkers, all the time under heavy fire.

5. **Sepoy Bhandari Ram – 10th Baluch Regiment – 1944, East Mayu, Arakan, Burma**
   Secured the position despite coming under heavy fire from the top of the hill and being wounded in the leg, chest, face and shoulder. Survived to receive his VC.

6. **Havildar Major Chhelu Ram – 6th Rajputana Rifles – 1943, Djebel Garci, Tunisia**
Ran through enemy fire armed only with a tommy gun and tin helmet killing all occupants of the machine-gun post. Also attended to officer in an exposed position though himself seriously wounded. Died on the field.

7. **Naik Fazal Din – 10th Baluch Regiment – 1945, Meiktila, Burma**
Was speared by an officer's sword but tore the sword out of his back and killed Japanese with it. Continued to help his colleagues and killed two more Japanese with the same sword. Then waved the sword rallying his men, who were so inspired they annihilated the garrison of 55 Japanese. He died soon afterwards.

8. **Havildar Gaje Ghale – 5th Royal Gurkha Rifles – 1943, Chin Hills, Burma**
Led his men through artillery and mortar fire though seriously wounded himself and secured the position storming the hill and slaying most of the enemy.

9. **Rifleman Ganju Lama – 7th Gurkha Rifles – 1944, Ningthoukhong, Burma**
Knocked out two enemy tanks with his Piat gun and would not stop, though seriously wounded, till he had had killed all the tank-men trying to escape.

10. **Naik Gian Singh – 15th Punjab Regiment – 1945, Kamye, Burma**
Secured the post while coming under anti-tank fire. Killed 20 Japanese and cleared the enemy from fox-holes and cactus hedges with his tommy gun.

11. **Sepoy Kamal Ram – 8th Punjab Regiment – 1944, River Gari, Italy**
Secured the bridgehead over River Gari single-handedly killing many Germans and covering a colleague.

12. **Lieutenant Karamjeet Singh Judge – 15th Punjab Regiment – 1945, Meiktila, Burma**
Wiped out ten bunkers single-handedly, allowing the tanks to get through and secure the area on the outskirts of Myingyan.

13. **Rifleman Lachhiman Gurung – 8th Gurkha Rifles – 1945, Taungdaw, Burma**
Fought for over four hours alone at his post despite his face, body and right leg being torn apart by a grenade. Firing with his left hand, he killed 31 enemy soldiers at point-blank range and 87 others lay dead in the vicinity. So inspired were his colleagues that they held and smashed every attack after that. He lived to collect his VC.

14. **Subedar Lal Bahadur Thapa – 2nd Gurkha Rifles – 1943, Rass-es-Zouai, Tunisia**
Secured a vital passage on a precipitous ridge.

15. **Sepoy Namdeo Jadav – 5th Mahratta Light Infantry, Senio River, Italy**
When his commanders were wounded and rest of his unit killed he waded through the river under enemy gunfire and carried two colleagues to safety one by one. Then giving a mighty war cry, he climbed to the top of the hill despite heavy mortar shelling and his own injuries, and took the post.

16. **Naik Nand Singh – 11th Sikh Regiment – 1944, Maungdaw-Buthidaung Road, Burma**
Commanded his platoon up a steep razor-edge ridge under heavy fire from the Japanese, taking three trenches single-handedly, though heavily wounded, allowing his platoon to follow him and seize the top of the hill.

17. **Subedar Netrabahadur Thapa – 5th Royal Gurkha Rifles – 1944, Bishenpur, Burma**
Fought bravely in pouring rain and with low reserves against the enemy and regained the crucial post of Mortar Bluff before being killed by a bullet in his mouth.

18. **Havildar Parkash Singh – 8th Punjab Regiment – 1943, Donbaik, Mayu Peninsula, Burma**
Single-handedly saved injured colleagues trapped in a disabled carrier vehicle by driving his own carrier straight to it through enemy fire. Then rescued the weapons from another carrier.

19. **Jemadar Prakash Singh – 13th Frontier Force Rifles – 1945, Kanlan Ywathit, Burma**
Drove off the enemy, rallying his men though his hands and legs had been smashed. Died when a grenade hit his chest after the post was secured.

20. **Second Lieutenant Premindra Singh Bhagat – Corps of Indian Engineers – 1941, Gallabat, Abyssinia (now Ethiopia)**
Cleared mines continuously for 48 hours without stopping even though both his eardrums were damaged.

21. **Subedar Ram Sarup Singh – 1st Punjab Regiment – 1944, Kennedy Peak, Burma**
Routed the Japanese with his brave charge, but died after being hit by machine-gun fire.

22. **Subedar Richhpal Ram – 6th Rajputana Rifles – 1941, Keren, Eritrea**
Led his men on a successful bayonet charge through two-way fire after his company commander was wounded, even though his right foot was blown off.

23. **Rifleman Sher Bahadur Thapa – 9th Gurkha Rifles – 1944, San Marino, Italy**
Fell fighting after rescuing two wounded comrades.

24. **Lance Naik Sher Shah – 16th Punjab Regiment – 1945, Kyeyebyin, Burma**
Killed 23 Japanese soldiers despite having his right leg blown off and secured the post.

25. **Rifleman Thaman Gurung – 5th Royal Gurkha Rifles – 1944, Monte San Bartolo, Italy**
Stood in full view of enemy and opened fire, allowing his platoon to withdraw without further loss.

26. **Rifleman Tulbahadur Pun – 8th Gurkha Rifles – 1944, Mogaung, Burma**
Fought single-handed in knee-deep mud after his commanders were killed. Secured railway bridge at Mogaung.

27. **Havildar Umrao Singh – Royal Indian Artillery – 1944, Kaladan Valley, Burma**
Beat back the Japanese though seriously wounded. He had collapsed from his wounds but the Japanese led a counter-charge. In a fanatical fight, Umrao Singh killed ten Japanese single-handedly and fought them back. He recovered in hospital.

28. **Naik Yeshwant Ghadge – 5th Mahratta Light Infantry – 1944, Upper Tiber Valley, Italy**
Captured a machine-gun post under heavy fire at zero range. Died after he was shot in the chest after securing the post.

B) Recipients of the George Cross for services in the Second World War

1. **Captain Ahmed Matreen Ansari – 7th Rajput Regiment, Indian Army – 18 April 1946**
Fortitude as POW.

2. **Sowar Ditto Ram – Central India Horse, Indian Armed Corps – 13 December 1945**
Helped wounded soldier. Memorial – Cassino Memorial, Italy.

3. **Captain Mahmood Khan Durrani – 1st Bahawalpur Infantry, Indian State Forces – 23 May 1946**
Fortitude as POW.

4. **Assistant Section Officer Noor Inayat Khan, WAAF sent to FANY – 5 April 1949**
Espionage. Memorial – Runnymede Memorial – Surrey, UK.

5. **Lance Naik Islam-ud-din – 6/9th Jat Regiment, Indian Army – 5 October 1945**
Grenade self-sacrifice. Memorial – Rangoon Memorial, Rangoon, Burma.

6. **Naik Kirpa Ram – 8th Battalion, 13th Frontier Force Rifles, Indian Army – 15 March 1946**
   Grenade self-sacrifice. Memorial – Rangoon Memorial, Rangoon, Burma.

7. **Subedar Major Pir Khan – Royal Engineers, Indian Army – 28 June 1940**
   Rebel ambush rescue.

8. **Havildar Abdul Rahman – 3rd Battalion, 9th Jat Regiment, Indian Army – 10 September 1946**
   Attempted crash rescue. Memorial – Singapore Memorial, Kranji War Cemetery.

9. **Subedar Subramanian – Queen Victoria's Own Madras Sappers and Miners – 30 June 1944**
   Bomb shield. Memorial – Sangro River Crematorium Memorial, Sicily, Italy.

Notes

1: Babuli

1 Elisabeth Keesing, *Hazrat Inayat Khan: A Biography*, p. 5; Musharraf Moulamia Khan, *Pages in the Life of a Sufi*, p. 22; and family sourccs.
2 Keesing, *Hazrat Inayat Khan*, p. 59.
3 Begum Inayat Khan, 'Woman's Seclusion in the East', *The Sufi*, September 1915.
4 Keesing, *Hazrat Inayat Khan*, p. 86.
5 Will Van Beek, *Hazrat Inayat Khan: Master of Life, Modern Sufi Mystic*, 1983.
6 Ibid.
7 Spasskaya Ye Yu, Memoirs of Spasskaya – chapter on 'Hindus of Moscow' (unpublished manuscript).
8 Sergey Moskalev, of the Emperor Society of Adherents of Natural Science, Anthropology and Ethnography, Moscow University, to author, May 2004.
9 Keesing, *Hazrat Inayat Khan*, p. 93.
10 Moulamia Khan, *Pages in the Life*, p. 123.
11 Vilayat to author, June 2003, Suresnes.
12 13 April 1919, when Gen. Dyer ordered his soldiers to open fire on a group of peaceful demonstrators in an enclosed area in Amritsar in Punjab, killing nearly 2,000 people including women and children. Many jumped into the well in the enclosed compound in complete panic. The troops did not stop till the last bullet had been fired.
13 Keesing, *Hazrat Inayat Khan*, p. 112.

2: Fazal Manzil

1 Jean Overton Fuller, *Noor-un-nisa Inayat Khan*, p. 38.
2 Elisabeth Keesing, *Hazrat Inayat Khan: A Biography*, p. 157.
3 Vilayat to author, Suresnes, June 2003.
4 Ibid.
5 Ibid.
6 Ibid.
7 Noor's letter to a friend from Switzerland, quoted in Overton Fuller, *Noor-un-nisa Inayat Khan*, p. 67.
8 Hidayat to author, letter, June 2004.
9 Vilayat to author, Suresnes, June 2003.
10 David Harper (Claire's son) to author, letter, November 2003.
11 Mahmood Khan, Noor's cousin, to author, telephone conversation from Suresnes, June 2004.
12 Maula Baksh's sons-in-law lived with him after their marriages, which made the family very large. This is why Inayat Khan's father stayed in the family house in Baroda after marrying Maula Baksh's daughter. The sole male heir of Maula Baksh was Ali Khan and it was to his son, Alladutt Khan, that Inayat wanted to marry Noor.

13 Vilayat to author, Suresnes, June 2003.
14 Ibid.
15 Keesing, *Hazrat Inayat Khan*, p. 176.
16 Vilayat to author, June 2003.
17 Mahmood to author, June 2004.
18 Ibid.
19 Noor's Personal File, HS9/836/5, National Archives, Kew. Handwritten notes by Noor about her background.
20 Mahmood to author, June 2004.
21 Noor herself would be referred to as a 'modern Joan of Arc who had refused to be subjugated and preferred death to slavery' by the Mayor of Suresnes, Monsieur Pontillon, on 17 July 1967 at the unveiling of a plaque in her honour at Fazal Manzil.
22 Mahmood to author, June 2004.
23 David Harper to author, October 2003.
24 Ibid.
25 The family could not remember his first name.
26 Mahmood to author, June 2004.
27 Vilayat to author, June 2003
28 Overton Fuller, *Noor-un-nisa Inayat Khan*, p 52.
29 Mahmood to author, June 2004.
30 Vilayat to author, June 2003.
31 Noor's Personal File, HS9/836/5, National Archives, Kew.
32 Vilayat to author, June 2003.
33 Vilayat to author, June 2003.
34 Noor's veena is now kept in the Sufi headquarters in the Hague along with other memorabilia.
35 Mahmood to author, June 2004.
36 Hidayat to author, May 2004.
37 Article by Alexis Danan in *Le Franctireur*, 17 February 1957, read out at a function in Suresnes to unveil a plaque in Noor's honour.
38 Overton Fuller, *Noor-un-nisa Inayat Khan*, p. 84.
39 Vilayat to author, June 2003.
40 Ibid.

3: Flight and Fight

1 Ian Ousby, *Occupation*, pp. 43–4.
2 Vilayat to author, June 2003.
3 Jean Overton Fuller to author, June 2004, Wymington, Northamptonshire.
4 Vilayat to author, June 2003.
5 Noor's service record, Personnel Management Agency, Royal Air Force, Innsworth.
6 Beryl E. Escott, *Mission Improbable*, p. 61.
7 Ibid.
8 Jean Overton Fuller to author, June 2004.
9 Jean Overton Fuller, *Noor-un-nisa Inayat Khan*, p. 97.
10 Ibid., p. 114.
11 Ibid., p. 101.
12 Vilayat to author, June 2003.
13 Patrick French, *Liberty or Death*, p. 162.
14 Bhagat Ram Talwar (codename Silver). WO/208/773 National Archives, Kew, and Mihir Bose, *Raj, Secrets, Revolution*, pp. 230–1.
15 Noor's Personal File, HS9/836/5, National Archives, Kew.

4: Setting Europe Ablaze

1 'History of SOE 1938–1945', 'SOE in Europe', Paper for VCSS lecture May 1946, File HS7/1, National Archives, Kew.
2 SOE Charter – WP (40) 271. Full copy of the charter is available as Appendix A; William Mackenzie, *The Secret History*.
3 M.R.D. Foot, *SOE in France*, p. 14.

4 History of SOE 1938–1945, 'SOE organisation', VCCS lecture July 1946, HS7/1, National Archives, Kew.
5 M.R.D. Foot, *SOE: The Special Operations Executive*, p. 22.
6 Later, Bickham Sweet-Escott borrowed the phrase as the title of his book on his own work in the SOE.
7 Germany invaded the USSR/Soviet Union (as it was known then) on 22 June 1941.
8 History of SOE 1938–1945, 'SOE in Europe', VCSS Lecture May 1946, HS7/1, National Archives, Kew.
9 Maurice Buckmaster, *Specially Employed*, p. 27.
10 Beryl E. Escott, *Mission Improbable*, p. 29.
11 M.R.D. Foot to author, October 2004, London.
12 Jean Overton Fuller, *Noor-un-nisa Inayat Khan*, p. 110.
13 Foot, *SOE*, p. 59.
14 Jepson's quotes in this section from Overton Fuller *Noor-un-nisa Inayat Khan*, pp. 110–11.
15 Noor's Air Ministry Records, Personnel Management Agency, RAF Innsworth.
16 Noor's Personal File, HS9/836/5, National Archives, Kew.
17 Patrick Howarth, *Undercover*, p. 20.
18 'SOE Organisation and Policy 30 Mar 1941–12 August 1941', WO 193/626, National Archives, Kew.
19 Jean Overton Fuller to author, June 2004, Wymington, Northamptonshire.
20 Ibid.
21 Ibid.
22 Ibid.
23 John Marais, Joan's son, to author, Cambridge, December 2005, and article by Joan Cubbin (Marais, née Canham), 'The Sixteenth of June', published in the *Ipswich Evening Star*.
24 Noor's Personal File, HS9/836/5 and Air Ministry records.

5: Codes and Cover Stories

1 Letter quoted in Jean Overton Fuller's *Noor-un-nisa Inayat Khan*, p. 121.
2 Noor's Personal File, HS9/836/5, National Archives, Kew.
3 Jean Overton Fuller to author, June 2004.
4 M.R.D. Foot to author, December 2004.
5 Security checks were often ignored by London, with disastrous results as we shall see in the following chapters.
6 Unfortunately, we do not know which one.
7 SOE agents in areas besides France were also affected. Almost the entire Dutch network was rounded up when a missed security check was not picked up in London.
8 M.R.D. Foot, *SOE in France*, p. 95.
9 Noor's Personal File, HS9/836/5, National Archives, Kew.
10 Maurice Buckmaster, *They Fought Alone*, p. 45.
11 Overton Fuller, *Noor-un-nisa Inayat Khan*, p. 127.
12 Buckmaster, *They Fought Alone*, p. 46.
13 Jean Overton Fuller to author, June 2004.
14 Flight schedule from Hugh Verity, *We Landed by Moonlight*, Appendix B, and Foot, *SOE in France*, p. 261.
15 M.R.D. Foot to author, October 2004.

16 Noor's Personal File, HS9/836/5, National Archives, Kew.
17 Noor's Personal File, HS9/836/5, National Archives, Kew.
18. Ibid.
19. Ibid.
20 M.R.D. Foot to author, October 2004, London.
21 Patrick Howarth, *Undercover*, p. 79.
22 Susan Ottaway, *Violette Szabo*, pp. 58–60.
23 Overton Fuller, *Noor-un-nisa Inayat Khan*, p. 132.

6: Leaving England

1 Noor's Personal File, HS9/836/5, National Archives, Kew.
2 Jean Overton Fuller, *Noor-un-nisa Inayat Khan*, p. 133.
3 Noor's Personal File, HS9/836/5, National Archives, Kew.
4 Leo Marks, *Between Silk and Cyanide*, pp. 307–21. Extracts and quotes in this section from two chapters in the book – 'Appointment with Royalty' and 'The Extended Briefing'.
5 Maurice Buckmaster, *Specially Employed*, p. 31.
6 Noor's Personal File, HS9/836/5, Instructions to Noor on her cover story. National Archives, Kew.
7 Letter to Hidayat from Patricia Stewart Bam.
8 Buckmaster, *Specially Employed*, p. 73.
9 Jean Overton Fuller to author, June 2004.
10 Ibid.
11 Hugh Verity, *We Landed By Moonlight*, p. 94.
12 Overton Fuller, *Noor-un-nisa Inayat Khan*, p. 139.
13 William Stevenson, *A Man Called Intrepid*, p. 224.

7: Joining the Circuit

1 William Mackenzie, *The Secret History of SOE*, p. 739.
2 Hugh Verity, *We Landed by Moonlight*, p. 94.
3 Ibid., p. 94.
4 Ibid., p. 94.
5 One or two daylight operations by Lysanders were undertaken in Italy in 1945 and a few in Burma in 1944 and 1945. M.R.D. Foot to author, February 2005.
6 M.R.D. Foot, *SOE in France*, Appendix D: Air Landing Notes, p. 434.
7 Verity, *We Landed by Moonlight*, Appendix B Summary of RAF pick-up operations in France, p. 191, and Noor's Personal File, HS9/836/5, National Archives, Kew.
8 Noor's Personal File, HS 9/836/5. Instructions given to her on 9/6/45, National Archives, Kew.
9 Francis Suttill's Personal File, HS9/1430/6 National Archives, Kew.
10 France Antelme's Personal File, HS9/42 Vol. 1, National Archives, Kew.
11 Francis Suttill's Personal File, HS9/1430/6, National Archives, Kew. Citation for his DSO.
12 Circuit summary by Eddie Boxshall (First SOE adviser), December 1960.
13 Foot, *SOE in France*, p. 231.
14 Noor's Personal File, HS9/836/5, National Archives, Kew.
15 Leo Marks once told M.R.D. Foot that Playfair was never used for operational messages, though agents were taught it as an exercise. M.R.D. Foot to author, February 2005.
16 Noor's Personal File, HS9/836/5, 'Instructions to Nurse' before Noor left for France. National Archives, Kew.

17 Quotes in this section from Jean Overton Fuller, *Noor-un-nisa Inayat Khan*, pp. 142–4.
18 France Antelme's Personal File, HS9/142 Vol. 1, National Archives, Kew.
19 Ibid.
20 Foot, *SOE in France*, p. 96.
21 David Stafford, *Secret Agent*, p. 154.
22 Noor's Personal Files, HS9/836/5, National Archives, Kew.
23 Overton Fuller, *Noor-un-nisa Inayat Khan*, p. 197. As told to her by Raymonde Prénat.
24 Leo Marks, *Between Silk and Cyanide*, p. 20.
25 Foot, *SOE in France*, p. 91.
26 Overton Fuller, *Noor-un-nisa Inayat Khan*, p. 146.
27 Ian Ousby, *Occupation*, p. 188.

8: The Fall of Prosper

1 Antelme's Personal File, HS9/42 Vol. 1, National Archives, Kew.
2 Francis Suttill (son of Suttill) to author, November 2004. From his conversations with Josette Bossard.
3 Culioli trial of 9 June 1949, quoted in French newspaper in HS6/426, National Archives, Kew.
4 Francis Suttill to author, Ross on Wye, March 2005, based on his conversations with Josette Bossard, Pierre Raynaud and Mrs Laurent.
5 Suttill to author, March 2005.
6 Suttill's Personal File, HS9/1430/6, National Archives, Kew.
7 Antelme Personal File, HS9/42, National Archives, Kew.
8 Suttill's letter in Lejeune Personal File, HS9/911, National Archives, Kew.
9 Ibid.
10 Antelme's Personal File, HS9/42 Vol. 1, National Archives, Kew. Report on events between 22 June and 1 July and notes on Prosper's arrest.
11 Ibid.
12 Ibid.
13 Alain Antelme, nephew of France Antelme, to author (February 2005 by e-mail) – as told to him by Madame Aigrain.
14 Gieules' Personal File, HS9/581/4, National Archives, Kew.
15 Antelme Personal File, HS9/42 Vol. 1, National Archives, Kew.
16 Ibid.
17 Ibid.
18 Alain Antelme to author, e-mail, October 2004.
19 Gieules' Personal File, HS9/581/4, National Archives, Kew.
20 Alain Antelme to author, February 2005, by e-mail. As told to him by William Savy.
21 Noor's Personal File, HS9/836/5, National Archives, Kew.
22 Ibid.
23 Antelme's Personal File, HS9/42, National Archives, Kew.
24 M.R.D. Foot, *SOE in France*, p. 281.
25 Maurice Southgate (SOE agent and fellow prisoner) who had heard the report in prison. Southgate interrogation dated 13.6.45 in his Personal File HS9/1395/3 National Archives, Kew.
26 Norman Personal File HS9/1110/5, National Archives, Kew.
27 Sworn statements by Josef Goetz and Kieffer in Noor's Personal File, HS9/836/5, National Archives, Kew.
28 Sworn deposition by Josef Goetz in Noor's Personal File, HS9/836/5, National Archives, Kew.
29 Jean Overton Fuller, *The German Penetration of SOE*, pp. 74–8.

30 Norman's Personal File, HS9/1110/5, National Archives, Kew. Letters/memos between Mott, Hazeldine and Buckmaster.
31 Armel Guerne's Personal File, HS9/631/5, National Archives, Kew.
32 William Stevenson, *A Man called Intrepid*, p. 228.
33 Benoist's Personal File, HS9/127 Vol. 1, National Archives, Kew.
34 Antelme Personal File, HS9/42 Vol. 1, National Archives, Kew.
35 Noor's Personal File, HS9/836/5, National Archives, Kew.
36 Noor's Personal File, HS9/836/5, National Archives, Kew.

9: Poste Madeleine

1 Antelme's Personal File, HS9/42, National Archives, Kew.
2 M.R.D. Foot, *SOE in France*, p. 286.
3 Robert Gieules' Personal File, HS9/581/4, National Archives, Kew.
4 Colonel Passy, head of Free France's intelligence and subversion services, lived at this address after the war.
5 Déricourt's Personal File, HS9/425, Vol. 5, National Archives, Kew.
6 Robert Benoist's Personal File, HS9/127, National Archives, Kew.
7 Antelme's Personal File HS9/43, National Archives, Kew.
8 Noor's Personal File HS9/836/5, National Archives, Kew.
9 Jean Overton Fuller, *Noor-un-nisa Inayat Khan*, p. 155.
10 Josef Goetz's sworn statement in Noor's Personal File, HS9/836/5, National Archives, Kew.
11 Overton Fuller, *Noor-un-nisa Inayat Khan*, pp. 157–9.
12 Ibid., p. 156.
13 Ibid., pp. 158–9.
14 Ibid., p. 175.
15 Ibid., p. 175.
16 Ibid., p. 171.
17 Ibid., p. 166.
18 Ibid., p. 169.
19 Noor's Personal File, HS 9/836/S. Instructions from HQ Signals Office, 15 August 1943.
20 Leo Marks, *Between Silk and Cyanide*, p. 399.
21 Overton Fuller, *Noor-un-nisa Inayat Khan*, pp. 171–2 (as told to Raymonde and Madame Aigrain by Noor).
22 Noor's Personal File, HS9/836/5, National Archives, Kew. Kieffer's sworn statement to Vera Atkins.
23 Overton Fuller, *Noor-un-nisa Inayat Khan*, pp. 178–9.
24 Gieules' Personal File, HS9/581/4, National Archives, Kew.
25 Ibid.
26 Gieules' Personal File, HS9/581/4, National Archives, Kew.
27 Overton Fuller, *Noor-un-nisa Inayat Khan*, p. 185.
28 Ibid., p. 195.
29 Danan's article of 17 February 1957 in the journal *Franc-tireur*. Read out at a ceremony in Suresnes to unveil a plaque to Noor.
30 Overton Fuller, *Noor-un-nisa Inayat Khan*, p. 196.
31 Marks, *Between Silk and Cyanide*, p. 399.
32 Werner Ruehl's sworn statement (November 1946) before Vera Atkins in Noor's Personal File, HS9/836/5, National Archives, Kew.
33 Overton Fuller, *Noor-un-nisa Inayat Khan*, Ernest's account, p. 207.
34 Noor's Personal File HS9/836/5 – Ruehl's sworn statement, National Archives, Kew.

10: Prisoner of the Gestapo

1 Eyewitness report by American journalist William L. Shirer, quoted in Ian Ousby, *Occupation*, p. 65.
2 The wagon-lit was apparently destroyed in an RAF raid on Berlin.
3 M.R.D Foot, *SOE in France*, p. 108.
4 Jean Overton Fuller, *Noor-un-nisa Inayat Khan*, p. 208, quoting Vogt. (Vogt knew about Noor's mother because he had read her photocopied mail provided by Déricourt.)
5 Norman's Personal File, HS9/1110/5, National Archives, Kew.
6 Overton Fuller, *Noor-un-nisa Inayat Khan*, p. 211.
7 Noor's Personal File HS9/836/5, Sworn statement of Ernest Vogt, National Archives, Kew.
8 Sworn statement by Josef Goetz in Vera Atkins' Personal File, HS9/59/2, National Archives, Kew.
9 Noor's Personal File, HS9/836/5, National Archives, Kew.
10 Leo Marks, *Between Silk and Cyanide*, p. 399 and Foot, *SOE in France*, p. 301. Conversation between Marks and Foot.
11 Overton Fuller, *Noor-un-nisa Inayat Khan*, p. 216.
12 Noor's Personal File HS9/836/S. Kieffer's sworn statement on Captain John Starr.
13 Overton Fuller, *Noor-un-nisa Inayat Khan*, p. 240.
14 Noor's Personal File, HS9/836/5. Kieffer's sworn statement on John Starr.
15 Noor's personal file HS9/836/S. Deposition on oath of Wilhelm Krauss, Governor of Pforzheim prison, sworn before a War Crimes Investigation Unit of 6.11.46.
16 Letter to Hidayat from Yolande Lagrave, fellow prisoner in Pforzheim, April 1982.
17 Krauss's sworn statement in Noor's Personal File, HS9/836/5, National Archives, Kew.
18 Overton Fuller, *Noor-un-nisa Inayat Khan*, p. 244.
19 Note in Noor's Personal File, HS9/836/5, National Archives, Kew.
20 Marks, *Between Silk and Cyanide*, p. 511.
21 Noor's Personal File, HS9/836/5. Yolande Lagrave's letter to War Office, National Archives, Kew.
22 Yolande Lagrave's statement to the War Crimes Investigation Team, Bordeaux, 26 January 1947.
23 Statement of Yolande Lagrave to War Crimes investigation team, Bordeaux, 26 January 1947.
24 Letter from Marcel Schubert, 11 July 1947. WO/309/282 National Archives, Kew.
25 Sworn statement by Goetz in Vera Atkins Personal File, HS9/59/2, National Archives, Kew.
26 Marks, *Between Silk and Cyanide*, p. 416.
27 Yolande Lagrave's sworn statement to the War Crimes Investigation Team at Bordeaux, 26 January 1947.
28 Ibid.
29 Guérisse earned a George Cross. He took charge of Dachau when the SD ran away and handed it over to the Americans.
30 Sworn statement by Josef Gmeiner in Vera Atkins' Personal File, HS9/59/2, National Archives, Kew.
31 Ott's deposition 27/5/46. WO/309/282, National Archives, Kew.

32 Sarah Helm, *A Life in Secrets*, pp. 328, 417.
33 Ott's deposition 16/2/48. WO/309/282, National Archives, Kew.
34 Foot, *SOE in France*, p. 373.

Aftermath

1 Noor's Personal File, HS9/836/5, National Archives, Kew.
2 Ibid.
3 Ibid.
4 Noor's Personal File, HS9/836/5, National Archives, Kew.
5 Jean Overton Fuller, *Noor-un-nisa Inayat Khan*, p. 253.
6 Noor's Personal File, HS9/836/5, National Archives, Kew.
7 Vilayat to author, June 2003, and Overton Fuller, *Noor-un-nisa Inayat Khan*, p. 216.
8 Vilayat to author, June 2003.
9 M.R.D. Foot to author, as told to him by Leo Marks.
10 Noor's Personal File, HS9/836/5, National Archives, Kew.
11 Sworn statement by Goetz in Déricourt's Personal File, HS9/422. Also sworn statement by Goetz in Noor's Personal File, HS9/836/5, National Archives, Kew.
12 Sworn statement by Goetz. Denunciation by Henri Frager (Louba) in Déricourt's Personal File, HS9/422, National Archives, Kew.
13 M.R.D. Foot, *SOE in France*, p. 307.
14 Overton Fuller, *Noor-un-nisa Inayat Khan*, p. 216.
15 Goetz interrogation in Noor's Personal File, HS9/836/5, National Archives, Kew.
16 Kieffer interrogation in Noor's Personal File, HS9/836/5, National Archives, Kew.
17 Hidayat to author.

Bibliography

Binney, Marcus. *The Women Who Lived for Danger: The Women Agents of SOE in the Second World War*, London, Coronet, 2002.

Bose, Mihir. *Raj, Secrets, Revolution: A Life of Subhas Chandra Bose*, London, Grice Chapman, 2004.

Buckmaster, Maurice. *They Fought Alone*, London, Popular Book Club, 1958.

—— *Specially Employed*, London, Batchworth Press, 1952.

Cave Brown, Anthony. *Bodyguard of Lies*, Guilford, CT, Lyons Press, 2002.

Cookridge, E.H. *Inside SOE*, London, Heinemann, 1966.

—— *They Came From the Sky*, London, Heinemann, 1965.

—— 'Four Roads to Dachau', (Article) HS6/629 National Archives, Kew.

Cunningham, Cyril. *Beaulieu: The Finishing School for Secret Agents*, Barnsley, South Yorkshire, Pen & Sword, 2005.

—— *The Beaulieu River Goes to War*, 2nd edn, Beaulieu, Montagu Ventures, 1997.

Escott, Beryl E. *WAAF: A History of the Women's Auxiliary Air Force in the Second World War*, Buckinghamshire, Shire Books, 2003.

—— *Mission Improbable: A Salute to the RAF Women of SOE in Wartime France*, Somerset, Patrick Stephens, 1991.

Foot, M.R.D. *SOE in France*, revd edn, London, Frank Cass, 2004.

—— *SOE 1940–1946*, 2nd edn, London, BBC, 1985.

Frayn Turner, John. *VCs of the Second World War*, Barnsley, South Yorkshire, Pen & Sword, 2004.

French, Patrick. *Liberty or Death*, London, HarperCollins, 1997.

Helm, Sarah. *A Life in Secrets: The Story of Vera Atkins and the Lost Agents of SOE*, London, Little, Brown, 2005.

'History of SOE 1938–1945', 'SOE in Europe', Paper for VCSS lecture May 1946, 'SOE organisation', VCSS lecture July 1976, File HS7/1, National Archives, Kew.

Howard, Michael. *Strategic Deception in the Second World War*, 3rd edn, London, Pimlico, 1994.

Howarth, Patrick. *Undercover: The Men and Women of the Special Operations Executive*, London, Phoenix, 2000.

Imperial War Museum, London, *Now It Can Be Told*, film on SOE training.

Keesing, Elisabeth. *Hazrat Inayat Khan: A Biography*, Munshiram Manoharlal, 2nd edn, East West Publications, Delhi, 1981.

Kramer, Rita, *Flames in the Field*, London, Penguin Books, 1996.

Mackenzie, William. *The Secret History of Special Operations Executive 1940–1945*, 2nd edn, London, St Ermin's Press, 2002.

Marks, Leo. *Between Silk and Cyanide: A Codemaker's War 1941–45*, New York, Touchstone, 2000.

Minney, R.J. *Carve Her Name With Pride*, London, George Newnes, 1956.

Moulamia Khan, Musharraf. *Pages in the Life of a Sufi*, revd edn, London, Sufi Publishing, 1971.

Nicholas, Elizabeth. *Death Be Not Proud*, London, Cresset, 1958.

Ottaway, Susan. *Violette Szabo: 'The Life That I Have'*, 2nd edn, Barnsley, South Yorkshire, Leo Cooper, 2003.

Overton Fuller, Jean. *The German Penetration of SOE*, revd edn, Maidstone, George Mann, 1996.

—— *Noor-un-nisa Inayat Khan*, revd edn, London, East West Publications, 1988. First published as *Madeleine*, London, Gollancz, 1952.

Ousby, Ian. *Occupation, The Ordeal of France 1940–44*, London, Pimlico, 1999.

Rigden, Denis (introduction). 'SOE Syllabus: Lessons in Ungentlemanly Warfare', London, Public Record Office, 2001.

Stafford, David. *Secret Agent: Britain's Wartime Secret Service*, London, BBC, 2002.

Stevenson, William. *A Man Called Intrepid*, Guilford, CT, Lyons Press, 2000.

Sweet-Escott, Bickham. *Baker Street Irregular*, London, Methuen, 1965.

Van Beek, Will. *Hazrat Inayat Khan, Master of Life, Modern Sufi Mystic*, New York, Vantage, 1983.

Verity, Hugh. *We Landed by Moonlight*, revd 2nd edn, Manchester, Crecy, 2000.

Wilkinson, Peter and Bright-Astley, Joan. *Gubbins and SOE*, London, Leo Cooper, 1993.

West, Nigel. *The Secret War: The Story of SOE, Britain's Wartime Sabotage Organisation*, London, Hodder & Stoughton, 1992.

Index

Note: Numbers in brackets preceded by *n* are note numbers (with chapter numbers, where necessary). Major entries are in chronological order, where appropriate.